Whole and Reconciled

"*Whole and Reconciled* speaks of the entirety of the gospel without discarding the uncomfortable truths and demands of biblical justice, peacemaking, and reconciliation. Tizon explains how the gospel necessitates the type of reconciliation that penetrates the deepest aspects of individual and community relationships with truth, love, and vulnerability. Read this important book to learn and be challenged to embrace what it means to be truly whole and reconciled."

—**Mae Elise Cannon**, executive director, Churches for Middle East Peace; author of *Social Justice Handbook: Small Steps for a Better World*

"In this engaging work, Tizon presents a powerful vision of the social implications of a genuine Christian commitment. As he masterfully weaves together themes that are both personal and universal, he names the integral connection between the healing of the human heart and the healing of the world. In doing so he speaks about not only the task of reconciliation but also the call to bring together the head and the heart, the grass roots and the academy, and the church and its mission to the modern world."

—**Daniel Groody**, Kellogg Global Leadership Program, University of Notre Dame

"Tizon's deep theological insights and comprehensive analysis of our present conditions make this provocative book a must-read. *Whole and Reconciled* brilliantly tackles the hard questions of colonialism, racism, empire, and Christendom. The book ushers readers toward the reconciliation, peacemaking, and wholeness that people and the world desperately need."

—**Grace Ji-Sun Kim**, Earlham School of Religion

"This book should be a blessing to the individual Christian, the church, and the theological academy. It brings fresh insight to old questions and offers an integrated approach that exemplifies wholeness. In this regard, it holds together virtually all aspects of theology—biblical, historical, systematic, and practical—and, of course, all of this comes from a missiologist. In its practical outlook, the book is an instrument for the mission of God, and its autobiographical flavor and down-to-earth style, along with questions meant to provoke further reflection, all underscore an inspiring and useful work. Any student of theology, practitioner, or aspiring practitioner of mission (and aren't all Christians supposed to be missionaries?) must get a copy of this book."

—**B. Y. Quarshie**, rector, Akrofi-Christaller Institute of Theology, Mission, and Culture, Akropong-Akuapem, Ghana

"A more timely book for this strategic moment in the life of the church cannot be imagined. This is what the global church needs in our divided and fragmented world. A godly thinker and superb writer, Al Tizon is directing us on the right path."

—Las G. Newman, global associate director for regions, Lausanne Movement

"Tizon provides not a new but a renewed orthodox theology of missions that brings all missiologists and theologians to the core of the *missio Dei*. In my home of Jerusalem, I have seen all kinds of gospels—what Al calls false gospels—affect my people badly, and they have been like stumbling blocks to the salvific knowledge of the Lord Jesus Christ. We are working on the ground to bring the whole gospel to transform our nation and bring true reconciliation with God. We are living in a changing world that has faced new trends of communication, including social media that broadcasts these false gospels. In the face of such false gospels, a true gospel of love and mercy and compassion for the nations is very much needed, a contextualized gospel that acknowledges the redeemable elements in culture. *Whole and Reconciled* points the way toward this gospel."

—Jack Y. Sara, Bethlehem Bible College; ordained minister with the Christian and Missionary Alliance Church in the Holy Land

"This book is a clarion call to the church to fully embrace the ministry of reconciliation. Our evangelism and social justice need reconciliation if they are to be part of a truly holistic mission. Tizon presents us with a prophetic call: to embrace a ministry of reconciliation that is at the heart of a whole mission and a whole gospel, and that transforms the whole church and the whole world. This is one of the most important books I've read in a very long time. There is no greater or more urgent work than reconciliation."

—Graham Hill, Morling Theological College; author of *GlobalChurch* and *Healing Our Broken Humanity*

Whole and Reconciled

Gospel, Church, and Mission
in a Fractured World

Al Tizon

𝕭

Baker Academic

a division of Baker Publishing Group
Grand Rapids, Michigan

Published by Baker Academic
a division of Baker Publishing Group
PO Box 6287, Grand Rapids, MI 49516-6287
www.bakeracademic.com

Printed and bound by CPI Group (UK) Ltd, Croydon, CR0 4YY

Library of Congress Cataloging-in-Publication Data
Names: Tizon, Al, author.
Title: Whole and reconciled : gospel, church, and mission in a fractured world / Al Tizon.
Description: Grand Rapids : Baker Publishing Group, 2018. | Includes index.
Identifiers: LCCN 2018005063 | ISBN 9780801095627 (pbk. : alk. paper)
Subjects: LCSH: Mission of the church.
Classification: LCC BV601.8 .T59 2018 | DDC 266—dc23
LC record available at https://lccn.loc.gov/2018005063

Unless otherwise indicated, Scripture quotations are from the New Revised Standard Version of the Bible, copyright © 1989, by the Division of Christian Education of the National Council of the Churches of Christ in the United States of America. Used by permission. All rights reserved.

Scripture quotations labeled KJV are from the King James Version of the Bible.

18 19 20 21 22 23 24   7 6 5 4 3 2 1

I dedicate this book to Tomas Alex Tizon, my Pulitzer Prize–winning journalist brother, whose untimely death in March 2017 has left what feels like a permanent void in my life. After reading one of his brilliant pieces, I paid him a compliment, saying that I wished I could write like him, to which he replied, "Brother, I may be a good writer, but you have something to write about."

Contents

Foreword *by Ruth Padilla DeBorst*   ix

Preface   xi

Introduction   xv

Part 1   Whole World   1

1. Globalization: Mission in a Reconfigured World   5

2. Post-Christendom: Decentered Church and Multidirectional Mission   21

3. Postcolonialism: Postcolonial Mission or Bust   37

Part 2   Whole Gospel   57

4. On False and Half Gospels   63

5. Gospel of the Kingdom: The Reconciliation of All Things   77

Part 3   Whole Church   91

6. Whole Persons: Reconciliation Beginning with Me   97

7. Church of the Trinity: Community, Diversity, and Reconciliation   111

8. Spirituality of Mission: The Church in the Power of the Spirit   129

Part 4 Whole Mission   145

9. Word and Deed: The Greatness of the Great Commission   155

10. Reconciliation and the Great Commission: Peacemaking as Mission, Part 1   171

11. Reconciliation and the Great Commission: Peacemaking as Mission, Part 2   183

Conclusion   211

Afterword *by Ronald J. Sider*   217

Author Index   219

Subject Index   223

Foreword

A bomb blast here. Summary executions there. Children recruited as soldiers. Students murdered at school. Wars and rumors of war. Violence in streets and in homes. While the weapons industry rules supreme, vulnerable people are forced to leave behind their home and land in search of safety, often finding nothing but rejection and further oppression. The current global scene is not unlike the one faced by the first followers of Jesus.

As Roman armies plundered conquered lands and people were taxed into grinding poverty, children, women, and men were forced to wander in search of safe haven. Vulnerable migrants traversed deserts, braved oceans, and were thrown together in unlikely mixes in haphazard cities. Anyone who dared to question the system was silenced. All this in the name of the Pax Romana, a repressed "peace" pounded precariously together by cross-nails.

In the midst of that reality, Jesus declared to his fear-filled disciples as he was preparing to return to the Father, "Peace I leave with you; my peace I give to you. I do not give to you as the world gives. Do not let your hearts be troubled, and do not let them be afraid" (John 14:27).

The peace of Christ, Pax Christi, contrasted starkly with imperial "peace." It was a peace brokered not by weaponry or economic oppression but by self-giving love. Through his life, death, resurrection, and loving rule, Christ embodied, made, and proclaimed true peace (Eph. 2). It was into this subversive peacemaking endeavor that Jesus called his followers. "Peace be with you! As the Father has sent me, so I send you" (John 20:21)—as peacemakers, reconcilers, wall-breakers, bridge-builders, and mediators in a fractured and violent world.

This calling is surely not new to the readers of this book. Since you've chosen this title among the many out there, you're surely acquainted with, or at least interested in exploring, the implications of this calling for your understanding and engagement with the gospel, church, and mission. You will not be disappointed!

What my dear friend Al manages in this deeply theological and creatively practical book is exactly what he sets out to do. Through solid biblical reflection and making heard the voices of followers of Jesus from around the world, he faces the bad news of colonialism, racism, Christendom, the false gospels of hate, prosperity, comfort, and empire, and the reduced gospels of personal salvation or social liberation, with the good news of God's reign of *shalom* and whole, healthy relations. In doing so, he provokes a hard reset in our understanding of the church and its mission. Broken and in constant need of confession, repentance, lament, and forgiveness for their complicity in the bad news, the people of the Triune God are called to wage reconciliation through whole-life evangelism, peacemaking, and stewardship. This book helps us see what that looks like in our everyday lives.

When tempted to respond to violence with further violence, to legitimize repression with religious veneers, to nourish conflict by denying the full humanity of the "other," followers of Christ, the Reconciler, moved by the Spirit of Truth, the Comforter, contribute to the Creator's purposes in the world when we wage reconciliation through all we are, say, and do as a community.

Thank you, Al, for helping us see this more clearly! And thanks be to God who reconciled us to himself through Christ and gave us the ministry of whole reconciliation (2 Cor. 5:18)!

Ruth Padilla DeBorst
Santo Domingo de Heredia, Costa Rica

Preface

This book reflects my attempt to make sense of God's mission as I have understood it via my messy lecture notes, personal experiences, and big ideas that have swirled around in my brain for far too long. It took about four years to write, and it completely consumed me. I am tired. To be honest, I thought it was going to be easier.

I set out to provide a fresh, updated volume on holistic ministry, a subject that has come to define "my thing," my life's purpose. By "fresh and updated," I mean that I wanted to enrich the vision of holistic ministry by developing the crucial practice of reconciliation, which in my estimation needed more missiological attention. I thought I could simply add reconciliation to my already-intact theology of the whole gospel. But as the study progressed, the bigness of reconciliation would not allow me to treat it as a mere addition. It in fact began to reshape, revise, and redefine my very understanding of holistic ministry. Throughout the writing of this book, I increasingly asked myself, How can we claim to be holistic if we continue to see God's desire to reconcile all things in Christ as optional to our practice of ministry in the world? So *Whole*, the one-word title I had in mind at the beginning, became *Whole and Reconciled*.

The world needs reconciliation—a contender for the understatement of the century! The world is broken, more broken in fact than ever before. Mass shootings. Civil wars. Religious wars. Racism. Genocide. Human trafficking. Grinding poverty. The threat of nuclear annihilation. The rise of dictators. The refugee crisis. Terrorism. Explosions in airports, restaurants, churches, synagogues, mosques, and concert halls. Hatred between peoples has intensified, and our technological ingenuity has not only enabled us to act on our hatred in unprecedented ways but also enabled us to watch the animosity, cruelty, and self-destruction in HD before our very eyes. We encounter evil acts so regularly that we have become numb to them.

I would not be a gospel minister/missionary/scholar/activist/pastor/leader if I did not believe that the church, at its best, has an important role to play in the healing of hearts and nations. God desires to heal, mend, and make whole again the very good world that God created, and humanity desperately needs to know this. Enter the church, which has good news to show and tell. Paul summed up God's project best when he revealed that in Christ, "all the fullness of God was pleased to dwell, and through him God was pleased to reconcile to himself all things, whether on earth or in heaven, by making peace through the blood of his cross" (Col. 1:19–20). We engage in holistic mission when we participate with God in putting the world back together in Jesus Christ: reconciliation as mission.

I need to thank some people. When I began this project, I served on the faculty of Palmer Theological Seminary of Eastern University and as president of Evangelicals for Social Action near Philadelphia. During that time, I had the privilege of working alongside Dr. Ronald J. Sider. Ron has been my primary model of Christian discipleship since college. I have done my best to follow Ron as Ron has followed Christ (1 Cor. 11:1). What an incredible honor, then, that he was willing to read and provide feedback on rough drafts of chapters as I finished them, as well as to write an afterword. If this book channels the theology of Ron Sider in some form, then it will have been worth the effort. Having said that, I own any and all heresies that may be found here.

Stefanie Wilson, a Palmer graduate who theologizes beyond her years, also slogged through awful rough drafts of chapters and provided invaluable input. As Ron's veteran holistic ministry insights informed the process, Stefanie's Millennial perspective made sure that the book will also speak to the next generation of reflective practitioners. A cofounder of a multiethnic church with her husband, Steve, in Coatesville, Pennsylvania, Stefanie's on-the-ground input on the practice of reconciliation was invaluable to the writing of this book. Thanks, Stefanie, for keeping me on track, not only with your insights but also with your periodic check-ins.

In the middle of this endeavor, I changed jobs. In my mind, at that point I had a legitimate reason to abandon the project; for part of its appeal, to be honest, was to write the next book on holistic ministry as president of Evangelicals for Social Action and thereby build on Ron's seminal work on the subject. As it has turned out, however, my new role as executive minister of Serve Globally (SG), the international ministries of the Evangelical Covenant Church (ECC), has required drawing from all my holistic ministry experiences. I therefore express sincere gratitude to my denominational colleagues, as well as to the faculty members at North Park Theological Seminary, for taking on someone with the baggage of an unfinished book.

I especially need to thank the SG office staff, whom I essentially forced to serve as an ad hoc advisory board to this project. I set up a monthly theological reflection time, shamelessly using my chapters as discussion starters. The input they gave me improved this book greatly. The SG team is large, so I won't name each person here. However, I do need to single out Chrissy Palmerlee, who helped me draft the discussion questions at the end of each chapter. To the entire SG team, please know how much I appreciate the inspiration each of you were to me as I chipped away at this book. SG's missionary personnel and ministry partners serving in over fifty countries also inspired this project, whether they know it or not, just by living out the whole and reconciled mission together, across cultures and around the world.

My good and brilliant friend Ruth Padilla DeBorst agreed to write the foreword, for which I am extremely grateful. Among other things, Ruth leads the networking team of the International Fellowship for Mission as Transformation (INFEMIT), of which I have been a part. We have been meeting monthly by Skype and annually in person as a team now for the past ten years and counting. These colleagues from all over the world keep me going: they regularly remind me that other holistic scholar-practitioners exist in the world. Thank you for existing, friends and partners, and thank you for leading us, Ruth. You are the global community of like-minded followers of Jesus through which I find my sustenance.

Speaking of sustenance, my deeply spiritual, but salt-of-the-earth friend Willette Burgie-Bryant has been nourishing my soul for years now, and I just need to thank her. There is a cost to taking on a project like this, especially when it is on top of a ridiculously busy schedule that includes Platinum Medallion–worthy travel on Delta Airlines. She has nicknamed me "Turbo," and from a distance she checks in on me, prays for me, encourages me, and exhorts me to slow down occasionally and breathe in the Spirit of God who loves me. Thanks for being *that* voice, Willette. When I listen to you (which is not always, to my detriment), I find myself in a better place.

Bob Hosack, Eric Salo, and the rest of the editorial staff at Baker Academic, thank you for essentially taking a lump of clay called a rough draft and painstakingly molding it into something readable. May your gamble on this project result in genuine service to the global church-in-mission. And yes, may you sell hundreds and thousands of copies!

I know at least five buyers: my wife, Janice, and our four children, Candace, Christian, Corrie, and Zoey. (Actually, I will likely buy them copies.) Thank you, Janice, for keeping it real for me. You see, book writing involves no small amount of ego. There, I said it: authors are egotistical. We think "we're all that" just because we wrote a book or two. Well, Janice brings this particular egomaniac down to earth, deflates his head, and reminds him that words don't amount to much if they do not take on flesh and serve people—especially the poor, oppressed, and marginalized. She does this not by preaching but by living out her call as a nurse practitioner at Lawndale Christian Health Center, located in the heart of the city of Chicago. Out among the sick, the addicted, and the poor, she lives what I think and write about and sometimes practice. She reminds me by her life that if our words, even published ones, do not ultimately imitate the Word made flesh, then, well, they're just words. Thank you, Janice, for your partnership in real life and concrete ministry. I love you. As for our kids, what an inspiration they are as they forge their own respective journeys of creative life and meaningful service in the world. As I said to you with my other books, you don't have to read this one either: just own a copy and be proud of your dad.

The photograph on the cover of this book shows Sarah Nyatuach Muon, a deaconess in the Evangelical Covenant Church of South Sudan and Ethiopia, blessing a group of visitors, including the author, as we left her village. May her outstretched hand bless all who read this book.

Solomon wrote, "Of making many books there is no end, and much study is a weariness of the flesh" (Eccles. 12:12). I do not interpret this as, "So don't make books, and don't study." Rather, I view scholarship as an all-consuming task, which, if done in the Spirit, can truly contribute to the inspiration of the church, the transformation of the world, and the glory of God. In that light, what's a little weariness?

Introduction

I wish that the words "gospel," "church," and "mission" had no need of additional adjectives to convey their compelling truths. I wish that when outsiders heard these words, they would imagine a community of ordinary but loving people who shine the light of God in a darkened world (Matt. 5:16). I wish these words would evoke an image of people who, by virtue of their claim to follow a revolutionary named Jesus, are living out peace, justice, freedom, and love for the good of the community and are announcing God's message of hope for a better world. I wish.

That "gospel," "church," and "mission" do not conjure up these kinds of images, that many of these words represent quite the opposite—a community marred by a colonial past, along with an intolerant, paternalistic, even scandalous reputation in the present—is profoundly disturbing. Although these awful descriptors do not tell the whole story, we as Christians would be foolish to become too defensive; for an honest critique of the church's past (and present, for that matter) would uncover a multitude of tragic sins in need of radical forgiveness.[1] So much evil has been done in the name of Jesus that, for some, the words "gospel," "church," and "mission" are beyond redemption. For those, however, who can see through (not past) the evil side of Christian history, for those who continue to take biblical teaching seriously, for those who can still see the good in the gospel, the relevance of the church, and the necessity of mission, it is not optional or desirable to abandon these words.

Because of the church's less-than-shiny witness, these words need something, though—perhaps an adjective such as "whole"—to help restore their

---

1. See Mae Cannon, Lisa Sharon Harper, Troy Jackson, and Soong-Chan Rah, *Forgive Us: Confessions of a Compromised Faith* (Grand Rapids: Zondervan, 2014), which courageously takes on the sins of the church, past and present.

reputation or at least enable us to have intelligent, nondefensive conversations about God and God's mission. Perhaps the language of "whole" can help recover the beauty and power of the truth that God so loved the world that Jesus pitched his tent among us to communicate that love personally and profoundly (John 1:14; 3:16–17). If, for example, the Lausanne Movement's slogan, "the whole church taking the whole gospel to the whole world," helps God's people embrace both evangelism and justice, then by all means let us use "whole" to the fullest.[2] "The divided church taking half the gospel to select parts of the world" may be more accurate, but it is not a very compelling slogan! Nor does it convey where we want to stay.

The New Whole in Holistic Mission

Those in touch with the debates in the last century over the nature of the Christian mission know that the language of "whole" has indeed been used at various times precisely to recover the glory of gospel, church, and mission. In chapter 9 I briefly sketch that history. For now, let me simply state my growing sense of the need to rethink what it means to engage in holistic mission, of the need for a new kind of whole, which is the impetus for this book.

We find ourselves living amid massive global changes, and contrary to the notion that holistic mission was forever settled and defined by the raging debates of the last hundred years concerning the relationship between evangelism and social concern, it is a dynamic reality that needs fresh formulations according to an ever-changing world. Indeed, a church that seeks to share good news amid increasingly volatile times faces new missional challenges.

In our diversifying, globalizing, and increasingly fracturing world, I have found it vitally important to consider the ministry of reconciliation as central to a contemporary understanding and practice of mission. I join others who have been urging the church to see reconciliation as the necessary paradigm of mission in the age of unprecedented global fragmentation. Since the turn of the twenty-first century, reconciliation has received renewed attention among missiologists and missionaries. After describing the sociopolitical, economic, and cultural consequences of colonialism, as

2. This is the slogan of the Lausanne Movement. For a detailed theology behind the slogan, see Theology Working Group, "The Whole Church Taking the Whole Gospel to the Whole World," Lausanne Movement, last modified June 1, 2010, http://www.lausanne.org/content/twg-three-wholes.

well as the ubiquitous, disorienting effects of globalization (more on these global realities in part 1), Robert Schreiter, one of the first among those who can be called reconciliation theologians, writes, "It is out of this miasma of violence and division that the theme of reconciliation began to surface as a compelling response to all that was happening in terms of mission." To show that reconciliation is emerging as a paradigm of mission for the twenty-first century, he cites the British and Irish Association of Mission Studies (2002), the Commission on World Mission and Evangelism of the World Council of Churches (2005), the International Association of Mission Studies (2008), and the Lausanne Movement (2010), all of which took up the theme in their respective annual meetings.[3]

I write this book, in part, simply to applaud this development and to reinforce the efforts of those who have seen the crucial importance of reconciliation as a way to think and do mission in today's world. I seek to explore the depths of reconciliation from my theological location—namely, as an Asian American Christian within the context of the global evangelical journey toward holistic mission—and thus hopefully add to the conversation. Historically, amid the infamous fundamentalist-modernist split in North American Protestantism, holistic mission has referred to efforts on the part of a group of courageous evangelicals who dared to challenge a myopic evangelism-only missiology.[4] Their efforts sought to reintegrate social justice into the evangelical missionary agenda, to make whole again the mission of the church, especially but not exclusively among evangelicals around the world.

I see a great need to advance the meaning of holistic mission, to build on the evangelism and social justice affirmation, by understanding the ministry of reconciliation as the new whole in (w)holistic mission. In the age of intensified conflict on virtually every level, it can no longer be just about putting word and deed back together again (though it will take ongoing effort on the part of the church to keep them together); holistic mission also needs to be about joining God in *putting the world back together* again. It needs to be about participating with God in the healing of the nations.

3. Robert Schreiter, "The Emergence of Reconciliation as a Paradigm of Mission," in *Mission as Ministry of Reconciliation*, ed. Robert Schreiter and Knud Jorgensen (Oxford: Regnum, 2013), 11–12. See also his definition of reconciliation in "Reconciliation," in *Dictionary of Mission*, ed. Karl Müller, Theo Sundermeier, Stephen B. Bevans, and Richard H. Bliese (Maryknoll, NY: Orbis Books, 1998), 381.

4. For an overview of this split as background for the development of holistic mission among evangelicals, see my chapter "Precursors and Tensions in Holistic Mission: An Historical Overview," in *Holistic Mission: God's Plan for God's People*, ed. Brian Woolnough and Wonsuk Ma (Oxford: Regnum, 2010), 61–75.

Reconciliation: What Is It?

From a biblical perspective, reconciliation flows out of God's big vision to transform—that is, mend, heal, restore, renew, re-create, and make whole—the world and everyone in it. Colossians 1:19–20 beautifully sums up God's agenda: "For in [Christ] all the fullness of God was pleased to dwell, and through him God was pleased to reconcile to himself all things, whether on earth or in heaven, by making peace through the blood of his cross."

God's vision of reconciliation only makes sense in light of the biblical story of creation and fall, when in the beginning God created *shalom*—that is, a social order wherein perfect harmony existed between the Creator, creature, and ecosystem—but also when that *shalom* was shattered by sin (Gen. 1–3). Theologically, then, reconciliation means God's initiative to restore wholeness to a shattered creation. The ministry of reconciliation to which God has called the church (2 Cor. 5:18–20), therefore, participates in God's big vision to reconcile all things in Christ. Brenda Salter McNeil defines "reconciliation" as "an ongoing spiritual process involving forgiveness, repentance and justice that restores broken relationships and systems to reflect God's original intention for all creation to flourish."[5]

We participate in God's vision of reconciliation as ambassadors. Emmanuel Katongole and Chris Rice explain what that means: "An ambassador is a representative who bears someone else's message in their absence. Ambassadors live in foreign countries, which they never really call home. Living within a country other than their own, their practices, loyalties, national interests and even their accent appear strange to the citizens of those countries where they are posted. So it is with Christ's ambassadors of reconciliation inside the world's brokenness."[6] Practically, as Christ's ambassadors, our ministry of reconciliation includes the hard work of overcoming distrust, misunderstanding, bitterness, and even hatred between deeply conflicted parties in the power of the gospel. Reconciliation as God's way of redeeming creation and the church's way of representing Jesus Christ, bringing a message of peace to a broken world, is clearly missiological at the core.

As we shall see, reconciliation has social, ecclesial, cultural, ethnic, and political implications, but any biblical treatment of this ministry sees the reuniting of humanity to God as the basis of all other levels of reconciliation. This vertical reconciliation between God and humanity in the death

5. Brenda Salter McNeil, *Roadmap to Reconciliation: Moving Communities into Unity, Wholeness and Justice* (Downers Grove, IL: IVP Books, 2015), 22.
6. Emmanuel Katongole and Chris Rice, *Reconciling All Things: A Christian Vision for Justice, Peace, and Healing* (Downers Grove, IL: IVP Books, 2008), 51–52.

and resurrection of Christ leads (or should lead) to horizontal reconciliation between warring factions within the human family. As the Cape Town Commitment plainly states, "Reconciliation to God is inseparable from reconciliation to one another."[7]

I am convinced that in today's fractured and fracturing world, if the church does not operationalize this understanding of reconciliation, then it cannot claim to be engaged in holistic mission. The whole church, which desires to bear witness to the whole gospel throughout the whole world, therefore needs to be gripped anew by the vision of reconciliation in Christ. It needs to discover the compelling image of being God's reconciled and reconciling people, modeling for a fractured world the power of God to mend, heal, and make whole even the most intense of enmities. For what does it mean to be the whole church engaged in God's whole mission if it does not include the goal of reconciliation between men and women, young and old, rich and poor, and black, white, and brown in a broken world?

Objections to Reconciliation as a Paradigm of Mission

Valid objections have been raised against reconciliation as a paradigm for mission today. On a conceptual level, as McNeil avers, "one cannot reconcile those who have never enjoyed conciliatory relationship in the first place."[8] In other words, if reconciliation means bringing back together the broken pieces of what was once whole, then in some cases (perhaps most cases), what exactly needs reconciling in a relationship that has never enjoyed any sense of oneness? There has not been a time, for example, in the history of black-white relations in the US that could be considered healthy and whole. What would the ministry of reconciliation look like in that context? The same can be asked by the formerly colonized around the world.

A sociological objection follows: when initiated by the church in power, the ministry of reconciliation and its kissing cousin, the multiethnic church movement, can represent yet another project of the dominant class conducted primarily to appease their collective Christian conscience. Their efforts may be sincere, evoked by a genuine move of the Spirit; but when an unwillingness to change power dynamics and racist structures accompanies the efforts, these efforts can amount to nothing more than tokenism. Those on the wrong end of injustice—the poor, oppressed, and marginalized—have valid reason to

---

7. Lausanne Movement, "The Cape Town Commitment: A Confession of Faith and a Call to Action," January 25, 2011, https://www.lausanne.org/content/ctc/ctcommitment.

8. McNeil, *Roadmap to Reconciliation*, 20.

interpret these reconciliation efforts "as assimilation, appeasement, a passive peace, a unity without cost, and maintaining power with only cosmetic changes."[9] Let us be reconciled . . . as long as you become one of us at the end of the process!

We must also raise a missiological objection—namely, whether the church has the right to practice reconciliation. Based on its historical collusion with colonialism and participation in other human-rights abuses through the ages, has the church disqualified itself? Emily Choge asks it this way: "What role does the church have as a minister of reconciliation in situations where it has been silent, or worse still, where it has been part of the oppressive system?"[10] Without sincere repentance on the part of the Western church, the objection—even outrage—of the formerly colonized toward any reconciliation efforts coming from the West would be understandable. Though historically missionaries have rarely repented, according to Choge, to humble themselves, confess their sins, and ask their victims for forgiveness would carry "a powerful message."[11] As we shall see in chapter 11, the possibility of reconciliation depends on the genuine repentance of those who have had the upper hand in situations of oppression.

These objections—conceptual, sociological, and missiological—are valid and must be taken seriously. However, I ultimately agree with McNeil, who writes, "Since reconciliation is a biblical concept that is rooted in and modeled by the reconciling work of Jesus, I have chosen to reclaim the term instead of replacing it. I want to redeem it and recover its holistic, mysterious and profoundly biblical meaning."[12] For the most part, these objections come from the historically oppressed who are tired of words with no actions to back them up. They are ultimately not against reconciliation, but their voices need to lead the way; for it is their voices that will "set free the word *reconciliation* to shock and overcome us by its power!"[13]

Whole and Reconciled

The obvious key words for this book are "whole" and "reconciled," as we seek to advance holistic mission by way of the ministry of reconciliation. Part 1

---

9. Allen Aubrey Boesak and Curtiss Paul DeYoung, *Radical Reconciliation: Beyond Political Pietism and Christian Quietism* (Maryknoll, NY: Orbis Books, 2016), 10.

10. Emily Choge, "Reconciliation," in *Dictionary of Mission Theology: Evangelical Foundations*, ed. John Corrie (Downers Grove, IL: InterVarsity, 2007), 330.

11. Choge, "Reconciliation," 330.

12. McNeil, *Roadmap to Reconciliation*, 22.

13. Boesak and DeYoung, *Radical Reconciliation*, 11.

analyzes the "whole world"—that is, it looks closely at significant realities today—globalization, post-Christendom, and postcolonialism—that pose both challenge and opportunity for the church-in-mission. Part 2 asks anew, "What is the gospel?" in the context of the new world. How must the whole gospel be understood and practiced in order to remain prophetically faithful in this new world? After identifying and critiquing false and half gospels that have unfortunately gained momentum in the context of today's global realities, part 2 seeks to articulate anew the gospel of the kingdom that Jesus preached—that is, the whole gospel—in terms of reconciliation. Part 3 necessarily follows up with a fresh ecclesiology, reminding us of the radical nature of the church in terms of both its personal and social wholeness, as well as in its spirituality, as the whole church takes its missional vocation seriously.

After sociological, theological, and ecclesiological analyses, part 4 provides a fresh formulation of the whole mission, as it first rehearses the history of the development of holistic mission (chap. 9) and then advances it by establishing the ministry of reconciliation as the new whole in holistic mission. What does it look like when the whole church is integrally engaged in evangelism, peacemaking, and stewardship (chaps. 10 and 11) as constitutive of the Great Commission to make disciples of all nations? This question lies at the heart of this book, and the church's missional relevance in today's world hinges on how we answer it.

Part 1

Whole World

Missiology and Culture

"What do you do?"

I can answer that question several ways: I am a professor, a denominational executive, a minister, a theologian. But to solicit the blankest of stares, I would say, "I am a missiologist." It is a conversational nonstarter, and what a travesty! Scholars should be passionate about their field, and I certainly am about mine. Missiology explores the intersection of active faith and culture, and therefore provides invaluable resources to those who seek to understand the interaction between God, the active church, and the cultures of the world.

Admittedly, it is confessional; that is, it would be difficult to be a missiologist if one did not profess faith in Christ and Christ's purposes in the world. I say this as a concession because missiology's confessional nature has made it suspect as a legitimate academic discipline in some circles.[1] But has not postmodernism debunked total academic objectivity, showing that every scholar of any discipline confesses something, that every scholar comes from a particular perspective? As an interdiscipline that sits at the intersection of theology and the social sciences, missiology assumes the essential missional

---

1. The academic objection to missiology is based on the assumption that true scholarship must be done dispassionately and "objectively." Therefore, the requirement that a scholar commit to a particular religion in order to engage in the discipline of missiology makes it illegitimate. For more on this debate, as well as a creative way to do missiology that is both legitimately academic and confessional, see Jan A. B. Jongeneel, "Is Missiology an Academic Discipline?," *Transformation* 15, no. 3 (1998): 27–32.

nature of the church while maintaining high respect for the cultures and societies in which the gospel drama plays out.

In addition to missiology's confessional nature as grounds for dismissal, some institutions have also found the historical missions-colonialism connection disturbing enough to question the ethics of mission at all and therefore also the inclusion of mission studies in the theological curriculum. Although to say that the church has simply colluded with colonizers oversimplifies the matter, history reveals enough missionary complicity in the colonial project that the church cannot escape the judgment of time.[2] Furthermore, like a tormented ghost, the colonial spirit has refused to go away, continuing to this day, albeit in subtler ways, to haunt the way some groups continue to engage in mission.[3] And if missiology keeps this spirit alive in any way, then I applaud the institutions that have eliminated the discipline from their course offerings.

If missiology, however, refers to the scholarly interdiscipline that affirms both the mission of the church and the value of culture, then it can potentially serve as an avenue for the healing of the nations from postcolonial trauma. It can provide resources in the service of reconciliation. Moreover, it can detect blind spots, prevent ill-advised alliances (with, say, neocolonizers and imperialists), and discern God's activities in the midst of a people. It can help the church maintain the dignity of cultures while remaining true to the gospel. It can help the church do mission right!

Global Contextualization: An Essential Task for Missiology Today

Missiology has this potential because of its commitment to contextualization. As Dana Robert points out, "The language and practices of contextualization

2. Elsewhere I interact with church historians such as Brian Stanley and others who make the case for a more sympathetic view of Christian missions as it relates to colonialism. It is true that a fuller historical picture would reveal altruistic motives in the work of missionaries alongside the blind motives that enabled them to take part in the colonial project. Nonetheless, in light of the lingering effects of colonialism in many countries today, I argue that anything less than resistance during that time makes the missionary enterprise as guilty as the rest. See F. Albert Tizon, "Remembering the Missionary Moratorium Debate: Toward a Missiology of Social Transformation in a Postcolonial Context," *Covenant Quarterly* 62, no. 1 (February 2004): 13–34.

3. The work of postcolonial theologians and missiologists does not just consist of calling out the sins of the colonial past; it also detects the colonial spirit that still operates today. For an excellent volume on the postcolonial challenge, see Kay Higuera Smith, Jayachitra Lalitha, and L. Daniel Hawk, eds., *Evangelical Postcolonial Conversations: Awakenings in Theology and Praxis* (Downers Grove, IL: IVP Academic, 2014).

appeared as a way to move beyond the tired colonialist frameworks for mission theology."[4] Contrary to the notion that contextualization simply seeks to dress up the gospel in culturally appropriate clothing to draw people of that culture to Christ, it means negotiating the complex and delicate balance between revelation and context; for while the good news comes "from God" (that is, it does not come from within but by revelation), it is also culturally conditioned in both its delivery and its reception. How we work out this dialectic in specific cross-cultural situations defines the task of missiological contextualization.

As a missiological study, this book necessarily begins with the contextualization question, as part 1 takes on the "whole world." It calls us to consider holistic mission anew in terms of reconciliation because the world pulsates with massive and rapid changes, the kinds that have created deeper, wider, and more violent rifts between peoples. These changes, rightly interpreted by way of the contextualization process, warrant rethinking the nature and practice of God's whole mission in terms of reconciliation.

Keen contextualizers would likely raise a red flag at this point, for by definition contextualization refers to a localizing, particularizing process. So the thought of contextualizing the whole world sounds like a contradiction in terms. However, due to the forces of globalization that have caused the unprecedented convergence of cultures, economies, politics, and religions everywhere, the world has become an experientially smaller, more integrated place.[5] A global culture has emerged, making it possible and necessary to apply the task of contextualization to the world as a whole.

An Understanding of "Whole World"

Part 1 seeks to understand several major global shifts that have massive implications for the church-in-mission. Chapter 1 takes on the phenomenon of globalization. If cultural and social interpreters have discerned correctly, then this global culture I speak of has primarily taken on the contours of the marketplace. An unprecedented coming together (some say a collision or clash) of cultures in the world marketplace, globalization offers both opportunity and challenge to the church-in-mission.

4. Dana L. Robert, "Forty Years of the American Society of Missiology," *Missiology* 42, no. 6 (January 2014): 13.

5. See Donald Hornsby's "The Incredible Shrinking World," Vision, February 2005, http:// www.vision.org/visionmedia/article.aspx?id=167. This is a three-book review of Thomas Friedman's *The World Is Flat*, Joseph Stiglitz's *Globalization and Its Discontents*, and Jagdish Bagwati's *In Defense of Globalization*.

So does an overlapping set of "post realities." Chapter 2 looks closely at a world that is no longer dominated by the Christian West, a reality that scholars have identified as a post-Christendom world. Whereas the Western church once shared the moral and political center of the globally dominant, cultural forces have begun to decenter it, relegating it to the margins, where, according to most post-Christendom scholars, the church is actually better positioned to be the prophetic people of God they were always meant to be. Furthermore, whereas the Christendom church took it upon itself to go out into all the world, mission today is now characterized by "*from* everywhere *to* everywhere," as missionaries from non-Western lands feel increasingly called to bear witness to the gospel around the world, including post-Christian peoples of the West. Indeed, life in the post-Christendom era affects the church and its mission both within and outside Western culture.

If post-Christendom describes a reorientation of the church and the development of a polycentric mission, then postcolonialism—the subject of chapter 3—describes in part a global reality wherein the formerly colonized nations of the non-Western world have begun to lift up their voices, seeking justice and demanding new ways to do church and mission. In light of such postcolonial demands, is mission so hopelessly tied to historical colonialism that the church simply needs to fold up its tents and abandon the practice of mission altogether, or is there such a thing as a postcolonial missiology?

Part 1 seeks to understand these global changes, believing that they greatly affect the way in which we understand and practice the faith—that is, gospel, church, and mission—in a diversifying, globalizing, and fracturing world.

ONE

Globalization

Mission in a Reconfigured World

. . . .

Ye cannot serve God and mammon.
—Jesus (Matt. 6:24 KJV)

I used to live in Upper Darby, Pennsylvania, a first-ring suburb that hits up against the western border of the city of Philadelphia. At least on the cultural front, Upper Darby could easily be the poster town for globalization.

I do not need to go any further than the block on which we used to live to illustrate this. A first-generation Greek Orthodox family lived directly to our right; next to them, an Indian Sikh family; a Tanzanian Christian family lived right next to them. A white, middle-aged couple with no particular religious leanings who provided housing for Japanese exchange students lived to their right; living next to them was a single white Christian woman and her adult son. An abandoned house sat next to them. Across the street on the same block at the corner lived a first-generation Chinese Buddhist family; then a Haitian Christian family; then a middle-aged, white, nominally Catholic couple with no kids. A family from Pakistan recently moved into the house next to them; next to them lived an elderly white Catholic couple. An alley lines the side of their house, separating them from a row of six small miscellaneous establishments, each accompanied by second-floor apartments where I saw a rotation of African American, Indian, Mexican, and white families living. Back on our side of the street, a Latino-Caribbean, nonchurchgoing

Pentecostal family lived directly to our left; and finally, going full rectangle, sat our own household, which was a racially mixed family, my wife being white and I being ethnically Filipino. Technically we had just entered the empty-nest phase of our lives, but a racially mixed community of students from Eastern University and Palmer Seminary made it decidedly full, as we all sought to live in intentional Christian community together.

The fact that less than twenty years ago our block consisted of nearly all white households attests to a remarkable demographic shift. A predominantly white community until the 1980s, Upper Darby "is [now] one of the most diverse communities in the [Philadelphia] region, . . . home to over 100 ethnic cultures. No wonder it has earned the nickname, 'The United Neighborhood.'"[1]

I have taken the time to describe one street in Upper Darby because globalization is coming to your street too, if it has not already, and with it an unprecedented convergence on all levels of life. In the diverse neighborhood in Chicago where we now live, for example, we can walk to many strange and wonderful multiethnic eateries, including a Japanese-Filipino restaurant, a Mexican-Korean restaurant (that's right, kimchi tacos), and an Ecuadoran restaurant that also serves sushi. Cultural globalization at its very best!

What Is Globalization?

If these demographic shifts alone were to define globalization, then we would have a much easier time understanding it. The coming together of cultures, however, describes but one aspect of this complex, interrelated, multilayered phenomenon. In a helpful article published in 2006, Nayef Al-Rohdan and Gerard Stoudman of the Geneva Centre for Security Policy provide an overview of many definitions of globalization. The eleven pages of definitions alone (of the twenty-one-page article) attest to globalization's complexity.[2]

Few, however, would question that the root of the contemporary globalization tree is economics. "What has been globalized," René Padilla plainly states, "is corporate capitalism."[3] Globalization's complex, multilayered, historically rooted nature notwithstanding, it entered into a new, intensified era when the

1. Meldon Jones, "Black Exodus: Part Three," *Metropolis: In-Depth News, Analysis & Commentary for the Philadelphia Region*, October 5, 2011, http://www.phlmetropolis.com/2011/10/black-exodus-part-three.php.

2. Nayef R. F. Al-Rohdan and Gerard Stoudman, "Definitions of Globalization: A Comprehensive Overview and a Proposed Definition," Geneva Centre for Security Policy, June 19, 2006, http://citeseerx.ist.psu.edu/viewdoc/download?doi=10.1.1.472.4772&rep=rep1&type=pdf.

3. C. René Padilla, "Globalization and Christian Mission," *Journal of Latin American Theology* 9, no. 2 (2014): 33.

Berlin Wall went down in 1989–90 and the Soviet Union collapsed in 1991, thus signaling the end of the Cold War and the triumph of capitalism over communism.[4] As Thomas Friedman notes, "Globalization means the spread of free-market capitalism to virtually every country in the world."[5] With no opposing economic system to hold it back, free-flowing, free-market capitalism broke the dam and began filling every nook and cranny of the world.

Economics affects everything, and, as such, globalization has come to include all areas of life. Globalization then refers first of all to a phenomenon that affects the totality of life. We cannot, therefore, see economics as just one aspect among many affecting globalization; economics drives it. Thus the world that contemporary globalization has made is money based; it is a global market culture that pervades all aspects of existence. "Welcome to life," quips Tom Sine, referring to today's world, "in the new imperial mall."[6]

Nevertheless, "globalization has evolved beyond its economic roots to refer to all forces that connect peoples and societies and shrink the distances between them."[7] The second part of this statement points out yet another important aspect of globalization: the unprecedented interconnectedness between peoples and cultures. Partly, no doubt, because of technological advances that have made intercontinental migration much more possible, the cultures of the world—their respective worldviews, philosophies, religions, values, and so on—have come together more than ever before. To be sure, human migration has been happening since time began, and the reasons people move—in search of a better life in general and economic advancement in particular—have not changed all that much. But with the ease of air travel, the word "unprecedented" characterizes migration patterns today in the age of globalization. According to a press release from the United Nations, "More people than ever are living abroad. In 2013, 232 million people, or 3.2 percent of the world's population, were international migrants, compared with 175 million in 2000 and 154 million in 1990."[8]

The miracle of the internet has also contributed greatly to this unprecedented interconnectedness. If unparalleled migration has enabled people

4. Robert Schreiter, *New Catholicity: Theology between the Global and the Local* (Maryknoll, NY: Orbis Books, 1997), 5–8.

5. Thomas Friedman, *The Lexus and the Olive Tree* (New York: Anchor, 2000), 9.

6. Tom Sine, *The New Conspirators: Creating the Future One Mustard Seed at a Time* (Downers Grove, IL: IVP Books, 2008), 67.

7. David Haugen and Rachel Mach, introduction to *Globalization: Opposing Viewpoints*, ed. David Haugen and Rachel Mach (Farmington Hills, MI: Greenhaven, 2010), 15.

8. "232 Million International Migrants Living Abroad Worldwide—New UN Global Migration Statistics Reveal," United Nations, last updated September 11, 2013, https://esa.un.org/un migration/documents/UNpressrelease_IntlMigrationFigures_11September2013.pdf.

and cultures to physically come together like never before, the internet has enabled them to do so virtually—that is, to share ideas and values, to collaborate on social causes, to make business transactions, and so on, without having to leave the comforts of one's home office. The internet, the greatest communications revolution since the invention of the printing press, can boast of 2.5 billion users as of 2012. According to World Internet Stats, internet usage has increased 1,052 percent since 2000.[9] Thus the internet has done its significant part in creating the greatest level of interconnectedness between people and cultures that the world has ever experienced.

Based on this brief look, we can generally see globalization as a new way of understanding the world primarily in terms of the all-pervasive market, a new way to live life by the rules of a global market culture, and a new way for people to interact with one another in a technologically sophisticated world through which languages, politics, values, religions, art, and other lifeways—in a word, cultures—have come together like never before.[10] In light of this definition, several important globalization truths emerge, which I will simply list here:

- The all-encompassing power of money is a fact of our time.
- Interconnectedness between regions of the world is such that what happens "over there" cannot help but affect us "right here" and vice versa.
- Exposure to ways of life, thought, and belief that are very different from ours is a regular or daily occurrence.
- There is heightened awareness that an imposing global culture is threatening local life and local economies.

Globalization as Process and Ideology

With this working definition, we necessarily move now to the crucial task of distinguishing the process of globalization from its ideological form.

Process: Intercultural Living, Human Solidarity, and Other Possibilities

As a process, globalization offers exciting possibilities "for the exchange of knowledge and ideas, for the expression of solidarity among peoples, for

9. "Internet Usage Statistics," Internet World Stats, last updated December 31, 2017, http://www .internetworldstats.com/stats.htm.

10. By "new," I mean relative to the age of the world. Although the beginning of the era of globalization is a matter of debate, the term has certainly been in usage at least for the last seventy-five years.

the sharing of human and material resources, and for fostering intercultural communication."[11] As a process (though certainly not morally neutral since it assumes the virtue of market economics), globalization can benefit humankind.

This should prevent any tendency to demonize the entire globalization phenomenon. As Bryant Myers reports, post–Cold War globalization "saw much of the developing world in the Global South adopt market systems and connect to global markets, leading to rapid increases in economic growth, a stunning increase in world trade, and a whole new generation of technology."[12]

Related to these facts, the process of globalization provides the potential to enrich human diversity and intercultural learning. Exposure to difference naturally opens the door to learn of and from other cultural experiences and perspectives. Rather than homogenizing the world, argues Michael Lynton, globalization can diversify it. Specifically countering Hollywood's alleged power to determine the world's entertainment tastes, he writes, "Instead of one voice, there are many. Instead of fewer choices, there are more. And instead of a uniform, Americanized world, there remains a rich and dizzying array of cultures, all of them allowing thousands of movies and television shows to bloom. . . . Hollywood is not simply a place in Southern California. It is a symbol of an entertainment culture which is becoming as diverse as it is universal."[13] Peter Berger argues similarly in the arena of religion, asserting that globalization has necessarily created a more tolerant, religiously pluralistic society in which different religions coexist and inform public life.[14]

The process of globalization can also mature from mere tolerance of difference to actually uniting for the common good. It can foster unity and solidarity among peoples, sometimes resulting in the mobilization of the masses across borders to rally around certain causes. For example, unified relief efforts in the aftermath of horrific natural disasters have been greatly facilitated by globalized processes. The immediate global response to the Haitian earthquake of 2010 stands out as an extraordinary coming together of the nations. The *Telegraph* reported that "the first aid to arrive was a US military assessment team tasked with determining the country's most pressing needs, followed just before dawn by an Air China plane carrying a search-and-rescue team, medics and tons of food and medicine and three French planes with aid

11. "The People of God among All God's People," in *The People of God among All God's People*, ed. Philip L. Wickeri (Hong Kong: Christian Conference of Asia, 2000), 14.

12. Bryant L. Myers, *Engaging Globalization: The Poor, Christian Mission, and Our Hyperconnected World* (Grand Rapids: Baker Academic, 2017), 11.

13. Michael Lynton, "Globalization Promotes Cultural Diversity," in Haugen and Mach, *Globalization*, 69.

14. Peter Berger, "Globalization Encourages Religious Pluralism," in Haugen and Mach, *Globalization*, 58–61.

and a mobile hospital."[15] The report describes the involvement of the UK, the Dominican Republic, Cuba, Brazil, Peru, Venezuela, Mexico, Colombia, Guatemala, Chile, and Canada. In addition to nations qua nations getting involved, international relief agencies such as the Red Cross, World Relief, and World Vision mobilized their forces almost immediately. The point is, processes of globalization greatly aided in the mobilization of relief efforts from around the world.

Beyond relief, citizens everywhere cooperate with development and activist organizations worldwide to alleviate poverty, challenge human trafficking, and call out human rights violations, as ideas, resources, and personnel have been exchanged more rapidly and efficiently through processes associated with globalization. For a small, concrete example, the website of One Day's Wages, a grassroots movement "impacting communities throughout the world in the fight to end poverty," reports that since it began in 2009 over twenty thousand people have joined the movement, and 5.7 million dollars has been raised to fund projects to provide water and sanitation, relieve global hunger, fight human trafficking, and deal with other areas of extreme poverty affecting over a half-million people around the world. "We are captivated by the idea that everyday people have the power to change the world."[16] The process of globalization makes possible the rallying of the masses around a common cause.

Ideology: Alternate Eschaton

Far from being just a morally neutral process, however, globalization can easily take on ideological dimensions, making it absolutely crucial to distinguish process from ideology and ideology from process. While we can affirm the potential good in the process, globalization as ideology (what we can call "globalizationism"—as if the already big word needs more syllables!) warrants our uncompromising resistance. Generally speaking, advocates of globalization tend to emphasize the process, while critics are concerned about and warn against its ideological form.

As ideology, globalization imposes its presence on all, demanding participation, commitment, and even loyalty to the vision of the marketplace. As ideology, it offers nothing less than human emancipation based on the

15. Aislinn Laing and Nick Collins, "Haiti Earthquake: Global Relief Effort Launched," *Telegraph*, January 14, 2010, http://www.telegraph.co.uk/news/worldnews/centralamericaandthecaribbean/haiti/6989532/Haiti-earthquake-global-relief-effort-launched.html.

16. "Our Story," One Day's Wages, accessed September 4, 2017, https://www.onedayswages.org/our-story.

pursuit of material wealth, a unifying future for humankind—an alternate *eschaton*—in accordance with a capitalist-based consumerist vision.

Sine's discussion of Enlightenment values captures this particular kind of *eschaton*. "Essentially," he explains, "the storytellers of the Enlightenment took the vertical quest for God's kingdom . . . and turned it on its side. It became the horizontal pursuit of Western progress, technological mastery and economic growth."[17] The Enlightenment vision not only has survived to this day but has bulked up and sped up through globalization. Globalizationism is Enlightenment values on steroids, and its pervasive, imposing nature gives critics such as Martin Khor occasion to define globalization as "what we in the Third World have for several centuries called colonization."[18]

Daniel Groody's clever use of "money-theism" profoundly calls out what we are dealing with here—nothing less than the idolatry of greed (Col. 3:5). Money-theism, he explains, idolizes capital, worshiping the gods of the marketplace "through the rituals of the stock market and the liturgies of global capitalism."[19] Post–Cold War globalizationism represents Mammon's strongest attempt to date to capture humanity's heart and dethrone God, and it has proved to be a formidable opponent.

Moreover, even though the process has opened the door for many economies and cultures to go global, the US still stands the tallest in the globalization arena, even among other economically booming nations such as China and Japan. James D. Hunter and Joshua Yates assert that "so much of what we know as globalization is, in both source and character, undeniably American." They explain further: "Whether McDonald's (serving 20 million people worldwide each year), MTV (reaching half a billion people per year), Coca-Cola (serving 1 billion people worldwide everyday), Hollywood (from which 85% of the most watched films in the world come), . . . and so on, the popular culture, food, and status symbols of America are ubiquitous."[20] They describe North America's dominance over the world's elite business, philanthropic, educational, and religious spheres. Even those who favor a more diverse approach to globalization concede North America's unmatched influence. For example, Jehu Hanciles, who

---

17. Sine, *New Conspirators*, 79.

18. Martin Khor, cited in Al-Rhodan and Stoudman, "Definitions of Globalization," 10.

19. Daniel G. Groody, *Globalization, Spirituality, and Justice* (Maryknoll, NY: Orbis Books, 2007), 22–23.

20. James D. Hunter and Joshua Yates, "In the Vanguard of Globalization: The World of American Globalizers," in *Many Globalizations: Cultural Diversity in the Contemporary World*, ed. Peter Berger and Samuel Huntington (Oxford: Oxford University Press, 2002), 325.

virtually sneers whenever he encounters Americanization theories, writes, "Undoubtedly, some vital aspects of contemporary globalization reflect American economic dominance."[21]

In the age of globalization, what has been hailed by some and decried by others as the American dream—a definition of the good life based on wealth, comfort, security, opportunity, and luxury—has become the global dream. This dream, however, does not deliver; it does not liberate; it is what Ruth Padilla DeBorst calls a "freedom myth."[22] The dream can easily turn into a nightmare of overwork, overstress, illness, and the devastating disappointment of empty promises for millions of people.

Backlash and Pushback

Both internationally and domestically, of course, this movement has met resistance, surfacing what has thus far only been inferred: antiglobalization reactions accompany globalization.

The 1999 protest of the World Trade Organization's meeting in Seattle marked only the beginning on the North American front, catalyzing similar protests at most, if not all, of the gatherings of the WTO, the World Bank, and the International Monetary Fund that followed.[23] Then the horrific attacks on September 11, 2001, on the Twin Towers in New York and the Pentagon in Washington, DC, happened. The attacks represented anti-Americanism of violent proportions, repudiating North America's perceived economic, political, and cultural dominance over the world with a ferocity and a vengeance that killed three thousand people. That al-Qaeda terrorists attacked the World Trade Center and the Pentagon—the commercial and military centers of the US—undeniably made this an act of antiglobalization.[24]

Predictably, the antiglobalization movement as a whole receded after 9/11. The attack was so violent and unjustifiable that even the most ardent antiglobalization activists took a step back, not wanting to be associated in the least with this brand of anti-Americanism. When some did continue

21. Jehu Hanciles, *Beyond Christendom: Globalization, African Migration, and the Transformation of the West* (Maryknoll, NY: Orbis Books, 2008), 34.

22. Ruth Padilla DeBorst, "On Being Set Free: Relational Truthfulness and Globalization," *Journal of Latin American Theology* 9, no. 2 (2014): 101–2.

23. Joseph Stiglitz, *Globalization and Its Discontents* (New York: Norton, 2002), 3.

24. As we know, a fourth plane was headed to an unknown destination before a passenger-led insurrection thwarted the terrorists' plans. The plane crashed in a field in central Pennsylvania, killing all forty-five on board. Theories abound as to its target; some say the White House, others say Camp David, and still others a nuclear power plant.

their activist work, the national sentiment for a few years after the attack was such that any form of protest "faced unprecedented hostility from the police."[25]

As long as globalization plods on, so does antiglobalization. Although the Occupy Movement, which began on Wall Street in October 2011, never clearly defined itself in terms of goals, objectives, and alternatives, it essentially protested social and economic inequality—that is, globalizationism. And, contrary to the notion that it was strictly a domestic protest, "rallies were held in more than 900 cities in Europe, Africa, and Asia, as well as in the US, with some of the largest occurring in Europe."[26] The movement did, however, flourish most demonstratively in the US, occurring in over seventy cities and six hundred communities across the land.[27]

The antiglobalization sentiment manifests in subtler forms as well. For example, various "buy local" campaigns ultimately attempt to subvert big business, multinational corporations, and the like, which destroy mom-and-pop stores, family farms, small businesses, and local economies. To say it more positively, Local First, an organization in Grand Rapids, Michigan, dedicated to boosting the local economy, articulates its mission statement this way: "We lead the development of an economy grounded in local ownership that meets the basic needs of people, builds local wealth and social capital, functions in harmony with our ecosystem, and encourages joyful community."[28]

On the cultural front, some regional and ethnic societies have felt a great need to assert their cultural identities against the imposing, homogenizing forces of globalization. If they fail to do this, they fear, then their cultures will eventually be absorbed into the looming market-based global culture that demands assimilation. It seems inadequate now, for example, to identify oneself as simply American; increasingly, people in the US describe themselves as Asian American, African American, Hispanic American, Native American, and so on. A heightened pride in one's cultural identity has also become chic: "*Pinoy* [Filipino] pride," "Black is beautiful," "Brown and proud [Mexican],"

25. Mimi Dwyer, "Where Did the Anti-Globalization Movement Go?," *New Republic*, October 25, 2013, http://www.newrepublic.com/article/115360/wto-protests-why-have-they -gotten-smaller.

26. Karla Adam, "Occupy Wall Street Protests Go Global," *Washington Post*, October 15, 2011, http://www.washingtonpost.com/world/europe/occupy-wall-street-protests-go-global /2011/10/15/gIQAp7kimL_story.html.

27. Joanna Walters, "Occupy America," *Guardian*, October 8, 2011, http://www.theguardian .com/world/2011/oct/08/occupy-america-protests-financial-crisis.

28. "Mission," Local First, accessed October 25, 2017, http://www.localfirst.com/who-we -are/history-about.

and so on. Moreover, in more and more cities across the US, Indigenous People's Day has replaced Columbus Day. How else can we interpret these cultural assertions but as reactions against the slow erosion of cultural identities by globalizationism?

Implications for the Church-in-Holistic-Mission

The question for the church now comes into focus: How, if at all, should the reconfiguration of the world called globalization inform the whole mission of the church? While I agree with Myers that no single program can address the complexities of globalization, I propose three theological commitments that should guide any missional effort.[29]

Embracing the Kingdom Dream

First, the church must see the global (American) dream for what it is—misguided, Mammon based, and idolatrous—and challenge it by embracing an alternate dream, the dream of the kingdom of God. A truly holistic mission offers nothing less than the good news of the kingdom dream. The compelling vision of God's universal reign of peace, justice, and freedom in Jesus Christ needs to captivate the imagination of the missional church like never before.

This will take repentance on a grand scale, for as Michael Budde and Robert Brimlow lament, the church in many ways has become a chaplain to capitalism, a sanctifier of the vision and goals of the global (American) dream.[30] The wrong dream, therefore, has captured the church's imagination, resulting in "Christianity Incorporated—a church that has bent to capitalism and economic power so long that its own practices and beliefs become shaped by the corporate form and spirit."[31]

If we accept this, then one word comes to mind: repent! For, as Jesus said, we "cannot serve God and wealth" (Matt. 6:24). The church must turn from the alluring but ultimately wicked way of the global (American) dream and imagine something bigger, more inclusive, and more reflective of God's desire for global *shalom*. "We are called to denounce the evils of 'Christianity Incorporated,'" Padilla declares, "to summon people to break away from 'the American Way of Life,' and to embrace an alternative lifestyle centered in

---

29. Myers, *Engaging Globalization*, 8.
30. Michael Budde and Robert W. Brimlow, *Christianity Incorporated* (Grand Rapids: Eerdmans, 2002).
31. Budde and Brimlow, *Christianity Incorporated*, 24.

the kingdom of God and [God's] community-restoring justice, which brings peace to the poor and oppressed."[32]

Embracing the kingdom dream in the age of globalization means, of course, a focused ministry among the poor, globalizationism's most vulnerable victims. Though poverty has many dimensions, I refer specifically to the economically deprived poor who suffer immeasurably and daily as a result of their inability to join the global market arena. Though globalizationism has an all-are-welcome mat at its entrance, the survival-of-the-fittest nature of the game quickly marginalizes the rural farmer, the uneducated, those born into underprivileged families or lower castes, and, generally speaking, women and children. These make up the majority of the world's population. Globalizationism makes the rich minority richer and the poor majority poorer. It has resulted in a "class polarization, the emergence of a transnational aristocracy of materially wealthy and politically powerful people over against increasing masses of poor and deprived people unable to satisfy their basic needs everywhere."[33]

To embrace the kingdom dream means to "bring good news to the poor" (Luke 4:18)—that is, to grow in our capacity to empower the poor to break the cycle of poverty through effective community and economic development initiatives in the name of Jesus and by the power of the Spirit. Christian organizations such as World Vision, Opportunity International, and the Asian School of Development and Cross-Cultural Studies have led the way in Christ-centered development that embodies the kingdom dream and by doing so have challenged globalizationism's negligence of the poor, oppressed, and marginalized.

In terms of the ministry of reconciliation, I contend that the first line of the church's work in the age of globalization must address the gap between the rich and the poor. I agree with Padilla's interpretation of the heart of the rich-poor divide. "In today's world," he writes, "the main reason for the material poverty that prevents millions and millions of people from covering their basic needs is the spiritual poverty of a small minority of Mammon worshippers in the transnational class generated by corporate capitalism."[34] The church engages in the ministry of reconciliation when it at once cares for and empowers the poor and exhorts the rich to denounce Mammon and to shift their gaze and resources toward the world's most vulnerable.

32. René Padilla, "Imperial Globalization and Integral Mission," *Princeton Seminary Bulletin* 27, no. 1 (2006): 22.

33. Padilla, "Globalization and Christian Mission," 38.

34. René Padilla, "The Globalization of Greed," *Journal of Latin American Theology* 9, no. 2 (2014): 43.

Developing Competencies in Reconciliation

Additionally, to operationalize God's kingdom dream, the church needs to develop competencies in reconciliation—at least the following four—if it desires to be relevant and effective in today's globalized world.

Intercultural Competence

The church needs to develop intercultural competence. It needs to enter boldly into the multicultural fray that increasingly describes our neighborhoods and communities today with a humility that is eager to learn and with enthusiasm for bearing witness to the gospel for all cultures. It needs to be intentional about meeting the new neighbors and serving them, as well as being served. Harvest Time Christian Fellowship (HTCF) in Philadelphia provides a prime example of developing this competence. A predominantly African American congregation, HTCF intentionally moved to a predominantly Hispanic neighborhood located just on the other side of a large park that separates the two communities. More than a geographical boundary, the park has symbolized the segregation between the two communities. Replanted now on "the wrong side" of the park, HTCF not only began to offer English as a Second Language classes but also recruited a number of residents from their new community to teach Spanish to church members as part of its efforts to bridge the two communities.

The times require this kind of reconciliatory intentionality to counter the divisiveness of our world. To continue to have monocultural churches, conferences, and other Christian gatherings should make less and less sense as the world becomes more and more globalized. These monocultural gatherings should feel as incomplete as attending an all-men's or all-women's church. As Padilla asserts, "The church as a homogeneous unit is a contradiction in terms."[35] This especially rings true in the age of globalization. We should develop an acute awareness that when we gather together in Christ's name for whatever reason, we need to model the multicolored gospel of reconciliation.

Interreligious Competence

The church also needs to develop interreligious competence as part of the ministry of reconciliation in a fractured world. Inevitably, as cultures come together, so do different religious belief systems. The interactions between different faiths has proved to be one of the most volatile in the age of

---

35. Padilla, "Imperial Globalization," 18.

globalization. Some scholars, such as Arun Pereira, argue compellingly that as mass migration blurs the lines between nationalities, religion will become the primary point of identity for people—and likely a point of sharp disagreement.[36] If Pereira is right, then the danger of religious wars can become more acute as religious fundamentalists dig in their heels.

It is all the more important, therefore, that "legitimate leaders of peace-loving religions . . . recognize this situation as an opportunity to effect positive change in our world and thwart the efforts of religious fanatics who are using it for their selfish and twisted goals."[37] It will become extremely important in the coming days—if not already urgent—for the church to learn how to dialogue with "the religious other," to know how to listen to and learn from them, as well as to know how to proclaim Jesus in word and deed in a confident but humble way. Christian-Muslim tensions, for example, have risen to disturbing heights. Myers keenly observes, "Learning to love our Muslim neighbor may be the biggest and most important missiological frontier Christians face in this century."[38]

I suspect that theology of religions—the specialized field in Christian theology that deals with the complexities posed by a plurality of religions in the world—will gain in prominence in the age of globalization, not just in the academy but also in lay training institutes and church adult education programs. For churches need to know how to understand, interact with, and work together with people of other faiths. Elsewhere I develop a number of postures that outline a practical theology of religions, which includes the practice of Christian hospitality, authentic dialogue, and humanitarian partnership with people of other faiths.[39]

Intergenerational Competence

In the age of globalization, we also need more than ever to develop intergenerational competence as the ministry of reconciliation addresses the perpetual rift between the young and the old. As Sam George asserts, "Globalization and the emerging culture are deeply intertwined subjects and have a reciprocal relationship. . . . Youth culture simultaneously shapes globalization and is shaped by it."[40] Our young have before them the largest smorgasbord of knowledge,

36. Arun Pereira, "Globalization Encourages People to Identify Themselves along Religious Lines," in Haugen and Mach, *Globalization*, 50–56.
37. Pereira, "Globalization Encourages People," in Haugen and Mach, *Globalization*, 56.
38. Myers, *Engaging Globalization*, 13.
39. Al Tizon, *Missional Preaching: Engage, Embrace, Transform* (Valley Forge, PA: Judson, 2012), 146–47.
40. Sam George, "Emerging Youth Cultures in the Era of Globalization: TechnoCulture and TerrorCulture," and "TerrorCulture: Worth Living for and Worth Dying For," in *One*

beliefs, values, and lifestyles ever known. To the extent that it can, the church needs to know the nature of the massive amount of information at the fingertips of the young and how they process it. It needs to be in touch with their thinking about life, God, church, sexuality, relationships, violence, and death more than ever before. And it needs to know how to share Jesus in a way that resonates with them, lest it completely lose the next generation to the globalization vortex.

Intergenerational competence depends largely on the church overcoming its propensity toward traditionalism, that is, its resistance to change. In the age of globalization, where change is the name of the game, church traditionalism (not to be mistaken for "tradition," which is a good thing) becomes much more pronounced. When the church easily dismisses technology as a legitimate vehicle for spiritual experience, for example, the youth begin to slip away. When it scoffs at their movie and musical icons as figures of antifaith, the youth begin to slip away. When the church refuses to at least have open conversations regarding outlooks, values, and philosophies that differ from church conventions, the youth begin to slip away. In order to develop intergenerational competence, the church "must change with the continually changing culture, yet preserve the truth of the gospel of Jesus Christ and the historic Christian faith."[41]

Internet Competence

Related to intergenerational competence, the church needs finally to develop internet competence. In the age of globalization, the World Wide Web is not just another means of communication but a hypermedium that subsumes, links together, and enhances all previous media. The internet is a culture all its own. While our children are natives to this culture, previous generations, including mine, are immigrants. We go to the young to help us navigate the new world. The question for the church is not so much "How do we share the gospel through the internet?" but rather "How do we share the gospel *in* the internet, or if you'll allow it, in Internet City?" Just as we would ask how best to share the gospel, say, in China, we should ask how best to share the gospel in Internet City. Understanding the internet as a virtual metropolitan culture in and of itself, we need to apply the principles of missionary contextualization and thus become competent in it with the gospel.

The church has always needed to be competent in crossing cultures, religions, generations, and technologies, but it is truer now more than ever before. These constitute the new frontiers of the church's ministry of reconciliation.

World or Many? The Impact of Globalisation on Mission, ed. Richard Tiplady (Pasadena, CA: William Carey), 33–34.
    41. George, "Emerging," 35.

Joining the Mustard Seed Conspiracy: Globalization of the Gospel

At least one other implication comes to mind in response to globalization: the church must act out mustard seed faith in the world. By that I mean the church committing to doable, local acts of service and believing that in the hands of God these small, seemingly insignificant, drop-in-the-bucket acts do their part in subverting and eventually toppling the Goliath of globalizationism.

I am indebted to the work of Tom Sine for giving me a lasting metaphor for holistic mission. As a young Christian in my early twenties, I providentially stumbled on his book *The Mustard Seed Conspiracy*, and in retrospect it probably has motivated me to lead an active, missional life more than any other.[42] By creatively developing Jesus's parable of the mustard seed (Matt. 13:30–32; Mark 4:29–31; Luke 13:17–19), Sine made "changing the world" seem doable as he invited the ordinary and unassuming to join in the subversive work of God. In *The Mustard Seed Conspiracy*, Sine tells story after story of ordinary people making realistic but profound decisions to live radically for Christ. I remember chapter 9 having a particular impact on me, as Sine highlights "seeds of righteousness," "seeds of justice," "seeds of peace and reconciliation," and "seeds of wholeness and love" planted by ordinary people who made small but profound decisions concerning their lifestyles, their budgets, their time, and their energy in the service of the gospel.[43] Since I am among the ordinary and unassuming, I reasoned, I too can take part.

Inspired by the truth of mustard seed faith, my wife, Janice, and I set a life trajectory that eventually led us to quit our jobs, sell our belongings, and head off to the Philippines with our two young children. For the next unforgettable decade of our lives, I engaged in community development and pastoral ministries in desperately poor squatter and disaster-stricken communities, while Janice applied her nursing skills to a ministry that served thousands of street children. As insignificant as our efforts may have been, we believe in the strength of mustard seed faith that they have contributed to the resources that God can use to reclaim the world from the clutches of lesser gods, or to say it positively, to reconcile all things in Christ.

In 1999 Sine's book *Mustard Seed versus McWorld* came out, wherein he applies mustard seed faith to challenge globalization, lending even greater and deeper meaning to the descriptor "mustard seed conspiracy." In this book Sine names the adversary "McWorld" or globalizationism, calling the church to

---

42. Tom Sine, *The Mustard Seed Conspiracy* (Waco: Word, 1981).
43. Sine, *Mustard Seed Conspiracy*, 194–207.

subvert it by way of the small.[44] Then, in 2008, Sine wrote *The New Conspirators: Creating the Future One Mustard Seed at a Time*, wherein he discusses emerging, missional, mosaic, and new monastic church movements as gospel-inspired attempts to undermine the objectives of the global (American) dream.

Privileged these days to call Tom and his wife, Christine, friends, I spent a few days with them in 2014 for the Inhabit Conference. An annual gathering, Inhabit is organized by the Parish Collective, a new way to understand, root in, and mobilize neighborhoods for peace and justice.[45] Its radically local nature and its call for Christians to commit to place and to the people living in that place decidedly makes it an integral part of the mustard seed conspiracy.

The cumulative effect of the works of Sine and others is the celebration of the truth that to engage in something as large as transforming the world in Christ in the age of globalization ironically requires a commitment to the small, the local, and the less than glorious. The saying "Everyone wants a revolution, but no one wants to do the dishes" should hang on the wall of any would-be revolutionary as a reminder of what is required to participate in the globalization of the gospel of reconciliation. And as God gathers the church's small mustard seed acts of faith happening all over the world, we can rest in the promise that Mammon will eventually be overtaken by the tree of God's *shalom*. The true *eschaton* belongs to Christ.

Embracing the kingdom dream over and against the global (American) dream, developing competencies in reconciliation, and committing to the bottom-up subversive work of the whole gospel—these actions position the whole church to be relevant and powerful in the age of globalization.

Discussion Questions

1. Where do you see globalization, in terms of both process and ideology, at work in your own world?
2. What is your definition of the good life?
3. How are you pursuing "competencies in reconciliation"? In what ways are you becoming more adept at crossing cultures, religions, generations, and technologies?

---

44. Tom Sine, *Mustard Seed versus McWorld: Reinventing Life and Faith for the Future* (Grand Rapids: Baker, 1999).

45. To learn more about the Parish Collective and the Inhabit Conference, go to http://www.parishcollective.org. The book *The New Parish* (Downers Grove, IL: InterVarsity, 2014), by Dwight Friesen, Tim Soerens, and Paul Sparks, is also indispensable in learning about this movement.

TWO

Post-Christendom

Decentered Church and Multidirectional Mission

. . . .

Give to the emperor the things that are the emperor's,
and to God the things that are God's.
—Jesus (Mark 12:17)

To equate Christendom with biblical Christianity is like equating Kool-Aid with water. About seventeen hundred years ago by way of imperial decree, the additives of position, privilege, and power were mixed into the pure water of the church, fundamentally changing its properties. Given that up to that point the church had only tasted the bitterness of marginalization and persecution in the Roman Empire, position, privilege, and power no doubt tasted incredibly sweet. Like Kool-Aid.

Another, more recent event involving the sweet drink comes to mind as we consider Christendom—namely, the Jonestown massacre of 1978, when 918 followers of the wayward religious leader Jim Jones "drank the Kool-Aid" to their disturbing, horrible deaths. Admittedly, evoking this atrocity reveals at the outset my view of Christendom. Indeed, I join a growing number of scholars who say that Christendom is a bittersweet but ultimately poisonous imposter institution that has resulted in unspeakable atrocities in the name of Christ.

Many of these same scholars bring good news, however. They claim that recent developments have signaled the demise of Christendom, that the signs of the times point to the fact that the world is entering, if not already in, a post-Christendom era. This chapter celebrates this fact. Our task to contextualize the world requires us to consider this development, for the shift from a Christendom to a post-Christendom context has tremendous implications for the church-in-mission.

To appreciate more fully the dawn of post-Christendom and its implications for mission, we need a basic knowledge of the history and meaning of Christendom. What is it? What are its characteristics? What is different about it from biblical Christianity? And how does, or should, the church engage in mission in a post-Christendom world?

What Is Christendom?

Few would disagree that the then-three-hundred-year-old, persecuted, marginalized community of Jesus people morphed into something different when it accepted the political privileges of the Roman Empire at the beginning of the fourth century. Emperor Constantine's alleged conversion to Christianity led to the Edict of Milan of 313, which legalized Christianity and thus put an end to the persecution of Christians. This opened the door, sixty-seven years later in 380, for Theodosius I to make Christianity the official religion of the Roman Empire. Then, in 528, Emperor Justinian made it illegal *not* to be Christian. If one accepts these events as markers of the maturation of Christendom (though the term was not coined until the ninth century[1]), then doing the math from Constantine's conversion to Justinian's outlawing of non-Christian allegiances, we can say that the solid establishment of Christendom in the Western world took about 215 years.

Christendom, Addison Hodges Hart explains, "is that historical merging of an institutional church with the government of a state, the alignment of religion with politics, and the alliance of clergy with ruling powers to share in those powers."[2] For the church, at least in the beginning, the alliance represented "sweet rescue" from persecution, and for the state, it was religious legitimation for the building up of the empire. But make no mistake: in Hart's succinct words, "Christendom [was not and] is not Christianity."[3] The term "Christendom" serves more accurately as a descriptor of Western civilization after Constantine. As Craig Carter explains, "Christendom is the concept of Western civilization as having a religious arm (the church) and a secular arm

1. Stuart Murray, *Post-Christendom: Church and Mission in a Strange New World* (Waynesboro, GA: Authentic, 2004), 23.
2. Addison Hodges Hart, *Strangers and Pilgrims Once More: Being Disciples of Jesus in a Post-Christendom World* (Grand Rapids: Eerdmans, 2014), 15.
3. Hart, *Strangers and Pilgrims*, 15–16.

(civil government), both of which are united in their adherence to Christian faith. . . . The essence of the idea is the assertion that Western civilization is Christian. With this Christian civilization, the state and the church have different roles to play, but, since membership in both is coterminous, both can be seen as aspects of one unified reality—Christendom."[4] Church and state depend on each other for their respective identities and functions in the context of Christendom. We can define the Christendom church, therefore, as a mixed spiritual-secular institution whose identity depends as much on its theology as it does on "the state of the union," and whose allegiance, whether consciously or not, is pledged to both the cross and the flag. As such, the Christendom church differs fundamentally from the church of the first three centuries.

This is not to imply that the pre-Constantinian church epitomized conflict-free, harmonious existence (like the "pure water/Kool-Aid" analogy at the beginning of this chapter might have suggested); to be sure, the early church had an array of problems, as the letters of Paul attest, but abuse of political power was not one of them because the church had no such power to speak of. The Jesus community in fact lived perilously on the sociopolitical margins of Roman society.

Although church historians differ in their overall assessment of Christendom, the church as a spiritual-secular institution has undeniably participated in great evils in the name of Christ throughout these last two millennia.[5] Citing a small sampling of Christendom's trail of tears and blood, Carter painfully rehearses the intense periods of anti-Semitism (the Holocaust being the most vivid in the minds of many), the persecution of Anabaptists in the sixteenth century, and the genocide of native peoples of the Americas.[6] Add to this list the burning of heretics, the Crusades, the Inquisition, witch hunts, and colonialism, and the obvious comes to light: Christendom—the marriage of church and state—was a very bad idea.[7] Whatever good came out of the marriage—for example, the establishment of educational institutions, hospitals, and magnificent cathedrals; the source of classical literature and art;

4. Craig A. Carter, *Rethinking Christ and Culture: A Post-Christendom Perspective* (Grand Rapids: Brazos, 2006), 14.
5. One of the most compelling arguments of the positive side of Christendom comes from Lesslie Newbigin. Ultimately a critic of Christendom, Newbigin nevertheless asserts that the church would have been irresponsible if it had not taken the offer from the state to become a part of the shaping of society. See Lesslie Newbigin, *Foolishness to the Greeks* (Grand Rapids: Eerdmans, 1986), 100–101. See also Joseph Back Nikolajsen, "Beyond Christendom: Lesslie Newbigin as a Post-Christendom Theologian," *Exchange* 41 (2012): 370–71.
6. Carter, *Rethinking Christ and Culture*, 86–92.
7. Carter, *Rethinking Christ and Culture*, 77.

and yes, even the global expansion of the faith through missions—it cannot ultimately offset the great evils that occurred in the name of Christ.

The Idea of Christian America: A Contemporary Example

A single chapter cannot adequately chronicle Christendom's developments and consequences throughout the ages. Besides, thorough historical works on Christendom have already been excellently done, so there's no need to attempt anything herculean here.[8] However, in order to appreciate the post-Christendom shift more fully, we need to consider at least one way in which Christendom has manifested in a particular place among a particular people. The fiercely passionate idea of Christian America immediately comes to mind. I know it well, as it has manifested most strongly in my theological tribe of North American evangelicalism, though the idea is not exclusive to evangelicals or even conservatives. As Greg Boyd, author of *The Myth of a Christian Nation*, asserts, "My thesis [that America was never and is still not Christian] applies as much to Christians on the political left as on the political right."[9]

Let me be crystal clear: the idea of Christian America is a direct descendant of historical Christendom. In fact, the idea of a Christian nation can only emerge out of a Christendom context, in which religion takes on a territorial dimension.[10] So any physical nation today claiming to be Christian does so in the spirit of Christendom. Full-orbed Christendom, however, requires political leverage; it stirs into one pot Christianity and the political culture of the most powerful and influential nation in the world. So while any nation can claim to be Christian, the most dominant "Christian nation" at any given time embodies Christendom most fully. In the fourth century, the Roman Empire held that position; in the twenty-first century (and the foreseeable future), the United States of America sits on that throne.

Being God's Chosen

At least four interrelated features of the Christian America idea bear the marks of Christendom. First, it derives its strength from the belief that the US is God's chosen people, a kind of new Israel. It asserts that *God has chosen the*

8. See, e.g., Peter Leithart's *Defending Constantine: The Twilight of an Empire and the Dawn of Christendom* (Downers Grove, IL: IVP Academic, 2010).

9. Gregory A. Boyd, *The Myth of a Christian Nation: How the Quest for Political Power Is Destroying the Church* (Grand Rapids: Zondervan, 2005), 14.

10. Andrew Walls, *The Cross-Cultural Process in Christian History* (Maryknoll, NY: Orbis Books, 2002), 35–47.

US to be and do great things. "The twin themes of chosen people and national covenant" defined a vision that possessed the English Puritans, who settled in North America. Richard Hughes writes, "New England Puritans typically understood themselves as God's new Israel—a people [that] God had chosen for Himself [and] had led out of Egyptian bondage (England) across the Red Sea (Atlantic Ocean) and into the Promised Land (the American wilderness)."[11]

Far from being a Puritan historical artifact, however, Christendom-based, North American exceptionalism is alive and well today. Besides the usual suspects espousing the idea of Christian America—such as Jerry Falwell (*Listen Up, America*), James Kennedy (*Can America Be Christian Again?*), and Pat Robertson (*America's Date with Destiny*)—recent presidents from Ronald Reagan to Barack Obama have all appealed to God's role in the founding and leading of the US.

Expanding the Faith Territorially

Related to its sense of chosenness, the idea of Christian America has also fed on the need for territorial expansion, of Manifest Destiny. North American Christendom proclaims that *God has chosen the US to do God's bidding, which is to engulf the whole world with God's truth, mercy, and justice.* As Israel felt called to occupy Canaan, Christendom-based colonists felt the providential call to claim the North American continent, coast to coast. This vision resulted in the decimation of millions who were insultingly lumped together under the designation "Indian" and continue today to be lumped together by the not-much-better "Native American."

Moreover, the expansion did not stop at the continental coastlines, as Manifest Destiny inspired the colonization of Puerto Rico, Hawaii, Guam, and the Philippines. Ironically and tragically, the sincere desire for all to experience the blessings of God justified the purging of indigenous peoples and the colonizing of civilizations beyond the continent. Although the US does not expand its borders in the same way today, some have argued compellingly, as we saw in chapter 1, that the globalization of its will in the cultural, economic, religious, and sociopolitical arenas continues today and can be seen as a new kind of colonization.

Keeping or Restoring the Faith

The idea of Christian America also carries with it the responsibility to "keep the faith," or, to those who feel like the country has lost its way, to

11. Richard T. Hughes, *Christian America and the Kingdom of God* (Urbana: University of Illinois Press, 2009), 23–24.

restore the faith in the land. According to this feature of North American Christendom, *God has called the US to be Christian and to safeguard its people against false religions*. This echoes Emperor Justinian's decree of 528 that made Christianity the only legal religion in the Roman Empire. The vision of Manifest Destiny sought precisely to replace pagan cultures with Euro-American Christian culture. It was "to spread the values of white civilization from the Atlantic to the Pacific."[12]

Once the colonists completed the "benevolent Christian invasion" of the Americas, the responsibility shifted to the retention of the nation's white Christian character. This posture has translated today into a keeper-of-the-gate mentality that tightly guards the nation's borders in an effort to keep intact the perceived Christian purity of the nation; for embedded deep within the Christendom psyche lies an all-pervasive but misguided belief that foreigners who enter the country will surely bring their strange gods with them.

Those who feel that the US has lost its Christian base see their duty as "taking America back for God."[13] Often invoking 2 Chronicles 7:14, they cry out against the sins of the nation (such as religious tolerance, liberalizing laws on homosexuality and abortion, and the outlawing of prayer in schools, to name a few) and call it to repentance, so that it cannot only avert God's judgment but also return to its purpose to be the city on the hill for the rest of the world.

The slogan "Make America Great Again," used effectively by Donald J. Trump during his successful bid for the White House in 2016, captures this spirit. His proposal to build a high wall at the US-Mexico border represents the misguided fear that it is foreigners who defile the purity of Christian America and its high morals. That Trump won the election, thanks in no small part to the 81 percent of white evangelicals who voted for him, shows the pervasiveness of this fear.[14] As true as the dawning of post-Christendom may be, Trump's presidency, especially the support he has continued to enjoy

---

12. Mae Elise Cannon, Lisa Sharon Harper, Troy Jackson, and Soong-Chan Rah, *Forgive Us: Confessions of a Compromised Faith* (Grand Rapids: Zondervan, 2014), 66.

13. Books and resources abound here, but to mention just a few, see David Barton and George Barna's *U-Turn: Restoring America to the Strength of Its Roots* (Lake Mary, FL: Charisma House / FrontLine, 2014); Todd Starnes's *God Less America: Real Stories from the Front Lines of the Attack on Traditional Values* (Lake Mary, FL: Charisma House / FrontLine, 2014); Woodrow Polston's *Preparing America for the Wrath of God: The Truth about America from a Christian Who Isn't Afraid to Say It* (Lake Mary, FL: Creation House, 2013); Newt Gingrich's *A Nation Like No Other: Why American Exceptionalism Matters* (Washington, DC: Regnery, 2011); James Kennedy's *What If America Were a Christian Nation Again?* (Nashville: Thomas Nelson, 2003).

14. Sarah Pulliam Bailey, "White Evangelicals Vote Overwhelmingly for Donald Trump, Exit Polls Say," *Washington Post*, November 9, 2016, https://www.washingtonpost.com/news/acts-of-faith/wp/2016/11/09/exit-polls-show-white-evangelicals-voted-overwhelmingly-for-donald-trump.

from the evangelical constituency, demonstrates that Christendom is surely not dead yet.

Depending on the Military

Last, the idea of Christian America also depends on the military to ensure that the North American way of life stays safe from hostile, non-Christian enemies of God and God's people. According to this feature of North American Christendom, *God is on the side of the United States of America*. This staple of historical Christendom, of course, justified the persecution of Jews, Muslims, and so-called Christian heretics such as the Donatists and the Anabaptists. Today many Christians believe that any threat to the safety of the nation (as well as other "freedom-loving" nations) should be quelled, by violence if necessary. If this means a preemptive strike, such as the one authorized in Iraq in 2003 as part of the US's war on terrorism, then so be it.

Christian America and the US military have enjoyed a strong relationship. Fueled by faith-inspired patriotism, church youth by the thousands join the military every year as an act of Christian duty. In the 2001 documentary *Constantine's Sword*, a segment depicts the pressure that non-Christians feel at the military bases in Colorado Springs (now a major hub of North American evangelicalism) to convert to Christianity.[15] The strong message emanating from the pressure goes something like this: if you are not a Christian, then you are not a true American and therefore not a trustworthy soldier.

These four interrelated aspects of Christian America—being God's chosen, expanding the faith territorially, keeping or restoring the Christian faith in the land, and protecting God's country by military might—capture the heartbeat of Christendom as it has manifested in a particular place among a particular people.

Christendom's Decline (Thank God!)

If we grasp just one main point from this brief treatment of North American Christendom, let it be that Christendom was and is a bad idea. Twenty-twenty hindsight acquits the ancient Donatists, the Waldensians, the Anabaptists, Søren Kierkegaard, Dietrich Bonhoeffer, and many other courageous souls who openly denounced, at great cost to themselves, the unholy marriage of church and state.

But, good news: Christendom is dying. Historians, theologians, and sociologists alike have rightly discerned that a shift has occurred, or is occurring,

---

15. *Constantine's Sword*, directed by Oren Jacoby (New York: First Run Features, 2008), DVD.

that threatens the very foundations of Christendom, thus ushering in a post-Christendom era. If they have discerned rightly, then we have reason to celebrate.

Unfortunately, a huge segment of the church has unwittingly accepted Christendom's assumptions and has felt its decline as cause for lament, as well as for preparing for battle to take the nation back for Christ. At the time of this writing, for example, a campaign has begun, led by David Lane, founder of the American Renewal Project, and endorsed by Colorado state representative Gordon Klingenschmitt, to recruit one thousand pastors to run for office as part of the effort "to take America back for the Kingdom of God."[16] Though I cannot disagree more with those who espouse this faulty "patriotic theology," their outcry actually verifies what the social commentators have discerned: the death knell of Christendom and the dawn of something new. Lane, Klingenschmitt, and many other champions of Christian America have sensed the loss of the once-assumed central power of the church to weave the moral, cultural, legal, and spiritual fabric of society, and they are fighting intensely to restore the church's and therefore the country's greatness. Their reactions verify the dawning of the post-Christendom era.

Stuart Murray describes post-Christendom as "the culture that emerges as the Christian faith loses coherence within a society that has been definitively shaped by the Christian story and as the institutions that have been developed to express Christian convictions decline in influence."[17] As part of the postmodern project, wherein certainty and authority have become suspect, "post-Christendom" refers to the marginalization of the church and the fragmentation of the church's mission. These words—"marginalization" and "fragmentation"—denote a negative, but to consider it alongside the negative of Christendom, we have before us a double negative, which, of course, grammatically constitutes a positive!

Church and Mission in the Post-Christendom Age

Several major shifts in church and mission emerged after Christendom. The church in the West feels them most acutely, but these shifts have tremendous implications for the whole global church.

---

16. Kellan Howell, "Evangelicals Launch Effort to Recruit 1000 Pastors to Run for Political Office," *Washington Times*, November 23, 2014, http://www.washingtontimes.com/news/201 4/nov/23/evangelical-david-lane-begins-effort-recruit-pasto. See also Kyle Mantyla, "Klingenschmitt Hopes Pastors Will Run for Office and 'Take Back America for the Kingdom of God,'" Right Wing Watch, February 9, 2015, http://www.rightwingwatch.org/content/klingenschmitt -hopes-pastors-will-run-office-and-take-back-america-kingdom-god.

17. Murray, *Post-Christendom*, 19.

Decentered Church

In a Christendom society, a church represents authority just as much as city hall; in a post-Christendom society, the church is just another institution, which may or may not have authority depending on what people give it. Granted, city hall does not hold as much sway either since postmodern sentiments have made it easier to question all types of authority, whether secular or religious. As for the church, an increasing number of the general population, especially in Europe and North America, no longer regard it as the keeper of truth and morality. The Pew Research Center, for example, confirms the rapid growth of the religiously unaffiliated, or "the Nones," in the US. It reports that "while nationwide surveys in the 1970s and '80s found that fewer than one-in-ten US adults said they had no religious affiliation, fully 23 percent now describe themselves as atheists, agnostics or 'nothing in particular.'"[18]

Significant indicators of the post-Christendom shift in the European and North American contexts would include a decline in traditional church attendance and an increase in commercial establishments being open for business on Sundays. In the US in particular the intensification of opposition to nativity scenes on government property, to "IN GOD WE TRUST" on currency, to the use of the Bible in courtrooms, and to the practice of prayer in schools signals the post-Christendom shift. In short, the church has been decentered in post-Christendom society; it has been marginalized.

To be pushed out of the center of sociopolitical and cultural dominance may not sound like a good thing, but it has begun to awaken the church to its true mission. As John Driver astutely observes, "When mission flows from centers of power and prestige, a certain kind of gospel is communicated, different from when the gospel is shared in weakness from the social periphery."[19] Driver and many other theologians and missiologists believe that when the church operates from the margins, its words and deeds have the ring of biblical, Christ-centered, Spirit-empowered authenticity.

The way Pastor Edwin Searcy describes his church's forced journey to the margins exemplifies this sense of authenticity. He reflects, "[University Hill Congregation in Canada] is a story of congregational dislocation and relocation. It is a story of how a congregation is re-discovering the gospel after being moved from mainline to sideline."[20] Because of steady membership

18. "Fact Tank," Pew Research Center, last updated September 14, 2016, http://www.pewre search.org/fact-tank/2016/09/14/the-factors-driving-the-growth-of-religious-nones-in-the-u-s.

19. John Driver, *Images of the Church in Mission* (Scottdale, PA: Herald Press, 1997), 227.

20. Edwin Searcy, "University Hill Congregation: From Dislocation to Relocation," unpublished presentation for Mid-Winter Convocation at Luther Seminary, St. Paul, MN, January 30–31, 2013.

decline, the once-prominent United Church of Canada congregation sold its building in the mid-1980s and eventually negotiated with the Vancouver School of Theology to use its chapel for Sunday morning worship, where it continues to hold services to this day.

The loss of place, Searcy continues, felt like a major setback when it first happened, but it has in time given the people of University Hill Congregation the opportunity to experience their faith afresh. He writes, "Three decades later [my church] looks back upon its painful dislocation from a propertied existence as the movement of the Holy Spirit. In giving up ownership of the church as a building the congregation was given the gift of rediscovering its identity as a people."[21]

The Whole Church on the Margins

Of course, I have thus far been speaking primarily about the white church in the post-Christendom West. I say "of course" because it has been the white church, and the white church alone, that has held political power through the ages and has therefore felt the impact of the post-Christendom shift most acutely. To be sure, immigrant and nonwhite churches have had a different experience with Christendom. Marginalized by race and culture, these churches have never "enjoyed" the center and have therefore been spared the experience of being decentered. As post-Christendom forces have pushed the white church out of the center, the white church has involuntarily joined the rest of the church on the margins.

As the church forever on the margins, nonwhite congregations have been in a position to have retained a powerful sense of Christ's lordship, identity, and mission. It therefore behooves the white church in these post-Christendom times, in the words of Soong-Chan Rah, "to submit to the spiritual authority of nonwhites,"[22] which will require significant adjustment. As Leroy Barber avers regarding nonwhite leaders, "We are not white people in red, yellow, black or brown skin. We bring a new approach to leadership, shaped by our cultures."[23] Post-Christendom times call the nonwhite church, which has always been on the margins, to lead the way in defining the identity and mission of God's people today.

In the post-Christendom era, the decentering of the white church has created an opportunity for the truly intercultural—that is, black, brown, and

---

21. Searcy, "University Hill Congregation."
22. Soong-Chan Rah, *The Next Evangelicalism* (Downers Grove, IL: IVP Books, 2009), 205.
23. Leroy Barber, *Red Brown Yellow Black White: Who's More Precious in God's Sight?* (New York: Jericho, 2014), 31.

white—church of Jesus Christ to be a prophetic presence in society, to model in word and deed gospel power, reconciliation, and unity across racial, ethnic, and cultural lines in a divided world. To the extent that the church makes good on this opportunity to be the whole global church from the margins, it positions itself to become the agent of reconciliation that its Lord has called it to be in a fractured world.

The Emergence of World Christianity

If "decentered church" describes post-Christendom's effects primarily in the West, then the emergence of Christianity as truly global and polycentric characterizes its positive effects on the global level. I say "emergence" not to convey that world Christianity represents something new on the scene, but rather that the post-Christendom age has enabled us to see anew the truly diverse, global nature of the Christian faith. As Allen Yeh notes, "This more recent phenomenon of world Christianity is a recovery not a discovery."[24]

Based on how this chapter has defined Christendom, Philip Jenkins's now-famous descriptor, "the next Christendom," is unfortunate.[25] By making "Christianity" and "Christendom" interchangeable, he inadvertently leaves the door open for misinterpretation. I am certain Jenkins did not mean to argue for this, but heaven forbid that Christendom has not died so much as it has simply moved to another part of the world! Giving him the benefit of the doubt, I interpret his thesis as verifying that a shift has indeed occurred in the world's Christian population from Europe and North America to Africa, Latin America, and Asia. "By 2050," he asserts, "only about one-fifth of the world's three billion Christians will be non-Hispanic whites." He continues: "The era of Western Christianity has passed within our lifetime, and the day of Southern Christianity is dawning. The fact of [this] change . . . is undeniable: it has happened, and will continue to happen."[26]

The church at large, however, has been slow to grasp this shift, despite the likes of Walbert Bühlmann, Andrew Walls, Kwame Bediako, and other scholars pointing it out for decades.[27] The 2011 Pew Research Report on Global

24. Allen Yeh, *Polycentric Missiology: Twenty-First Century Mission from Everywhere to Everywhere* (Downers Grove, IL: IVP Academic, 2016), 37.
25. Philip Jenkins, *The Next Christendom: The Coming of Global Christianity*, rev. ed. (Oxford: Oxford University Press, 2007).
26. Jenkins, *Next Christendom*, 3.
27. Walbert Bühlmann, *The Coming of the Third Church* (Maryknoll, NY: Orbis Books, 1977); Kwame Bediako, *Christianity in Africa: The Renewal of Non-Western Religion* (Maryknoll, NY: Orbis Books, 1996); Andrew Walls, *The Missionary Movement in Christian History* (Maryknoll, NY: Orbis Books, 1996). See also the Festschrift for Walls: William Burrows, Mark Gornik, and

Christianity documents this shift, reporting that out of the two-billion-plus Christians in the world, "1.3 billion . . . live in the Global South," that is, Africa, Latin America, and parts of Asia. Whereas in 1910, some 82.2 percent of Christians worldwide resided in the Global North (North America, Europe, Australia, New Zealand, and Japan), only 39.2 percent did so in 2010.[28] Jenkins suggests that "if we want to visualize a 'typical' contemporary Christian, we should think of a woman living in a village in Nigeria or in a Brazilian *favela*."[29] Indeed, an unprecedented world Christianity characterizes the post-Christendom age.

This should go without saying, but the idea of world Christianity should still include Europe and North America. The weight of Christianity may have shifted, but it would be misguided to believe that the Western church has somehow been replaced or left behind by non-Western forms of Christianity. Rather, other centers have been formed. Whereas the Western church was at some point *the* center, it is now one of many centers of Christianity around the world. "Christians are . . . geographically widespread," states the Pew Report, "so far-flung, in fact, that no single continent or region can indisputably claim to be the center of global Christianity."[30]

Multidirectional Mission

To be sure, Christianity has not disappeared in the West, but now that it makes as much sense to talk about Global South Christianity as it does Western Christianity, it stands to reason that mission flows multidirectionally. In a post-Christendom age, mission happens *from* the West, East, North, and South *to* the West, East, North, and South—from everywhere to everywhere. Multidirectional mission corresponds with the recovery of world Christianity. That being said, now that the majority weight of Christianity lies in the Global South, the South sits in prime position to lead the way. As Cardoza-Orlandi and Gonzalez qualify, "[The] missionary movement . . . moves in all directions yet with a major protagonist role coming from the South."[31]

Janice Beals, eds., *Understanding World Christianity: The Vision and Work of Andrew F. Walls* (Maryknoll, NY: Orbis Books, 2011).

28. "Global Christianity—A Report on the Size and Distribution of the World's Christian Population," Pew Research Center, December 19, 2011, http://www.pewforum.org/2011/12/19/global-christianity-exec.

29. Jenkins, *Next Christendom*, 1–2.

30. "Global Christianity—A Report on the Size and Distribution of the World's Christian Population."

31. Carlos F. Cardoza-Orlandi and Justo L. Gonzalez, *To All Nations from All Nations: A History of the Christian Missionary Movement* (Nashville: Abingdon, 2013), 449.

In the Christendom age, the Western church dominated the world scene and therefore claimed responsibility to evangelize the rest of the globe. Missions, therefore, appeared unidirectional from the dominant Western center to the ends or the outer "margins" of the earth. The editors of the important volume *Mission after Christendom*, however, provide a picture of the future trajectory of the church's global mission. They write, "Though previously mission was uni-directional, moving from the Western hemisphere to what were called mission territories, today mission seems to be from everywhere to everywhere."[32]

This phrase "from everywhere to everywhere" refers to a way of viewing mission as an enterprise of the global church scattered throughout the earth, not only enriching and growing itself in and through its diversity but also demonstrating the whole gospel of reconciliation for our broken, desperate world to see. Such a picture of the intercultural, missional, united, global church as reconciler becomes a viable possibility in a post-Christendom world.

"From everywhere to everywhere" also refers to flexible and resilient mission, shaped and reshaped by the various cultures involved in any given missionary encounter. Mission in a post-Christendom age has become a holy, beautiful mess! It does not have clearly defined messengers and recipients, or a one-way flow of personnel and finances, or a clear leadership structure. "The missionary movement is not a one-way street," assert Cardoza-Orlandi and Gonzalez, "but is rather a network with multiple intersections and crossings, so that one cannot point to a particular center or to an established pattern of lineal, cumulative, and progressive movement. The fuller picture presents a much freer and fragile movement with success and failure, enthusiasm, frustrations, ambiguities, and perplexities."[33]

The collapse of Christendom enables us to see more clearly the multidirectionality of the growth of the church through mission. Furthermore, it enables us to bear witness to the truly diverse, global nature of the Christian faith and thus inch closer to becoming an agent of reconciliation in a fractured world.

"From everywhere to everywhere" refers to one more crucial point: the deemphasis on territorial expansion. The post-Christendom age compels us to go beyond thinking of mission in primarily geographical terms; after all, mission is from everywhere to everywhere. As mentioned earlier, territorial expansion bears the mark of mission practice under Christendom. As Walls contends, in contrast to Christianity, Christendom suggests "an entity with

32. Peter Vethanayagamony and Edmund Kee-Fook Chia, introduction to *Mission after Christendom*, ed. Ogbu Kalu, Peter Vethanayagamony, and Edmund Kee-Fook Chia (Louisville: Westminster John Knox, 2010), xvii.
33. Cardoza-Orlandi and Gonzalez, *To All Nations from All Nations*, 434.

temporal dimensions, something that can be plotted out on a map."[34] So as Christendom began to colonize the globe, missionaries went hand in hand with armed explorers (conquistadors) to grow the church. In a Christendom context, "to spread the gospel" virtually meant the same as the goal of adding to the list of Christian territories throughout the world. As post-Christendom takes hold, territorial expansion takes a backseat (if it should be allowed in the car at all!) in favor of genuine multidirectional mission by God's whole church among all populations. From everywhere to everywhere.

In a post-Christendom world, the whole church together has the unprecedented opportunity to engage in the whole mission of God as the intercultural body of Christ. This is what Walls calls "the Ephesian moment," a coming together of cultures in Christ that demonstrates what God desires—the healing of the nations and the reconciliation of all things. Whereas the original situation in Ephesus (Eph. 2) involved the coming together of two cultural blocs—Jew and gentile—many cultures now make up today's worldwide church.[35] "Perhaps the most striking single feature of Christianity today," Walls celebrates, "is the fact that the church now looks more like that great multitude whom none can number, drawn from all tribes and kindreds, people and tongues, than ever before in its history."[36] To take full advantage of our Ephesian moment in a post-Christendom age will require a posture of intercultural learning and mutual partnership.

The church in the West in a post-Christendom world has been decentered, creating an opportunity for the whole church to take full advantage of "the Ephesian moment." The time is now for the global church to demonstrate racial, ethnic, intertribal, international reconciliation and unity; to be a prophetic presence in society based on God's peace, justice, and freedom; and to preach the good news of the kingdom of God from everywhere to everywhere.

Postcolonialism, post-Christendom's close cousin, constitutes yet another global phenomenon that will require new thinking and new practices on the part of the whole church. To this we now turn.

Discussion Questions

1. What is the difference between Christendom and biblical Christianity?
2. Is Christian America a form of Christendom? Why or why not?

34. Walls, *Cross-Cultural Process*, 36.
35. Walls, *Cross-Cultural Process*, 78.
36. Walls, *Cross-Cultural Process*, 47.

3. What would be characteristic of a "church on the margins," compared to a church sharing political power in the center?

4. Global mission today can be described as "from everywhere to everywhere," meaning that traditionally mission-sending countries are now also receiving missionaries. Could the US be considered a mission field to which churches in other countries send missionaries? In what ways?

THREE

Postcolonialism

Postcolonial Mission or Bust

. . . .

What God has made clean, you must not call profane.
—A voice from heaven (Acts 10:15)

My doctoral studies at the Graduate Theological Union in Berkeley, California, began with a jolt. I met with a well-known theology professor, hoping he would resonate with my dissertation idea and consider being my supervisor. Just a few months removed from a decade of mission work in my native country of the Philippines, I expressed my excitement at the prospect of contributing to the field of missiology, necessarily saying "mission-this" and "mission-that" in my telling. I went on for several minutes when he suddenly interrupted me midsentence and said, "Al, I'm sorry to say this, but we don't use that language around here."

"I don't know what you mean," I responded quickly, ready to own whatever foul language I might have inadvertently blurted out.

"Mission, missionary, and the like. We don't use those words here."

I was taken aback, even slightly offended. I was literally at a loss for words for the rest of the conversation. The man took this missionary's language away! My first encounter with a critical spirit toward mission from a Christian theologian left me speechless and a little defensive. Generally speaking, evangelical missionary types have no tools to deal with criticism leveled against the most holy task of world evangelization (that is, apart from criticism from non-Christian antagonists), and I was no exception.

In time, however, I began to understand that professor's kind retort as my sustained and honest study of mission inevitably led me down the historical path of colonialism and the undeniable role that Christian missions played in it. My eyes opened to the underside of mission history, revealing the systematic and brutal eradication of whole cultures, yes, in the name of the crown and in the service of the Westernization of the world, but also in the name of Jesus Christ and in the service of the so-called Great Commission to make disciples of all nations. Indeed, as part of the colonial project, "the missionaries viewed the Great Commission as the mandate to convert the indigenous people to Christianity, and they dedicated all their efforts and the means at their disposal, including coercion, to make this happen."[1]

The formerly colonized and their succeeding generations, "the victims of the Great Commission," long muted by dominant histories that painted the indigenous as uncivilized, unintelligent, and inarticulate, have begun to raise their voices and to tell their stories as the world enters a postcolonial era. We come to the last global reality—postcolonialism—that we will analyze in this book as we conclude our attempt to contextualize the world for the sake of mission. As Jorge Rieger asserts, "The quality of international encounters, if not the future of theology and mission, depends on how we deal with colonialism, neocolonialism, and postcolonialism."[2]

What is postcolonialism? What does it call for? How does it challenge Christian mission? And assuming that the missionary enterprise survives the crucible of postcolonial critique, what might be included in what we can call a postcolonial missiology?

The Idea of Colonialism

Understanding postcolonialism, which, according to R. S. Sugirtharajah, refers more to a criticism than a theory,[3] necessitates gaining a basic grasp of the object of its critique, namely, the phenomenon of colonialism—its motives,

1. Beatrice Okyere-Manu, "Colonial Mission and the Great Commission in Africa," in *Teaching All Nations: Interrogating the Matthean Great Commission*, ed. Mitzi J. Smith and Jayachitra Lalitha (Minneapolis: Fortress, 2014), 24.
2. Jorge Rieger, "Theology and Mission between Neocolonialism and Postcolonialism," *Mission Studies* 21, no. 2 (2004): 202.
3. R. S. Sugirtharajah, quoted by Robert S. Heaney, introduction to *Evangelical Postcolonial Conversations: Global Awakenings in Theology and Praxis*, ed. Kay Higuera Smith, Jayachitra Lalitha, and L. Daniel Hawk (Downers Grove, IL: IVP Academic, 2014), 31.

justifications, implementation, and consequences. For our purposes, it will be especially important to understand the role of Christian missions in the colonization of the world.

To speak of a colonial era belies that people have been dominating other people since time immemorial, or, from a biblical perspective, since sin entered the world in Genesis 3. In the very next chapter, Cain kills Abel, and by chapter 6, "the earth was corrupt in God's sight, and the earth was filled with violence" (v. 11). One simply needs to think of ancient conquests led by the likes of Alexander the Great, Genghis Khan, Attila the Hun, Shih Huang-ti, Montezuma, and many more to validate the biblical text that the subjugation of some peoples by other peoples has been a staple of postfall human existence. In this light, we can say that "colonialism" existed long before Christopher Columbus set sail in 1492 CE and accidentally discovered what we now call the Americas.

Nonetheless, the conquest of the Americas marked the beginning of modern colonialism. Melvin Page defines that era as "the development of particular patterns of settlement, control of external lands, and associated ideologies of domination that first found expression in Europe during the fifteenth and sixteenth centuries."[4] In a span of approximately five hundred years—from the late fifteenth to the mid-twentieth century—European nations and, later, North America used their religiopolitical power and military superiority to extend their respective empires in the Americas, Africa, and Asia on a grand scale never before experienced in human history. Economic gain (commerce) and the quest for world dominance (crown) obviously drove the colonial project, and one could make a case that greed and the desire to be on top of the world sufficiently explain the logic of colonialism. Indeed, commerce and crown represent indomitable forces.

However, the way colonizers executed the vision methodically, thoroughly, and with great cruelty compels us to see beyond the obvious, to go below the surface of commerce and crown, and to understand the deeper factors that made colonialism possible. Why was it acceptable to claim already-occupied lands, raze peaceful and high-functioning villages, destroy well-established family structures, take away people's names, enslave and torture millions, kill the uncooperative, decimate entire populations, and extinguish whole cultures? "I am talking about societies drained of their essence," laments Aimé Césaire, "cultures trampled underfoot, institutions undermined, lands confiscated, religions smashed, magnificent artistic creations destroyed,

4. Melvin Page, preface to *Colonialism: An International Social, Cultural and Political Encyclopedia*, ed. Melvin E. Page (Santa Barbara, CA: ABC-CLIO, 2004), xxi.

extraordinary possibilities wiped out."[5] The expansion of European and
Euro-American empires throughout the world occurred by means of cultural genocide, "the effective destruction of a people by systematically . . .
destroying, eroding, or undermining the integrity of the culture and system
of values that defines a people and gives them life."[6]

Is it enough to pin these atrocities on the base pursuits of greed and power?
Could the motives behind colonialism have been that overtly and consciously
evil? Today we can see with 20/20 hindsight the evil of colonialism, but what
blinded the colonizing nations, good Christian people—missionaries, no
less—from seeing it? Beyond commerce and crown, two worldview-defining
narratives explain more clearly the atrocities committed in the colonial era:
civilization and Christianization. These two intertwined worldviews made
the idea of colonialism morally justifiable; they actually convinced colonizing
nations and their churches that remaking people in the civilized and Christianized image of the West was a good thing. This speaks to the power of
grand narratives.

To Civilize: Racism's Contribution to Colonialism

The responsibility to bless the rest of the world with the "gift of civilization" constituted the first sincere but tragically misguided narrative. Eu-
ropeans/Euro-Americans truly believed that Providence had endowed them
with superior intelligence, universal values, and more sophisticated culture,
as advances in industry, education, military might, and urban development
could attest. This Providence was first based primarily on religious grounds;
for whatever reason, God made them superior over the rest. But later, lest
religion be wholly blamed, secular Enlightenment thinking, particularly Darwinism and the concept of the survival of the fittest, became the ideological
basis of the notion of Western cultural superiority.[7]

A sense of moral obligation, therefore, virtually required "the superior"
to enlighten the darkened (physically and spiritually) cultures of the world.
Paternalism was palpable. Black and brown peoples needed to be civilized,
which meant, from the perspective of the colonizing nations, that they had
to become European or Euro-American in their lifeways and worldview. Of

5. Aimé Césaire, *Discourse on Colonialism*, trans. Joan Pinkham (New York: Monthly
Review, 2000), 43.
6. George Tinker, *Missionary Conquest: The Gospel and Native American Cultural Genocide* (Minneapolis: Fortress, 1993), 6.
7. Peter Kivisto, "Racism," in *Encyclopedia of Religion and Society*, ed. William H. Swatos Jr.
(Walnut Creek, CA: Altamira, 1998), 400.

course, given their alleged inferior makeup (not just physically but psychologically, emotionally, and spiritually), they could never be as European as Europeans, or as Euro-American as Euro-Americans, and thus they would forever occupy a subordinate place in society.

The inextricable link between colonialism and racism comes into full view here. According to Peter Kivisto, "The impetus for [racial divisions] revolved around the question of what kinds of policies Europeans ought to enact in establishing relations with the indigenous peoples they encountered."[8] However, Europeans did not determine human variation neutrally, as if they created race language simply to distinguish one kind of human from another; on the contrary, the categories of white and nonwhite (Negro, colored, black, yellow, Oriental, Indian, and so on) conveyed domination. Race became (and remains) a social construct that placed European and Euro-American at the top of the heap (of course, considering who did the constructing!), establishing white mastery over "inferior," nonwhite peoples. The very categories of race, therefore, were (and are) inherently racist.

Colonization's relationship to slavery also comes into full view. Though they differ in nature, colonization and slavery are joined at the hip by the racist ideology that drove the colonial project. While colonization was the overall aim of civilizing the world, necessarily subjugating native populations, the advancement of civilization depended on the institution of slavery. In the case of the United States, the new European settlers colonized First Nations peoples, while they imported and enslaved Africans to advance civilization on the North American continent. Both First Nations peoples and African Americans, however, share the historical experience of being on the wrong side of racism for the sake of civilization.

In any case, the religioscientific social construction of race—or, in Robert Sussman's more succinct descriptor, the "myth of race," along with the inherent myth of white superiority[9]—resulted in an obligation to civilize nonwhite cultures, even if the task meant pain, suffering, destruction, enslavement, and death to the people of these inferior cultures. Within such a racist framework, to civilize, even by way of conquest, was not only morally justifiable, it was also the responsible thing to do. Colonizers saw the great suffering endured by the native populations of Africa, Asia, and the Americas as the necessary price for the gift of civilization!

8. Kivisto, "Racism," 399.
9. Robert W. Sussman, *The Myth of Race: The Troubling Persistence of an Unscientific Idea* (Cambridge, MA: Harvard University Press, 2014), 2.

To Christianize, Part 1: Religion's Contribution to Colonialism

Part of "this gift" entailed the privilege of Christian conversion. Christendom could not fathom civilization without Christianization, the second narrative that drove the colonial project. Related inseparably to the civilization narrative, the Christianization narrative went something like this: these people, inferior, unenlightened, and uncivilized as they may be, need to adhere to the one true religion to be saved from the fires of hell, even if against their will in this life. Europeans/Euro-Americans thought of themselves as superior in large part because they believed that God revealed the one true religion to them and therefore called them to serve as its keepers and evangelizers. In this light, to Christianize these hell-bound savages, to baptize them as "new believers" into the church, which also meant razing their idolatrous temples and outlawing their religious practices, became the responsibility of the church of the colonial project. To Christianize, or to engage in missions, was necessary to civilize the people, but more than that, it was necessary for the salvation of their souls.

It made sense in this light to engage, if need be, in what Luis Rivera calls a "violent evangelism." Rivera quotes the Requerimiento of 1513, a document read by the conquistadors to the natives of the Americas, compelling them to submit to Spain and Spain's God. It reads in part:

> I beg and require of you . . . to recognize the church as lady and superior of the universe and to acknowledge the Supreme Pontiff, called Pope . . . and the king and queen . . . as lords and superiors. . . . If you do not do it, . . . then with the help of God I will undertake powerful action against you. I will make war on you everywhere and in every way that I can. I will subject you to the yoke and obedience of the church and of your Highnesses. I will take you personally and your wives and children, and make slaves of you, . . . and I will take away your property and cause you all the evil and harm I can.[10]

Christendom—the unholy alliance of church and state, cross and flag, Bible and gun—made this method of evangelism (if we can call it that) conceivable. And although some missionaries spoke out against the Requerimiento and other similar decrees, the missionary enterprise on the whole did not challenge the Christianization narrative, and therefore could not avoid taking part in the evil of colonialism. Referring to missionaries among the First Nations people, George "Tink" Tinker writes, "They surely did not intend any harm to Indian people, yet their blindness to their own inculturation of European

10. The Requerimiento, quoted in Luis Rivera, *A Violent Evangelism: The Political and Religious Conquest of the Americas* (Louisville: Westminster John Knox, 1992), 24.

values and social structures meant that complicity was unavoidable."[11] This complicity and the evangelistic methods it produced have enabled church critics over the last few centuries to speak of missions, racism, and colonialism in the same historical breath; they were and are not wrong!

To Christianize, Part 2: Missions' Contribution to Colonialism

Nevertheless, missions contributed in morally mixed ways to the colonization of the non-Western world. It did, for example, temper the cruelty of conquest. Many missionaries, Bartolomé de Las Casas perhaps the best known among them, "defended the humanity [of the natives], their capacity to receive the faith, to practice self-government and to exercise reason."[12] We can only speculate as to how much worse colonialism would have been if missionaries such as de Las Casas had not denounced the maltreatment of the native population, as well as the enslavement of imported Africans. These missionaries, despite not challenging the Christianization narrative itself, advocated for the humanity of the native population, as well as their ability to come to faith in Christ. For example, David Bosch quotes a French governor of Madagascar as accusingly saying to the missionaries, "What we want is to prepare the indigenous population for manual labor; you turn them into people."[13]

In a fascinating, against-the-grain political-scientific study, Robert Woodberry makes a series of bold claims related to the theory that the work of "conversionary Protestant missionaries" during the colonial period played a central role in the formation of democratic societies.[14] We cannot analyze his full argument here, but at the center of his assertions lies the bold claim that such missionaries as Alice Seeley Harris in Congo, John Mackenzie in Botswana, Ida Sophia Scudder in India, and others who did their significant part in contributing to colonial reform represented the majority rather than the minority of missionaries in the colonial era.[15] In other words, according to Woodberry, the evidence shows that the missionary enterprise on the whole

11. Tinker, *Missionary Conquest*, 15.
12. Scott W. Sunquist, *Understanding Christian Mission: Participation in Suffering and Glory* (Grand Rapids: Baker Academic, 2013), 56.
13. David J. Bosch, *Transforming Mission*, 20th anniv. ed. (Maryknoll, NY: Orbis Books, 2011), 311.
14. Robert D. Woodberry, "The Missionary Roots of Liberal Democracy," *American Political Science Review* 106, no. 2 (May 2012): 244–74.
15. Woodberry, "Missionary Roots," 253–55. To read more on the missionaries listed in the context of Woodberry's study, see Andrea Palpant Dilley, "The World the Missionaries Made," *Christianity Today*, January/February 2014, 38–39.

did more to reform colonialism than to help it along. Whether this and other related claims will stand the test of follow-up studies remains to be seen. However, at minimum, Woodberry's research shows that colonial cruelty against native populations did not go unchecked by courageous missionaries.

Second, and related to the first point, missions certainly contributed to the worldwide spread of the gospel, thus paving the way for contextual "Christianities" to break away from Eurocentric and Americentric cultural captivity. Though the ends certainly do not justify the means, something resembling authentic Christian faith emerged from the interaction between missionaries and the peoples of the Americas, Africa, and Asia, creating enduring non-Western expressions of Christianity. So despite the evil soil of colonialism in which the gospel was planted, genuine non-Western versions of the faith found their way to the surface. This is no small miracle, attesting to the Spirit-led ability of native peoples to extricate truth from its racist, paternalistic wrappings. "Through twenty centuries in which diverse empires have risen and fallen," writes Samuel Escobar, "the Holy Spirit has continually driven Christians to obedience, so that today we have a global church."[16]

The previous two contributions described how missionaries challenged colonialism; the next two describe how they helped to advance it. Missions undoubtedly enabled the success of the colonial project by subduing the native population—embarrassingly, in retrospect—through catechesis (or "teaching all nations") with what passed for gospel. Missionaries taught and preached peace in Christ, respect for one's master, present endurance of suffering in anticipation of future bliss, and other such lessons, thereby domesticating the native population in the name and power of Christendom. By accepting this gospel, the colonized went from being warriors and defenders of their ways of life to docile subjects of the colonial system. For example, the specialized catechisms written for slaves by North American Protestant churches taught

> that God, the Great Creator, spoke to them commanding them to accept white Christian norms; that God was their heavenly master whom they should obey; that they have a moral duty to obey their earthly masters too; that God spoke to them in the Bible, even though they were forbidden to or unable to read the Bible; that God sees and hears everything so that attempts to commit any sins (i.e., acts of resistance) would be futile and would result in God's wrath; and that any trouble that afflicts them should be considered an act of God.[17]

16. Samuel Escobar, *The New Global Mission: The Gospel from Everywhere to Everywhere* (Downers Grove, IL: IVP Academic, 2005), 13.
17. Mitzi J. Smith, "US Colonial Missions to African Slaves: Catechizing Black Souls, Traumatizing the Black Psyche," in Smith and Lalitha, *Teaching All Nations*, 85.

Furthermore, missions aided in not just subduing the native and enslaved populations by way of a procolonial, domesticating gospel; it also "educated" them. I put quotation marks around the word because today education conveys self-actualization and empowerment. The schools established in colonial lands, on the other hand, had opposite aims: to replace identity and to disempower—that is, to assimilate. While the government sponsored these schools, such as the ones established for First Nations peoples in the US and Canada, the church ran them in many cases as part of its mission in the late nineteenth and twentieth centuries.[18] These schools sought to "kill the Indian in the child." Separated from their parents and required to stay at faraway boarding schools, native children endured the process of being "remade" in the image of a people they could never become. The curriculum undermined native lifeways as it sought to indoctrinate students into white religion, white values, and white ways of life. The teachers forbade the children to speak in their native tongue or to engage in any form of native practice. If they did so, forms of punishment included food deprivation, solitary confinement, and sometimes severe beatings. These schools exemplified the ultimate in white colonial assimilation, which Tinker and others rightfully call nothing less than ethnocide and ultimately genocide.[19]

Undoubtedly, commerce and crown provided the base motives for colonialism, but the coterminous worldviews of civilization and Christianization made it entirely possible, morally responsible, and spiritually justifiable. Indeed, colonialism became "the white man's burden; colonial officials and missionaries alike gladly but consciously took it upon themselves to be the guardians of these incapable, less-developed races."[20] Commerce and crown, undergirded by the civilization and Christianization narratives, proved a lethal combination for millions of people all over the world.

The Postcolonial Critique

In light of the obvious evil of what we can call the four Cs of colonialism—commerce, crown, civilization, and Christianization—we cannot overcelebrate the dawning of the postcolonial age. Scholars identify the period following World War II, when nations in Africa, Asia, and Latin America started to gain their independence, as the beginning of this age. So "postcolonial" can simply mean the world after colonialism, a periodization that indicates

18. Gregory Lee Cuellar and Randy S. Woodley, "North American Mission and Motive," in Smith, Lalitha, and Hawk, *Evangelical Postcolonial Conversations*, 68.
19. Cuellar and Woodley, "North American Mission and Motive," 68.
20. Bosch, *Transforming Mission*, 308.

a beginning point of dramatic change in sociopolitical relationships between nations, as well as a specific point in history that marks the culmination of centuries of resistance against colonial domination.[21]

But the word does more than just mark time; it also conveys a perspective, a critique, a powerful school of thought that has arisen from the bottom up. It refers to a space wherein the formerly colonized have found their voices to lament the tremendous loss they incurred through centuries of colonial rule. It also refers to a platform from which they raise awareness of colonialism's ongoing influence today via ideological globalization and neocolonialisms, as well as forge new ways of relating to the formerly colonizing white world as free and equal peoples.

The postcolonial critique naturally tends to make the white world uncomfortable and even angry since this critique calls for an accounting of colonial sins and calls out practices today that resemble colonialism. Moreover, it seeks to reclaim identities, ways of life, and values destroyed by the colonial project, and thus feels threatening to some. The late Richard Twiss, for example, recounts a time when he and a group of First Nations Christian leaders tried to book a space at a Christian retreat center. They received a reprimanding rejection letter, which read in part, "In your effort to 'restore culture' you are taking the indigenous people back into paganism, shamanism, false gods and the occult. You are leading them away from the Gospel message of the Bible." A brief exchange ensued between the center registrar and Twiss, ending in the registrar's final decision: "I hear what you're saying, but we still cannot support what your group [is] teaching. No retreat at our facility."[22]

Postcolonialism deconstructs, interrogates, and challenges these sorts of lingering biases. It detects and calls out any manifestation of any of the four Cs of colonialism. In light of missions' collusion with colonialism, one can argue that "postcolonial mission" constitutes an oxymoron. Tinker does exactly that, questioning the legitimacy of continuing the missionary enterprise at all. He writes, "Given the disastrous history of euro-western mission practices—to the culture and the peoplehood of those missionized—it would seem that there are no missiological projects that we might conceive that would have legitimacy of any kind."[23]

21. Robert J. C. Young, *Postcolonialism: A Very Short Introduction* (Oxford: Oxford University Press, 2003), 3.

22. Richard Twiss, *Rescuing the Gospel from the Cowboys: A Native American Expression of the Jesus Way* (Downers Grove, IL: InterVarsity, 2015), 18–20.

23. Tink Tinker, "The Romance and Tragedy of Christian Mission," in *Remembering Jamestown: Hard Questions about Christian Mission*, ed. Amos Yong and Barbara Brown Zikmund (Eugene, OR: Pickwick, 2010), 26–27.

However, an authentic expression of the gospel inherently includes a fundamental call to participate in the transformation of the world, that is, mission. Herein lies the dilemma: the impulse to disassociate completely from the history of colonial-stained missions while knowing that mission lies at the very heart of the Christian faith. The church today should struggle with this dilemma; it should let the ghosts of the colonial past disturb our sleep, for in the wrestling, something resembling postcolonial mission might emerge.

My own experience of wrestling with the church's colonial past bears this out. This wrestling led me to a crossroads, with one way—the way of disassociating from missions altogether and quitting being a missionary—strongly beckoning me. But I realized that by abandoning mission I would be abandoning the Christian faith as I understood it, which I was not ready to do. The other way—the way of doing mission radically different—also beckoned me. I eventually chose the latter, but not without serious soul-searching and learning what that might look like. This book, in fact, reflects much of what I am learning, and it gives me hope that we can and must engage in postcolonial mission.

Indeed, this kind of wrestling leads most Christians (including Tinker[24]) to believe that the church cannot throw the proverbial baby out with the bathwater. The whole gospel—the very good news of Jesus Christ—compels us to engage the world in mission. But how does it do so while avoiding the bathwater of colonialism?

As Sathianathan Clarke asserts, "Ruptures and wounds caused by misdirected Christian mission [via colonialism] must be attended to, but terminating all mission activity cannot repair them." He even goes so far as to say that, ultimately, "mission inaction is an irresponsible cop-out and a form of escapism."[25] A Christian postcolonial perspective decries the domination, violence, ethnocentrism, racism, paternalism, and cultural genocide of the colonial past and nurtures "a holy suspicion" of missionary postures or activities that resemble that past; but ultimately, Christian postcolonialism calls for a reimagining, not an abandoning of mission. This reimagining that must occur needs to go through, not around, the postcolonial critique. By trying to go around it, the church risks committing the same mistakes under different guises. Let the church's missionary mantra be "Postcolonial mission or bust!"

How should postcolonial sensibilities reshape the church's global mission? I see two distinct sets of characteristics in answer to this question.

24. Tinker, "Romance and Tragedy," 27.
25. Sathianathan Clarke, "World Christianity and Postcolonial Mission: A Path Forward for the Twenty-First Century," *Theology Today* 71, no. 2 (2014): 200.

Postcolonial Implications for the Western Church-in-Mission

What postcolonialism demands of the once-dominant missionary force of the formerly colonial North and West makes up the first set.

Confession, Repentance . . . and Restitution

The need for the Western church to confess and repent of its colonial past sits at the top of this set. Confession, which leads to repentance, is a natural part of the Christian life, as sinful people bow down to a holy God. Consistent with hyperindividualism, however, Western Christians tend to see confession as a strictly personal matter.

For example, several years ago I called a group of North American Christians to repent of the sin of racism at an interchurch gathering. My words upset at least two people in the audience, who later proceeded to challenge me vehemently in stereo (at least they waited until question-and-answer time). That they themselves did not individually enslave black people, and that they did not consider themselves racist, fueled their argument. Several others in the audience seemed to nod in approval. Individually they did not commit the sin of racism (so they believed!), so it was offensive to them that I would make them feel guilty about it and call them to repentance.

The Bible, however, rebuts their solely personal view of sin and repentance, for it often calls for community confession and repentance. A few examples include the Lord's famous words to Solomon the night after the dedication of the temple (2 Chron. 7:14), Nehemiah's lament and confession on behalf of Israel (Neh. 1:5–6), Isaiah's call for corporate repentance and justice (Isa. 1:4–31), Jesus's prayer of confession (Matt. 6:12), and Peter's charge against the entire house of Israel, which led many to repent (Acts 2:36–38).

The sins of colonialism, or more specifically the sins of colonial missions, run quite consistently with the type of transgressions for which the Bible calls God's people to corporate repentance. Jeremy Bergen's excellent work on ecclesial repentance commits a whole chapter to the efforts of various church bodies to repent of their colonial past. These include the "Apology to First Nations," issued in 1986 by the United Church of Christ of Canada; Pope John Paul II's public acknowledgment of the need of the Catholic Church "to make an act of atonement for the sin, injustice and violence done on the American continent and [to ask] forgiveness first of Indians [Native Americans], then of black slaves"; the "Sand Creek Apology," delivered in 1996 by the United Methodist Church in the US for the 1864 massacre of "200 Cheyenne persons at the hands of a militia led by a lay Methodist minister"; the "Service of Memory and Reconciliation" held in 2007 by the Baptist World

Alliance in Ghana, in which the statement "An Apology for the Transatlantic Slave Trade" was delivered; and the list goes on.[26] At the time of this writing, Pope Francis apologized to indigenous peoples gathered together in Bolivia "for the sins and offenses committed by the Catholic Church . . . during the colonial-era conquest of the Americas."[27]

Bergen's work reflects a fundamental aspect of the nature of repentance, which involves a long process in contrast to a onetime act. He notes that the First Nations people responded to the 1986 apology issued by the United Church of Canada by acknowledging the apology but not accepting it; for, as UCC aboriginal minister Alf Dumont stated, "[It] must be lived out if it's to be a real apology." That sentiment challenged the UCC "to see an apology not primarily as closure but an ongoing task."[28]

The notion of repentance as an ongoing task more than hints at an aspect of postcolonial missionary repentance that needs to be considered—namely, the need for restitution wherever possible. Genuine repentance has with it a desire to make things right; it "requires an about-face in our actions and a deep change in our way of life."[29] For example, Bergen reports that the official apology from UCC leaders to First Nations people included the following concrete steps: "the establishment of the All Native Circle Conference, programmes of aboriginal theological education, a healing Fund especially for the legacy of residential schools, and an initiative to explore the relationship of Traditional and Christian spiritualities."[30]

The land reform program that has been implemented in postapartheid South Africa provides another example. Jakobus Vorster reports that provisions have been made not only for all to have access to the land (not just white South Africans, as was the case in colonial times) but also for the dispossessed (the former colonized and their children) to be assisted by the government in obtaining the needed resources for the acquisition of land.[31] The point is, genuine corporate repentance on the part of the Western church should

26. Jeremy Bergen, *Ecclesial Repentance: The Churches Confront Their Sinful Pasts* (New York: T&T Clark, 2011), 57–85. Bergen also provides a comprehensive list of statements of confession and repentance in the appendix, on 319–26.

27. Nicole Winfield and Jacobo Garcia, "Pope Apologizes for 'Offenses' against Indigenous Peoples," *Huffpost Religion*, July 10, 2015, http://www.huffingtonpost.com/entry/pope-francis-apologizes-for-catholic-churchs-offenses-against-indigenous-peoples_559f02aae4b096729155dd59.

28. Bergen, *Ecclesial Repentance*, 59.

29. Mae Elise Cannon, Lisa Sharon Harper, Troy Jackson, and Soong-Chan Rah, *Forgive Us: Confessions of a Compromised Faith* (Grand Rapids: Zondervan, 2014), 25.

30. Bergen, *Ecclesial Repentance*, 245.

31. Jakobus Vorster, "The Ethics of Land Restitution," *Journal of Religious Ethics* 34, no. 4 (2006): 699–700.

result in supporting policies and practices of restitution wherever, whenever, and however possible.

The authors of *Forgive Us*, though not specifying the Western church's sins under colonialism, do write the following words that apply: "As Christians, we are guilty before God and before the world. God sees it. The world sees it—and because the world sees our sin and perceives that we have not removed the log from our own eye before calling out the specks in the eyes of others, our hypocrisy has been exposed. We have damaged our own witness to the world."[32] Confession that leads to genuine repentance that leads to restitution would do much to reverse the church's damaged witness.

Corporate Humility

The sincerity of confession, repentance, and restitution depends on genuine humility on the part of the Western missionary community. Christian faith requires humility of all Christians, but once again, because of the Western tendency toward individualism, humility remains exclusively within the realm of personal virtue. Postcolonialism, however, demands genuine humility of corporate proportions. This will take nothing less than radical culture change in churches and missionary-sending agencies in the West.

It would likely require "deconstruction projects" to dislodge deep-seated, lingering notions of superiority. Like bad tattoos, missionary condescension, paternalism, and cultural arrogance do not go away by the mere passage of time. Practices and policies linger, not just of the colonial past but also of the postcolonial present. Current realities that come to mind include missionaries openly criticizing the lifeways of host cultures; nationals, even ones who are older, addressing missionaries by titles such as "mother," "father," "aunt," or "uncle"; policies preventing nationals from applying as missionaries (i.e., this is reserved only for Westerners); policies against cross-cultural courting and marrying; and the list goes on.

To remove these colonial tattoos requires intentionality (and surgical pain, to be consistent with the metaphor). For example, what if rehearsing colonial missions history became a mandatory part of missionary training? What if the church began to change its missionary language, steering clear of words such as "crusade," "marching orders," "furlough," and other military-related terms?[33] What if listening and learning came to be valued just as highly as speaking and teaching? Seriously addressing questions of this sort can help

32. Cannon et al., *Forgive Us*, 21–22.
33. E.g., Campus Crusade for Christ changed its name to Cru in 2011 in part to disassociate itself from the negative connotations of "crusade." See Sarah Bailey, "Campus Crusade Changes

the Western church to begin replacing colonial missionary condescension with a disposition that resembles genuine, Christlike humility.

Power Dynamics

The granddaddy of postcolonial questions has to do with the complex issue of power. The effort to change the power dynamics between Western missionaries and non-Western churches indicates a maturing missionary humility. However, seventy years of "officially" living into the postcolonial age have only proved that, generally speaking, the relationship between Western missionaries and the formerly colonized remains unequal.

What if, instead of defaulting to being trainers and imparters of Western knowledge, approaches, technologies, and systems (which, subconsciously or not, Westerners think are better than those of the respective host countries), missionaries went with a posture of subordination to the leadership of the national church? Missionaries must intentionally pull back from assuming the role of leader/trainer/teacher. "Please," Melba Maggay urges, "no more missionaries with an awful teacher complex."[34]

Furthermore, in light of the undeniable relationship between power and money, the Western missionary community needs to reconsider the wealth that it represents and actually brings into very poor contexts. Jonathan Bonk, in his classic *Missions and Money*, describes the devastating consequences of affluence in terms of strained interpersonal relationships with the much poorer host peoples, ineffective and distorted communication of the gospel, and unsustainable strategies, not to mention the dissonance of affluence with biblical teaching on wealth and poverty.[35]

Elsewhere I suggest four principles of what I call "whole-life stewardship," which applies perhaps more urgently for Western missionaries than anyone else. I plead for God's people to practice biblical stewardship (1) by having a careful view of wealth, (2) by demonstrating kingdom generosity, (3) by committing to simple living, and (4) by living as if the physical creation—the earth—itself mattered.[36]

Its Name to Cru," *Christianity Today*, July 19, 2011, http://www.christianitytoday.com/ct/2011/julyweb-only/campus-crusade-name-change.html.

34. Melba P. Maggay, "Some Do's and Don'ts," in *Communicating Cross-Culturally: Toward a New Context for Missions in the Philippines*, ed. Melba P. Maggay (Quezon City, Philippines: New Day, 1989), 27.

35. Jonathan Bonk, *Missions and Money: Affluence as a Western Missionary Problem* (Maryknoll, NY: Orbis Books, 1991), 43–107.

36. Al Tizon, *Missional Preaching: Engage, Embrace, Transform* (Valley Forge, PA: Judson, 2012), 106–11.

Obviously, we can say much more about the complex nature of money, leadership, and power dynamics in the missionary/national church relationship. The important point is that postcolonialism demands ongoing conversations regarding these matters, with a trajectory toward understanding the proper way to practice power in the cross-cultural encounter, power that ultimately comes from God alone.

Toward a Postcolonial Missiology for the Whole Church

We are addressing the question, How should postcolonial sensibilities reshape the church's global mission? The first set of answers begins to address what postcolonialism demands of the Western missionary community as a former colluder with colonialism; the second set applies to the whole, global, intercultural, missional church.

Proclaiming Good News

Postcolonialism compels the whole and reconciled global church to be mindful of the obvious—that the gospel of the kingdom should be *good* news; that is, it cannot be experienced, either in content or form, as bad news by anyone or any people. Violent evangelism, its cousins manipulation and extortion, and any other means that violate the dignity of people or belittle cultures different from the missionaries' have no place in postcolonial missiology.

We could have easily discussed this point in the first set, but as churches from non-Western nations increasingly send out missionaries, paternalisms that frighteningly resemble the practices of colonial missions go with them. Darrell Whiteman, for example, while celebrating the increase of non-Western missionaries today, also laments the absence of insights from anthropology in their training programs and the consequent lack of tools for distinguishing between gospel and culture. He writes, "This pattern of confusing the gospel with one's culture is being repeated throughout the non-Western world, and missionaries from these cultures are making the same mistakes that Western missionaries made in the age of colonialism."[37] Indeed, Christ's commission to bear witness to the *good* news of the kingdom, the whole and reconciled gospel (which part 2 will flesh out), applies to all who engage in mission.

To proclaim good news does not just mean steering clear from colonial malpractices, however; there is also a positive side to this call—namely, to

37. Darrell Whiteman, "Anthropology and Mission," in *Mission & Culture: The Louis J. Luzbetak Lectures*, ed. Stephen B. Bevans (Maryknoll, NY: Orbis Books, 2012), 82.

bear witness to the whole gospel and all that it entails. After reviewing the historical colonial application of the Great Commission in Africa, ethicist Beatrice Okyere-Manu calls for something different in the postcolonial age. She writes, "The message of the Great Commission is not about elevating teaching but also about restoring justice and equality. We are being challenged to understand how our interpretation and response to the Great Commission are to be redeemed and appropriated in postcolonial Africa in a way that presents a holistic ministry to all."[38]

Racial Righteousness through Reconciliation

As established earlier, racism played a significant part in the unfolding drama of colonialism and slavery. It thus stands to reason that as long as racism exists, colonialism and slavery in some form remain possible. The International Convention on the Elimination of All Forms of Racial Discrimination (ICERD) defines racism as "any distinction, exclusion, restriction, or preference based on race, colour, descent, or national or ethnic origin which has the purpose or effect of nullifying or impairing the recognition, enjoyment, or exercise, on equal footing, of human rights and fundamental freedoms in the political, economic, social, cultural or any other field of public life."[39] Let us note that this definition does not speak of racism as a thing of the past, and rightfully so. Anyone inclined to believe that racism no longer poses a problem today in mission circles needs only to listen openly to the experiences of many non-Western "partners" who work with (and for) missionaries. Indeed, as Petersen observes, "Mission is still located in the context of global racism."[40] Postcolonial missiology calls us to denounce racism, to call it out when it rears its ugly head, to stand up for its victims, and to work to dismantle racist social structures that still may be in operation.

Positively, racial righteousness calls the global church to engage in the ministry of reconciliation. Kingdom justice does not just demand the eradication of global racism; it also calls for reconciliation between Tutsis and Hutus in Rwanda, the Dutch and the people of color in South Africa, Congolese and Belgians, Israelis and Palestinians in the Holy Land, Euro-Americans and First Nations peoples in North America, and the list goes on. This, of course, is

38. Okyere-Manu, "Colonial Mission and the Great Commission in Africa," 31.
39. ICERD, quoted in Rodney L. Petersen, "Mission in the Context of Racism, Restorative Justice and Reconciliation," in *Antioch Agenda: Essays on the Restorative Church in Honor of Orlando E. Costas*, ed. Daniel Jeyaraj, Robert W. Pazmiño, and Rodney L. Petersen (Boston: Andover Newton Theological School and the Boston Theological Institute, 2007), 277.
40. Petersen, "Mission in the Context of Racism, Restorative Justice and Reconciliation," 261.

central to this book, so we will gradually unfold the ministry of reconciliation in these pages, culminating it in part 4. For now, let us grasp that the ministry of reconciliation—the hard work of overcoming distrust, misunderstanding, bitterness, and hatred between former colonizers (and their descendants) and the formerly colonized (and their descendants) in the power of the whole gospel—centrally defines holistic mission in a postcolonial age.

Global Partnership

In the previous chapter, we established mission in the post-Christendom age as "from everywhere to everywhere." One would think that a natural development of multidirectional mission would be genuine, intercultural partnership, but, alas, this kind of partnership remains elusive.[41] Although partnership has been an official ecumenical ideal at least since 1928 at the Jerusalem meeting of the International Missionary Council, ministry relationships between churches that can be characterized as equal, mutual, intercultural, and respectful, while sharing a vision, goals, and leadership—that is, relationships that are genuine partnerships in mission—have been difficult to forge. This would be understandable (though still not acceptable) during the colonial era, but it is intolerable today. We need to keep trying, for global partnership in mission across the colonial divide will surely help to establish the church's credibility in the ministry of reconciliation. Postcolonial global partnership would demonstrate that the reconciliation the church offers to the world actually works!

We could have also discussed this point of global partnership within the first set of postcolonial demands for the Western church, but I intentionally locate it in the second set because kingdom partnership will take the whole global church to be committed to it. By that I mean it imposes requirements on both sides of the colonial relationship. For the Western church, postcolonial partnerships require serious grappling with the issues of the first set— confession, repentance, restitution, humility, and a shift in power dynamics, especially with regard to money. It will mean avoiding paternalism. In their helpful book *When Helping Hurts*, Steve Corbitt and Brian Fikkert identify five areas of paternalism: resources (including monetary), spiritual, knowledge, labor, and managerial—all of which we need to avoid if the global church desires to experience true partnership in mission.[42] As for the non-Western

---

41. See, e.g., Jonathan S. Barnes, "The Ambivalence of Partnership: A Colonial and Contested History," *Encounter* 74, no. 3 (2014): 27–44.

42. Steve Corbitt and Brian Fikkert, *When Helping Hurts: How to Alleviate Poverty without Hurting the Poor* (Chicago: Moody, 2009), 115.

church, it will take assertiveness in the Spirit to assume a posture of equality and leadership in mission initiatives.

Both Western and non-Western churches need to resist default dominant/ subservient positions, which solidified during colonial times. I share the vision of partnership in mission Paul Borthwick describes when he writes, "The image I prefer is that of an interdependent team. . . . The global church needs to work together, incorporate our respective strengths, accommodate our re-spective weaknesses and move forward as a family."[43] Missiology informed by a postcolonial perspective will strive toward this vision of partnership, which reflects the rise not just of world Christianity but also of Jesus's upside-down kingdom. The global church in mission together across the colonial divide positions itself to be the church as the reconciler that God has called it to be.

These two sets of implications only begin to guide the church-in-holistic-mission in the postcolonial age. In humility and openness, the whole and reconciled church must be agile to do whatever it takes to bear witness to the whole and reconciled gospel in a world desperate to see genuine expressions of justice, peace, and freedom for all, especially the downtrodden. Postcolo-nial mission or bust!

Discussion Questions

1. Under the colonial model of mission, in what ways can we view receptor cultures as "victims of the Great Commission"?
2. Should Christian mission be abandoned altogether in our postcolonial world? If not, what might missiology look like in a postcolonial world?
3. In what ways has the "colonial mentality" endured in missions today? How can the church challenge this?

43. Paul Borthwick, *Western Christians in Global Mission: What's the Role of the North American Church?* (Downers Grove, IL: IVP Books, 2012), 193.

Part 2

Whole Gospel

Part 1 sought to contextualize the world, that is, to understand major, discernible global shifts that have affected the human family as a whole and to interpret them for mission. Part 2 seeks to understand anew the good news of Jesus Christ and its full implications amid these global shifts. The quest to redefine holistic mission for the new world requires asking once again the crucial question, "What is the gospel?"

"Asked and answered a thousand times over!" some might say, and legitimately so, for there is no shortage of articles, books, lectures, and sermons on the gospel. And yet, whenever I pose this question—whether with a group of academics, ministry peers, students, or laypeople—the answers vary widely and sometimes wildly. This should not ultimately surprise us; after all, the New Testament itself has at least four different versions, five if we count Paul's (and we should). The gospel is at once simple and complex. It refers simply to the good news from God, announced, demonstrated, and embodied most definitively in Jesus Christ, that salvation has come and is still coming in its fullness; but it also refers to a living and dynamic reality that is complex, requiring translation in every age and in every context.

Up Close and Personal

As a missiologist, I interact with the gospel as regularly as a banker deals with money or a dentist with teeth or a schoolteacher with children. But as for encountering it existentially—that is, profoundly, at the core of my being—I have had two such experiences (so far) that have changed the course of my life. I share them here to say that these two ways of gospel encounter more than hint at the scope of God's transforming work; they demonstrate the gospel's transforming power in sinful human hearts and broken social systems that cause inequity, poverty, and injustice.

The Gospel and Me

I first experienced the gospel as the good news of personal salvation from my chaotic, self-destructive lifestyle during my adolescent years. In response to massive upheaval in my family that eventually resulted in the divorce of my parents, my fourteen-year-old self decided that God did not exist—if indeed the idea of God represented goodness, rightness, and order. If anyone was going to bring meaning to life, I would have to step up, for no benevolent deity was coming to save me, much less all of humankind. I carried this resolve to an extreme by cleverly creating a humanist-based religion that essentially espoused a spiritual version of "If you want something done, you have to do it yourself."

The conviction that I alone could bring meaning to my life led to an intense (if not frenetic) pursuit of self-betterment as I overachieved in academics, sports, and popularity. The confusion and pain within, however, also led me to self-medicate almost daily. I pursued a life of drugs and parties like I did everything else—fully and with excellence! Martin Luther's famous dictum "Be a sinner and sin boldly" comes to mind as I think about that period in my life.[1] In short, I was a popular, above-average athlete with a 3.8 GPA, but I had a serious substance abuse problem. In retrospect, the need for affirmation and a sense of meaning tied all these pursuits together, though none of them satisfied the need.

But then I encountered something called the gospel—the good news that God is real, that God can be known in Jesus Christ, and that God in Christ loves me/us. Surrendering to these gospel truths, I repented; that is, I turned from former ways, and I began heading in a new direction, setting my sights on Christ and Christ's purposes. This left many of my friends scratching their heads. What happened to Al?

---

1. Martin Luther, *Let Your Sins Be Strong: A Letter from Luther to Melanchthon, Letter no. 99*, August 1, 1521, From the Wartburg (Segment), trans. Erika Bullmann Flores, from Martin Luther's *Sämmtliche Schriften*, ed. Johannes Georg Walch (St. Louis: Concordia, 1880–1910), vol. 15, cols. 2585–90. Of course, debate continues regarding Luther's true intent in this quote, which reads in full, "Be a sinner and sin boldly, but believe and rejoice in Christ even more boldly, for he is victorious over sin, death, and the world."

The Gospel and Beyond Me

After that gospel encounter profoundly changed the course of my personal life, a second encounter caused me to go beyond the personal: I caught what I believed (and believe) was a glimpse of the way God sees the world. This second encounter terrified me to my core as the suffering of the poor, oppressed, and marginalized broke my heart. It opened my eyes and broadened my mind to the social, cosmic dimension of God's mission, and it began to give shape to my sense of vocational call.

Early in my faith journey I intuitively understood that the good news did not apply just to me; it applied to everyone and everything. I knew that the gospel somehow pointed to the answer to all of life's problems—personal, social, and political. The strong desire to share this good news with others resided within me before I ever heard the word "evangelism." I did finally learn of it, but unfortunately from those espousing a fundamentalist theology who believed the world to be irredeemable, meaning that from this perspective social justice efforts ultimately held little value. Based on evangelist D. L. Moody's famous metaphor of the sinking ship called planet Earth and the lifeboat of Christ in which the church had to rescue as many of the drowning as possible, I set out to "save souls" passionately and aggressively as part of the evangelism-only missionary movement.[2]

But when I encountered the compassion and justice of the gospel, when I discovered that God cares not only for our souls but also for our bodies and our social situation, when I came to the truth that God cares, yes, for all, but especially for the poor, oppressed, and marginalized, then I realized that my earlier notions of justice were not off after all. I realized that the good news meant much more than my own personal transformation (as profound as that was). I realized that my personal conversion was but a part of a larger, broader, and greater project, as I encountered the gospel of the now-and-not-yet kingdom of God. Discovering that the gospel did not just point to a future hope for saved individuals but also to God's liberating, healing presence in the here and now for all, especially the downtrodden, changed everything. This awakening of God's radically present love for the world registered such an impact on my life that I often refer to it today as my born-again *again* experience.

It occurred in part as a result of a multipunch combination of books that included George Eldon Ladd's *The Presence of the Future*, Ronald J. Sider's

---

2. D. L. Moody, quoted in Randall Balmer, *Encyclopedia of Evangelicalism* (Louisville: Westminster John Knox, 2002), 389. The full quote is, "I look upon this world as a wrecked vessel. God has given me a lifeboat and said, 'Moody, save all you can.'"

Rich Christians in an Age of Hunger, Gustavo Gutiérrez's *A Theology of Liberation*, John Perkins's *Let Justice Roll Down*, and Tom Sine's *The Mustard Seed Conspiracy*.[3] It was, however, a graduate travel course called Contemporary Issues in Missiology: Latin American Practicum that forever opened my eyes for mission and wrecked any possibility of leading a safe and normal life, at least the one defined by the American dream.[4] Each morning began in the classroom, but after lunch, the class resumed via observation and/or engagement in hands-on ministry with, for, and among the poor. This daily schedule over a period of three weeks in the countries of Nicaragua, El Salvador, and Costa Rica exposed me to the blessings of the intercultural experience, the unromantic reality of poverty, and the joy of service—in short, whole mission—on both the theoretical and practical levels.

During those three weeks the impact of the gospel on my life cannot be overstated. It eventually led me back to my homeland of the Philippines as a missionary to engage in community-transforming and pastoral ministries among the poor for almost a decade. But beyond simply defining those ten years, that class catalyzed in me a lifelong commitment to holistic ministry— that is, to a practical theology of mission that will forever include both evangelism and social justice. And finally, it defined my future pedagogy: as a teacher-practitioner of church and mission, I have committed always to engage the heads, hearts, and hands of my students in the classroom.

A gradual progression of my "worldly reawakening" has led to a growing sensitivity to the unevenness of power and privilege (read: injustice) based on gender, race, and ethnicity. I was born in the Philippines, and when I was two years old, my family moved to the US. In immigrant language, I would be counted among the "1.5 generation."[5] As a 1.5er, I have had my share

---

3. George Eldon Ladd, *The Presence of the Future* (Grand Rapids: Eerdmans, 1973); Ronald J. Sider, *Rich Christians in an Age of Hunger* (Downers Grove, IL: InterVarsity, 1977); Gustavo Gutiérrez, *A Theology of Liberation* (Maryknoll, NY: Orbis Books, 1972); John Perkins, *Let Justice Roll Down* (Ventura, CA: Regal, 1976); Tom Sine, *The Mustard Seed Conspiracy* (Waco: Word, 1981). I realize with a little embarrassment the all-male cast of authors that influenced me early on. Feminist theologians Elsa Tamez, Miriam Adeney, and most profoundly Melba Maggay came later.

I cannot overstate the importance of these and a handful of other voices that essentially saved my faith. In retrospect, I am not sure whether my faith would have survived if it had remained solely in the personal realm. So when I describe this encounter as my "born-again *again*" experience, it goes beyond just trying to be cute!

4. This course was offered by Southern California College, now Vanguard University of Southern California, in June 1985, and cotaught by Dr. Murray Dempster and Dr. Douglas Petersen.

5. The descriptor "1.5" refers to people who moved to another culture as children. As such, they live in between their cultures of origin, which they experience in their households, and the culture into which they were transplanted. See Alisa Reznick, "Between Two Worlds: America's 1.5 Generation," *Seattle Times*, November 18, 2013, http://blogs.seattletimes.com/race-awsd /2013/11/18/race-project-between-two-worlds-americas-1-5-generation.

of being on the short end of racism, from being labeled and teased (named affectionately as "the Chink," for example, in my elementary school in the Bronx) to being passed over for a job because my ethnicity was deemed not conducive for fundraising.[6]

My keenness to racial injustice began to focus, however, ironically enough, while I served as a missionary in my homeland of the Philippines in the 1990s. I began to discover all too personally that, as a colonized people, first by Spain, then by the United States, and then briefly (but brutally) by Japan, Filipinos pervasively view foreigners, especially Americans, as higher than themselves (which is not uncommon, of course, among formerly colonized peoples around the world).

My eyes began to open to this reality when I was with white fellow missionaries who were given seats of honor while I was passed over (not that I wanted to be seated there, but why them and not me?); or when my white wife would walk right past a security guard at the entrance of a bank or a mall while I would be stopped and searched without fail; or when I would take out white visitors to dinner and the waiter would hand the dinner check afterward to one of them (most of the time, I would welcome that!). Such minor incidents of "brown-on-brown racism," which I experienced repeatedly in the Philippines, marked the beginning of justice consciousness and the redefining of the whole gospel to include advocacy: speaking out against unjust social structures and fighting for equality in solidarity with the oppressed. In time, my sense of justice expanded to include the need to challenge sexism, classism, homophobia, and other forms of injustice as part of living out the ministry of reconciliation.

The Whole and Reconciling Gospel

Some might argue that personal testimony has no place in a book such as this. If my story were an isolated, exceptional case, then they would have a valid point. But I share my story as empirical evidence, as a testament to faith, for my story is but one of those that could be told by billions of people around the world over the last two thousand years who have attested to the power of the gospel to transform broken lives.[7] So while such testimonies are admittedly

---

6. For more of my own reflections on my cultural journey, see Al Tizon, "I Am Asian, Hear Me Roar," *Evangelicals for Social Action*, January 14, 2015, http://www.evangelicalsforsocial action.org/reconciliation-and-dialogue/i-am-asian-hear-me-roar.

7. A collection of stories that I often use for courses and that demonstrate the varied ways that people have come to faith in Christ is Sharon Gallagher's *Finding Faith: Life-Changing Encounters with Christ* (San Francisco: Council Oak, 2001).

subjective or up close and personal, their sheer numbers throughout time would stand up in court as proof of the transforming truth of the gospel.

My born-again *again* experience of being reawakened to the poor and oppressed is not isolated either. In putting together a Festschrift for our mentor and friend Ronald J. Sider, for example, Paul Alexander and I heard story after story of how God used Ron Sider to wake them up to a broader understanding of the gospel that includes justice. To quote just one contributor, Shane Claiborne writes, "I remember reading *Rich Christians in an Age of Hunger* and feeling a fire for justice start to rage in my bones."[8] Indeed, many Christians around the world can testify to an awakening that has ignited them for holistic mission.

These two ways, personal and social, in which I and countless others around the world and throughout time have experienced the gospel, point to the scope of God's redeeming work—namely, the transformation of the world and every single person in it. The gospel has both personal and social dimensions, and to the extent that we live out both in our missionary engagement, we bear witness to the fullness of the coming kingdom. To burn with the fire of God's justice for the suffering and oppressed poor around the world without losing the fire of God's desire for all to come to personal faith through Jesus Christ is the essence of the missionary call in the service of the whole gospel.

Part 2 seeks to rehear this good news in and for a world that offers an unprecedented smorgasbord of thought, belief, and lifestyle, and it does so first by identifying and calling into account pseudo-gospels (chap. 4). I see these gospels as coming into prominence in large part as a consequence of the global changes that we analyzed in part 1. To distinguish truth from falsehood, authenticity from counterfeit, and biblical soundness from subtle deviance will require keen discernment.

Chapter 5 follows, arguing that today the whole gospel is best understood in terms of a kingdom theology of reconciliation. Indeed, John the revelator's image of the coming kingdom of God includes all tribes and nations and peoples and tongues (Rev. 5:9; 7:9–12). This is the good news of the kingdom of God for our globalizing, post-Christendom, postcolonial world.

---

8. Shane Claiborne, "Simplicity and the Poor," in *Following Jesus: Journeys in Radical Discipleship; Essays in Honor of Ronald J. Sider*, ed. Paul Alexander and Al Tizon (Oxford: Regnum, 2013), 83.

FOUR

On False and Half Gospels

Beware that no one leads you astray.
—Jesus (Matt. 24:4)

Several years ago, while visiting a university campus in central Pennsylvania, I encountered a group of Christians distributing tracts. I involuntarily received one, as a member of the crusade zealously shoved one into my hand. Not a fan of tracts in general, I was ready to be my silent, cynical self as I began to read it. It only took a few seconds, however, to go beyond cynicism to anger, then to outrage. At the top of the threefold tract sat the large, bold letters, "WWJD," but instead of "What Would Jesus Do?" it confronted the reader with the question, "Who Would Jesus Damn?" As I opened the first fold, the word "YOU!" in even larger, bolder font hit me right between the eyes like a bullet, warning me against the fires of hell if I have ever committed any sin on a list, which included fornication, adultery, homosexuality, and the like (evidently sexual sin angers God the most). Finally, at the bottom of the third fold, the tract urged me to repent to avoid the eternal fiery fate that awaited me.

I felt victimized—by "the good news," no less. Beyond my personal reaction, however, my blood boiled against this troop of evangelists for assaulting countless others with hate in the name of God. This sincere, zealous group proclaimed the bad news of judgment and did so under the banner of the church of Jesus Christ. I fought off the temptation to follow them around, urging all not to listen to this rubbish, but that would have just added to the fiasco. Instead, in my anger, I crumpled up the tract and slam-dunked it into the trash, where it belonged.

As cultures, religions, political affiliations, and ideologies come together—or clash—more than ever before, the church needs to know more than ever before what it believes with precision and conviction. It needs sharp competence to discern truth from falsehood and wholeness from halfness. It requires spiritual keenness in identifying false and half gospels that have emerged (or reemerged) in force in a pluralistic, confusing world. We cannot overstate this, for deviant ideologies that claim to stand for gospel truth lead millions of people around the world away from the fullness of life found in Jesus Christ. As bearers of the gospel of the kingdom, we need to be aware of such gospels and to speak prophetically against them.

False Gospels

Gospel of Hate

The opening illustration points to the first of these false gospels: the gospel of hate. False gospels, more often than not, grow out of a biblical truth that a group focuses on, develops, and proclaims at the expense of other biblical truths. At the base of the gospel of hate lies the truth of God's holiness. The Scriptures certainly attest to a holy God becoming angry when evil occurs. Unquestionably, God hates sin. When not marred by human pathology, this dimension of the gospel simply points to the holiness of God that calls all to repentance.

This holy call, however, becomes the gospel of hate when human rage against all who disobey God replaces divine righteous anger. Unfortunately for champions of this gospel, the Scriptures teach that all have disobeyed, that our righteousness is like filthy rags (Isa. 64:6), and that all fall short of the glory of God (Rom. 3:23). As a line from a Phil Madeira song goes, "We all give God the blues."[1] Seemingly blind to this truth, proponents of this gospel set up an "us versus them" world, in which they act as self-appointed judges to mete out condemnation on unholy sinners.

Furthermore, this gospel feeds on the fear of God's judgment now and in the life to come. Rather than a holy, loving God calling us to repentance, it portrays God as a ruthless judge, who in this life punishes the wicked by way of calamities such as the AIDS epidemic, natural disasters, or economic

1. Phil Madeira, "Give God the Blues," *Mercyland: Hymns for the Rest of Us* (Tone Tree Music, 2012).

downfalls, and in the life to come by way of everlasting torment. The gospel of hate is fear-based, arrogant self-righteousness in the shape of a gun.

Westboro Baptist Church in Topeka, Kansas, and the Phelps family who founded it, make for easy targets with which to associate this gospel. According to the late pastor Fred W. Phelps, "The gospel message, from the mouth of the Lord, is that God hates fags. That's a profound theological statement that America and the world need more than they need food to eat, water to drink, and air to breathe."[2] To reduce the gospel to God's judgment is distorted enough, but to reduce it to judgment against one group of people and one type of alleged sin reveals how hatred can truly impair clear thinking, good judgment, and sound doctrine. Westboro Baptist Church's notoriety rose to great heights when the members brought its message to the funerals of military personnel who had died in action, as part of their "Thank God for Dead Soldiers" campaign.[3] Their reasoning was to let America know that God is punishing it "for its immorality including tolerance for homosexuality and abortion."[4]

Fortunately, Westboro Baptist Church represents a fringe group, registering only forty members and fewer than a hundred followers. However, it is but one loud proponent of the gospel of hate among many; others exist around the world, including the Qur'an-burning Dove World Outreach Center; the National Liberation Front of Tripura, a "Christian" terrorist group in India that threatens to kill participants in certain Hindu festivals;[5] and Anti-balaka, a group in central Africa that formed originally to defend themselves from Muslim-based terrorists but that now commits terrorist acts themselves in an effort to cleanse central Africa of Muslim presence.[6]

We can easily dismiss groups such as these as misrepresenting Christ. But lest we fall prey to self-righteousness ourselves, it behooves us to know that any notion of the gospel that is primarily motivated by fear, pharisaical legalism, and/or hellfire-and-brimstone preaching dangerously flirts with the gospel of

2. Fred Phelps, "God Hates Fags," May 16, 2012, https://www.youtube.com/watch?v=_LSMdol5Bz0.

3. This campaign is but a part of a larger "Thank God for . . ." campaign, which includes 9/11, AIDS, IEDs, Katrina, and other disasters. See their reasoning at "FAQ," God Hates Fags, accessed October 25, 2017, http://www.godhatesfags.com/faq.html#Thank_God.

4. "Supreme Court Weighs Arguments over 'Thank God for Dead Soldiers' Funeral Protest," NBC News, October 6, 2010, http://www.nbcnews.com/id/39531700/ns/politics/t/supreme-court-weighs-arguments-over-thank-god-dead-soldiers-funeral-protest.

5. "National Liberation Front of Tripura," Christian Aggression, April 29, 2016, http://christianaggression.org/2016/04/29/national-liberation-front-of-tripura-nlft.

6. "Anti-Balaka," Tracking Terrorism, accessed January 20, 2018, https://www.trackingterrorism.org/system/files/chatter/Anti-Balaka.pdf.

hate. I do not know this for certain, but the evangelistic group preaching "the good news," with which I began this chapter, likely hailed from a more typical evangelical (albeit fundamentalist) church than we would like to believe. The church should not avoid declaring God's judgment on sin—because, again, at the base of this gospel lies the holiness of God and the call to repentance—but listeners need to hear it in the larger context of the truly good news that God so loved the world that God decided to dwell among us in Jesus Christ for our salvation (John 1:1–3, 14; 3:16). It is this gospel, and not the gospel of hate, that God in Christ has called us to embody and proclaim for the sake of the world.

Gospel of Prosperity

The gospel of prosperity, another insidious false gospel, has captured the imagination (and pocketbooks) of countless people around the world. The Lausanne statement on the prosperity gospel defines it "as the teaching that believers have a right to the blessings of health and wealth and that they can obtain these blessings through positive confessions of faith and the 'sowing of seeds' through the faithful payments of tithes and offerings."[7] Prosperity preachers assert that God's children qua God's children are entitled to every divine blessing. They simply need to "name it and claim it," as well as to trust God to bless them a hundredfold if they give generously and sacrificially. The more we give, the more of God's blessings we will receive, which more than implies that material abundance, or even excess, indicates right standing with God. Robert Franklin tells of a time when he visited a megachurch in Atlanta, Georgia. During the sermon, the well-known preacher of that church boasted of a friend who had given him a Rolls Royce and then followed it up with, "Now that's not the Rolls that you all gave me years ago. See, so don't get mad. This was a gift from a friend. It's good to have friends." What appalled Franklin even more, however, was the "manner in which the congregation seemed to affirm this testimony of personal indulgence and excess."[8]

According to the gospel of prosperity, the opposite also holds true: simplicity, poverty, and sickness indicate at best a limited outlook on life; at worst, sin and disobedience. Again, false gospels grow out of a scriptural truth; prosperity has emerged out of the truth that God desires no one to be poor and sick, and that God desires all to flourish. But that truth goes tragically awry when

7. "Lausanne Theology Working Group Statement on the Prosperity Gospel," *Evangelical Review of Theology* 34, no. 2 (2010): 99.
8. Robert Franklin, *Crisis in the Village: Restoring Hope in African American Communities* (Minneapolis: Fortress, 2007), 116.

preachers teach that while prosperity indicates faithfulness, poverty indicates unfaithfulness. The gospel of prosperity not only puts undue spiritual burden on the poor and the sick (what am I doing wrong that I find myself in such deprivation, O Lord?); it also uses that same guilt to manipulate the masses to give all they have as the means to change their situation. The gospel of prosperity Christianizes the formula, "The rich get richer while the poor get poorer." The Lausanne statement decries this: "[The gospel of prosperity] vastly enriches those who preach it, but leaves multitudes no better off, with the added burden of disappointed hopes."[9]

Moreover, the gospel of prosperity goes tragically awry when it takes the truth of God's desire for human flourishing and turns it into an insatiable hunger for material wealth. To equate having not one but two Rolls Royces with the kind of prosperity God desires for all should sound the alarm in our souls. The googly-eyed desire for shiny things exposes the gospel of prosperity for what it is: a Christianized glorification of materialism, consumerism, and greed. According to Franklin, it conveys the idea that "greed is good," and therefore it is "diametrically opposed to Christian faith . . . and merits the church's vigilant opposition."[10]

Though greed is universal, the prosperity gospel as a movement originated in the US with people such as E. W. Kenyon, Kenneth Hagin, and Kenneth Copeland as its leading figures.[11] Today US-based prosperity preachers, such as Joel Osteen, Fred Price, Creflo Dollar, and Joyce Meyer have done their part in globalizing their brand of prosperity. Largely a fringe outgrowth of Pentecostalism, the prosperity movement spread dramatically along with the exponential growth of Pentecostalism in Africa, Asia, and Latin America, particularly after the 1980s.[12] Expressions of the movement vary widely depending on where it grows. Though the following churches vary in many ways, the Universal Church of the Kingdom of God in Brazil, Deeper Life Christian Ministry in Nigeria, City Harvest Church in Singapore, and the Lakewood Church in the US are considered part of the global prosperity movement.

We need to warn the world of this false gospel, but we would be remiss if we did not recognize the subtle power of wealth in our own lives and in our own churches. If indeed the gospel of prosperity represents the Christianization of

9. "Lausanne Theology Working Group Statement on the Prosperity Gospel," 100–101.

10. Franklin, *Crisis in the Village*, 124.

11. J. N. Saracco, "Prosperity Theology," in *Dictionary of Mission Theology*, ed. John Corrie (Downers Grove, IL: IVP Academic, 2007), 322.

12. Matthew Sharpe, "Name It and Claim It: Prosperity Gospel and the Global Pentecostal Reformation," in *Handbook of Research on Development and Religion*, ed. Matthew Clarke (Northampton, MA: Edward Elgar, 2013), 170–71.

materialism, consumerism, and greed, then many Christians and churches, especially those in wealthier nations, participate in the gospel of prosperity even as they denounce it. Money, material wealth, church edifices, the expansion of property, and possessing nice things hold more power over us than we care to admit. The global dream (defined in chap. 1 as globalizationism) provides the context for the abnormal growth of the prosperity gospel. Christians and churches that unreflectively participate in that dream around the world can be critical of the prosperity gospel with their words while promoting it with their lives. Rich Christians—which, relative to the rest of the world, probably includes most of the readers of this book and certainly this writer—beware!

Gospel of Comfort

The gospel of prosperity has a close cousin, what I call the gospel of comfort. Although I do not believe this belongs decidedly on the list of false gospels, it bears such an undeniable resemblance to the prosperity gospel that I speak of it here. While the gospel of prosperity raises wealth to idolatrous heights, the gospel of comfort raises security, safety, and ease just as high. Based on this gospel, comfort becomes a nonnegotiable. The "right to be comfortable" is endemic to a culture of wealth in general, but when Christians unthinkingly claim this right for themselves, comfort becomes gospel, or at least becomes the logical result of this gospel. Security, safety, and ease in life—that is, comfort—become signs of divine favor.

The gospel of comfort represents painless Christianity. As with the prosperity gospel, God's desire for human flourishing and not human suffering underscores this gospel. No one should desire to suffer, but to live sacrificially for the sake of others is central to the Christian faith. "Comfortable Christians" tend to forget that the one we call Savior and Lord suffered and died on a cross for us, and furthermore that Christ calls all who follow him to carry one (Luke 14:27). Dietrich Bonhoeffer captured the truth of redemptive suffering when he said famously, "When Christ calls [us], he bids [us] come and die."[13] The gospel of comfort, in contrast, teaches a crossless Christianity.

"Comfortable Christians," however, do not necessarily see the woes of the underprivileged as signs of divine disfavor, as in the case of the prosperity gospel toward the poor. In fact, they are even willing to help the less fortunate, as long as it does not impinge on their own comfort. I remember years ago, for example, friends sincerely trying to discourage us from moving to Vietnam to work with the church there. "It's dangerous." "What about your kids?" "Why

13. Dietrich Bonhoeffer, *The Cost of Discipleship* (New York: Macmillan, 1963), 99.

don't you just go for a few weeks, get it out of your system, and then come back?" One friend even reprimanded us, saying that it would be irresponsible of us to take our kids into a dangerous situation. These sentiments had the ring of Peter's rebuke aimed at Jesus for planning to go to Jerusalem despite the dangers facing him there (Matt. 16:22). For various reasons, we ended up remaining in the Philippines where we were serving, but shame on us if it was because we lacked the courage to love dangerously for the sake of the whole gospel! The point is, while our Christian friends expressed genuine concern for us, they spoke from the perspective of the gospel of comfort.

The gospel of comfort ultimately produces safe Christians, who may or may not engage in God's mission, depending on life's circumstances. If time permits, and if it does not impinge too much on the pursuit of wealth, security, and comfort, then perhaps we can consider participating. The church must call out and challenge this gospel; it must see that its message to the world does not just entail comforting the afflicted, as the adage goes, but also afflicting the comfortable.

Gospel of Empire

"Empire" has become a metaphor for dominant political and/or economic power that extends itself throughout the world.[14] When Christians and churches participate in the extension of politico-national and/or economic dominance, something that can be called the gospel of empire is at play. This gospel grows out of the biblical truth of God's future in which Jesus will reign as King of kings and Lord of lords. Its malformation comes when its advocates use worldly power to expand their version of the kingdom of God. The gospel of empire is where ideological globalization meets Christendom (see chaps. 1 and 2), and it manifests today in at least two ways.

Opportunism

The church riding the coattails of the global influence of a dominant nation to accomplish its own religious ends constitutes the first way. If this sounds much like when missionaries marched in lockstep with colonizers during the colonial period, then we hear it correctly. The evil offspring of classical Christendom and colonialism, the gospel of empire represents opportunism that seeks to take advantage of the political and economic power of a dominant nation in the name of extending the kingdom of God.

---

14. See Bruce Benson and Peter Heltzel, introduction to *Evangelicals and Empire*, ed. Bruce Benson and Peter Heltzel (Grand Rapids: Brazos, 2008), 11–21.

For example, when former US president George W. Bush declared war on
Iraq in 2003 and then occupied it for the next eight years, some US-based
evangelistic organizations "declared war" on the souls of Muslims in Iraq.[15]
As independent US missionary Tom Craig succinctly proclaimed, "God and
the president have given us an opportunity to bring Jesus Christ to the Middle
East."[16] This conviction, widespread among North American evangelicals
during the occupation, clearly communicates the notion that the US's attempt to establish its version of freedom and democracy in Iraq paved the
way for gospel work. In other words, as in the colonial period, to evangelize
the region—to make the occupied territory Christian—went hand in hand
with the project to civilize it.

Megachurch

Second, the gospel of empire also manifests itself through the worldwide
growth of the megachurch phenomenon. Rather than taking advantage of a nation's dominance to accomplish the *missio Dei*, the megachurch movement—
human, economic, and territorial expansion of the body of Christ—can be
seen as the building up of the church itself as its own powerful empire. According to the Hartford Institute for Religion Research, "megachurch" generally
"refers to any Protestant Christian congregation with a sustained average
weekly attendance of 2000 persons or more in its worship services, counting
all adults and children at all its worship locations."[17] Although the roots of the
modern-day global megachurch phenomenon can be traced to megachurches
in the US, the largest megachurches in the world have developed in South
Korea, Brazil, and Nigeria.

To be clear, that a church has grown massively does not necessarily mean
that it has preached the false gospel of empire. Indeed, as Kwabena Asamoah-
Gyadu states, "There are living testimonies of God using megachurches and
their leaders in doing great things in mission." But he qualifies this by saying,
"In equal measure there are stories of failure and shame due to the pursuits
of religious empire mindsets."[18] Megachurches devolve into "empire mind-

15. See David Rennie, "Bible Belt Missionaries Set Out on a 'War for Souls' in Iraq," *Telegraph*, December 27, 2003, http://www.telegraph.co.uk/news/worldnews/northamerica/usa/14
50359/Bible-Belt-missionaries-set-out-on-a-war-for-souls-in-Iraq.html.
16. Quoted in Charles Duhigg, "Evangelicals Flock to Iraq on a Mission of Faith," *Los
Angeles Times*, March 18, 2004, http://articles.latimes.com/2004/mar/18/world/fg-missionary18.
17. "Mega-Church Definition," Hartford Institute for Religious Research, accessed October
25, 2017, http://hirr.hartsem.edu/megachurch/definition.html.
18. Kwabena Asamoah-Gyadu, "Megachurches and Their Implications for Christian Mission," Lausanne Global Analysis, September 2, 2014, https://www.lausanne.org/content/lga/20
14-09/megachurches-and-their-implications-for-christian-mission.

sets" when they operate with the assumption that their megastatus indicates gospel success, when they believe and proclaim that bigger is always better.

The gospel of empire is also at play when influences less than the Spirit, such as marketing tactics, entertainment, and/or social prestige, have caused their expansion. What is it about megachurches that attracts hundreds of thousands of people into extravagant, stadium-like edifices regularly? Is it the compelling power of the death and resurrection of Christ that leads to sacrificial service for the sake of others, or is it the allure of wealth, worship entertainment, charismatic personalities, and Christian superstars?

Many megachurch advocates believe that all churches should strive toward megagrowth, necessarily implying that satisfaction with smallness indicates a lack of faith and therefore a lack of commitment to God's global expansion project. Dag Heward-Mills, founder and bishop of the Lighthouse Chapel International in Accra, Ghana, for example, begins his book *The Mega Church* with the following words: "You must desire to have a megachurch because that is the most appropriate vision and goal for a pastor."[19] He lists twenty-five reasons why this is true and then proceeds to teach his readers—most probably pastors of smaller churches—how to get on the road toward megachurch-dom. Though he tells his readers not to be discouraged with their small churches,[20] disappointment and frustration are inevitable for millions of church leaders around the world who will never see megagrowth in their churches, especially those who faithfully serve in contexts of poverty, oppression, and/or persecution.

These two ways of church presence in the world—(1) opportunism in the context of national dominance to accomplish its mission and/or (2) efforts to establish its own dominance by way of a bigger-is-better theology—reflect the gospel of empire, which woefully misses the mark of the kingdom of God. God's people should not only guard their own hearts against the alluring power of empire, but they should also in the power of the Spirit call out these imperial manifestations for what they are: caricatures of the church of Jesus Christ that mislead millions of people around the world.

Half Gospels

I hesitate to identify the next two gospels as false, but I do not hesitate to describe them as "half," or dangerously reduced. Whereas the previous gospels

19. Dag Heward-Mills, *The Mega Church: How to Make Your Church Grow* (Seattle: Amazon Digital Services, 2011), Kindle version, loc. 36 of 2431.
20. Heward-Mills, *Mega Church*, loc. 49 of 2431.

have the ring of falsehood to them (though they grow out of biblical truths), the next two have more the ring of incompleteness. At the end of the day, however, false and half gospels are not so different in that they both prevent people from experiencing the fullness of the kingdom of God. Nevertheless, let us maintain the distinction for the sake of precision and consider a few half gospels that have led many astray around the world.

Gospel of Personal Salvation

I begin with the one closest to my evangelical tribe: the gospel of personal salvation. This gospel proclaims the love and forgiveness of God for sinners who have looked to the cross of Christ for their redemption. That God has made a way for broken, sinful people to be reconciled to God is wonderfully and beautifully and biblically true. However, preachers of this gospel more often than not proclaim this at the expense of the clarion call of Scripture to love mercy, do justice, and make peace.

Despite scores of scriptural passages that attest to God's desire for the redemption of broken, unjust social structures, which result in mass poverty, injustice, war, oppression, and marginalization,[21] preachers of the gospel of personal salvation either neglect to attend to the social dimension of the gospel (to give them the benefit of the doubt), or, fueled by a faulty one-sided missiology, they willfully preach against social justice work as a distraction from the real work of the gospel.

With such preachers in mind, Ronald J. Sider asks provokingly, "Are evangelical leaders on their way to hell?" In light of Ezekiel 3, where leaders are divinely judged because they fail to warn people and point them in the right direction, Sider prophesies that God will hold many evangelical leaders accountable "for their widespread failure to teach their people about God's concern for the poor." He calls a gospel that neglects the poor and oppressed for what it is, heresy—and those who proclaim it for what they are, heretics.[22]

According to the gospel of personal salvation, to prepare souls for the life to come constitutes the primary (if not sole) task of the church. The unsaved are destined to an eternity of torment unless the church fulfills its mission to win their souls for Christ. This gospel operates on a faulty theology of disembodiment that separates the body from the soul—the soul being that which lasts forever, while the corrupt body eventually dies and rots. Such theology reeks

---

21. See Ronald J. Sider, "God Wills Justice," in *For They Shall Be Fed*, ed. Ronald J. Sider (Dallas: Word, 1997), 157–90. In this section, Sider comprehensively compiles the Scriptures that speak of God's justice in relationships and societies.

22. Ronald J. Sider, *I Am Not a Social Activist* (Scottdale, PA: Herald Press, 2008), 115–17.

of Gnosticism, a philosophy that believes, among other things, that what we generally call real, including the flesh, is ultimately evil.

We cannot overstate that this aspect of Gnostic thought does not square with Scripture. In direct opposition to a Gnostic type of gospel being proclaimed in the churches, the apostle John wrote, "By this you know the Spirit of God: every spirit that confesses that Jesus Christ has come *in the flesh* is from God, and every spirit that does not confess Jesus is not from God" (1 John 4:2–3). The early church fathers followed suit and officially condemned Gnosticism as heretical. Nonetheless, Gnostic disembodiment theology, in which the material world is evil, has made quite a comeback among Christians today. Western Christians in particular, N. T. Wright laments, "have embraced something worryingly similar to second-century Gnosticism when they think of the present world as evil and the only solution being to escape it and to go to heaven instead."[23] To the extent that the church embraces this heresy, it makes sense to define the sole mission of the church as saving souls and to view the work of social justice as having little or no eternal value. At the core of the gospel of personal salvation lies a Gnostic theology of mission.

The gospel of personal salvation may sound good to those who enjoy a level of wealth and comfort in this life in that it adds a sense of assurance for the afterlife. But for the poor, oppressed, and destitute, who need the good news of justice now, this gospel amounts, at best, to a promissory note for a heaven they will enjoy later. Meanwhile their suffering continues while proponents of this gospel teach the church worldwide that social ministry holds little eternal value. The cruelty of this reduction of the gospel, unintended as it may be, should be self-evident. The gospel of personal salvation is missiological heresy.

David Platt's challenge to the Southern Baptist leadership in 2013 reinforced this conviction when he courageously condemned phrases such as "Accept Jesus into your heart" and "Invite Jesus into your life" as superstitious and unbiblical.[24] He expressed grave concern that by overreliance on trite formulas such as the sinner's prayer, evangelists around the world have deceived countless people into believing they are now sharers in the life of Christ when in fact they are not. According to Platt, surface affirmations such as the sinner's prayer can actually keep people from experiencing the full, abundant life found in Christ. That full, abundant life, according to Platt, includes

23. N. T. Wright, *Surprised by Hope: Rethinking Heaven, the Resurrection, and the Mission of the Church* (New York: HarperCollins, 2008), 197.

24. David Platt, "Why Accepting Jesus in Your Heart Is Superstitious and Unbiblical," Verge Network, accessed October 25, 2017, http://www.vergenetwork.org/2012/04/12/platt -why-accepting-jesus-in-your-heart-is-superstitious-unbiblical.

sacrificial generosity of time, resources, and our very lives in the service of the poor and suffering in the world.[25]

The gospel of personal salvation attempts to simplify the message of the gospel so as to make it easier for people to come to Christian faith. But this convenience truncates the power and fullness of genuine, life-changing commitment to Christ and his purposes. If evangelical leaders have been preaching this oversimplified, justice-less gospel to make the message of Jesus more palatable, it is time to repent. It is time to recommit to the whole and reconciled gospel, the good news of God's reign of peace, justice, and freedom for all, especially the poor, oppressed, and marginalized around the world.

Gospel of Social Liberation

The second half gospel represents the other side of the missiological heresy: the gospel of social liberation. This gospel focuses on sociopolitical reform, proclaiming Christ as emancipator of the poor and oppressed; but more often than not its proponents preach it at the expense of personal transformation. The gospel of social liberation grows out of the all-pervasive theme in Scripture of God's desire for justice, for making all things right.[26] This necessarily includes the social order, which, with everything else, has been marred by sin. Preachers of this gospel cry out against broken and corrupt social systems that create poverty, war, oppression, racism, and marginalization.

It goes awry, however, when they do so at the neglect of proclaiming God's saving love for individuals and God's desire to have personal relationships with people. Does God care about the individual person? Does God care about you and me and our life circumstances? Does the sinful human heart need Christ's redeeming forgiveness? Do persons need to repent and change their destructive ways? Advocates of this gospel do not typically ask these kinds of questions, and as a result, they proclaim a truncated message that keeps desperately lost people from experiencing a personal relationship with God that results in divine forgiveness, freedom from addictions, transformation from selfishness to selflessness, and the willpower to restore broken relationships with spouses, children, friends, and neighbors.

While some advocates of this gospel unintentionally neglect dealing with personal sin because of their passion to address human need, many others

25. David Platt, *Radical: Taking Back Your Faith from the American Dream* (Colorado Springs: Multnomah, 2013).
26. See *God's Justice* (Grand Rapids: Zondervan, 2016), a study Bible that draws out the theme of justice from the Bible by way of introduction and commentary by scholar-practitioners from around the world.

maintain a conscious disdain toward the ministry of evangelism. "Maybe [missionaries] can lay off a bit about preaching their religion," writes a blogger. "I commend them for going into countries and helping the sick but why do they have to put in their opinions on religion while doing so? Can't people just help for the damn sake of helping or is that too hard to ask without some other reason for doing so?"[27]

WindListener, the name of the blogger, reflects the sentiments of a humanitarian approach to mission that can be traced back to the 1932 publication *Rethinking Missions* by William Hocking.[28] "The 'shocking Hocking report,' as it came to be called, . . . challenged what were then basic Protestant missionary tenets, such as the uniqueness of Christianity among the religions of the world and the necessity of preaching personal conversion to Christ."[29] This no-conversion theology continued to grow through the decades. Mission historians see the 1968 Assembly of the World Council of Churches in Uppsala, Sweden, as the maturation of this humanitarian approach to mission theology.[30] Commenting on the findings of the WCC Assembly in Uppsala, David J. Bosch quipped, "It was hard to find exactly how mission differed from the ethos and activities of the Peace Corps."[31]

Ironically, this generation of evangelicals has increasingly expressed this disdain for evangelism. Evangelicals against evangelism. Whereas justice was absent in previous generations, necessitating the work of organizations such as Evangelicals for Social Action (US), Latin American Theological Fraternity (Argentina and throughout Latin America), and others to restore justice on the evangelical missionary agenda, now we can identify evangelism as the endangered species. Ajith Fernando expresses well this concern:

> I hear evangelicals talking a lot about justice and kingdom values but not proclaiming the gospel to those of other faiths and winning them for Christ. Of course, if someone asks them about Christianity, they will explain the gospel. . . . But that is a woefully inadequate strategy. Most of the billions of people in the world who do not know Christ will not come and ask us. We need to take the initiative to go to them. . . . I fear that many evangelicals have fallen into Satan's trap of upholding kingdom values [doing social

---

27. Quoted in Elmer Thiessen, *The Ethics of Evangelism* (Downers Grove, IL: IVP Academic, 2011), 3.

28. William E. Hocking, *Rethinking Missions* (New York: Harper, 1932).

29. Al Tizon, *Transformation after Lausanne: Radical Evangelical Mission in Global-Local Perspective* (Eugene, OR: Wipf & Stock, 2008), 26.

30. Tizon, *Transformation*, 28.

31. David J. Bosch, *Transforming Mission*, 20th anniv. ed. (Maryknoll, NY: Orbis Books, 2011), 354.

justice work] to the diminution of God's call to proactively go after the lost and proclaim the gospel.[32]

Fernando calls the church to get back on course, to do both justice and evangelism, to practice the whole and reconciled gospel. We would do well to heed his advice lest we reduce the gospel to political, social liberation, neglecting to share the greatest story ever told with those who desperately need it.

More false and half gospels undoubtedly exist out there, but consider this partial list as a reminder of the prophetic dimension of our mission—namely, the call to identify movements that mar the name of Jesus and thus mislead millions of people away from the fullness of the kingdom. In our globalizing, fracturing world, where the intersection of diverse cultures, theologies, and ideologies is at its unprecedented busiest and most volatile, the church's prophetic ministry of reconciliation needs to be sharper than ever before. The world needs to know what the gospel is *not*.

As this chapter has warned us against at least some of the false and half gospels that have reasserted themselves in the world, the next chapter seeks to understand anew the true and whole gospel. The time has come to articulate afresh the very good news of the kingdom of God that Jesus preached.

Discussion Questions

1. Should we be responsible for pointing out theological errors that try to pass as the gospel? Why or why not?
2. Is there a difference between a false gospel and a half gospel?
3. Have you encountered any of the false or half gospels discussed in this chapter? How did it affect you?
4. Would you add any false or half gospels to the list?

32. Ajith Fernando, "Getting Back on Course," *Christianity Today*, November 2, 2007, http://www.christianitytoday.com/ct/2007/november/16.40.html.

FIVE

Gospel of the Kingdom

The Reconciliation of All Things

. . . .

The time is fulfilled, and the kingdom of God
has come near; repent, and believe in the good news.
—Jesus (Mark 1:15)

I first encountered the strange phrase "kingdom of God" in the form of a song. Having never heard the song before as a new Christian in my late teens, I sat with a group of peers who obviously knew it very well. "Seek ye first the kingdom of God," they sang as if they meant it, "And . . . his righteousness, . . . and all these things shall be added unto you . . . hal-le-lu . . . hallelu . . . jah."

The words were simple and the tune catchy enough that I learned them fairly quickly. In due time, I got over the embarrassment of singing publicly with others (a practice alien to an unchurched, "cool" teenager like me) and began to sing "Seek Ye First"—and many other faith-affirming songs—along with my new friends whenever we gathered together.[1] The positivity, simplicity, and God-orientation of those songs served as refreshing alternatives (and here, I date myself) to *Saturday Night Fever*, Funkadelic, and KISS, though we also continued to listen to "the devil's music," to the chagrin of our youth pastors.

1. "Seek Ye First," composed by Karen Lafferty, was on the original *Praise Album* (Maranatha! Music, 1974).

77

In retrospect, "Seek Ye First" served as a kind of anthem that reminded us of the faith commitment we shared, but in truth we had little to no idea what we were singing about. It took several years before my mind caught up with my heart. When it did, when the deep meaning of the reign of God began to take root in my being, my relationship with gospel, church, and mission changed forever. Far more than the blissful, heavenly place where we go when we die, the kingdom of God, I began to realize, was an all-encompassing alternate reality that challenged all that was wrong with the universe. So when we declared in song that we "seek it first," we pledged allegiance to the government of God, to topple broken, corrupt systems of sin, violence, oppression, and injustice. Innocently, sweetly, we sang to join a revolution of personal, social, and cosmic proportions!

I blame young, adolescent faith for not understanding the power and glory of the kingdom in those days. What then of the many adult Christians—pastors, teachers, and missionaries, no less—who have seemingly never taken seriously the centrality of the kingdom of God to gospel, church, and mission? This should concern us greatly since Jesus preached the gospel of the kingdom and nothing else. With Mortimer Arias, I ask sadly, "Why is it that we, the preachers and evangelists who are supposed to proclaim the gospel of Jesus the Christ, seem to have missed the central aspect of [his] teaching?"[2]

In light of the tectonic shifts that define and endanger our world today, as well as the emerging mutations of the gospel that masquerade as truth, the church needs to be gripped anew by the truth of God's reign or kingdom like it never has before.[3] I have come to define it as the biblical vision of God's *shalom*—the world whole, reconciled, and full of life—reflected most profoundly and completely in the person of Jesus Christ and made possible today by the power of the Holy Spirit. To the extent that God reigns over existence, reconciliation between God and people, between people and people, and between God, people, and creation happens. The good news of the reign of God heralds the incarnated truth that God has set in irreversible motion the reconciliation of all things. The reign of God has a boundless and all-encompassing effect on the whole of existence, from the domain of the human heart to the cosmos and everything in between.

2. Mortimer Arias, *Announcing the Reign of God: Evangelization and the Subversive Memory of Jesus* (Eugene, OR: Wipf & Stock, 2001), 9.

3. I am aware of the arguments against using "kingdom" language—such as its obvious masculine bias and the fact that monarchies are just not as prevalent in today's world as they were in Jesus's day. "Reign of God" is the preferred descriptor. I will use both phrases in this chapter (and the rest of the book), which is probably an indication that I myself am in transition from the beloved phrase "kingdom of God" to the more acceptable "reign of God."

The Gospel of the Biblical Kingdom

The Gospel Jesus Preached: The Kingdom of God

Biblical scholars across the liberal-conservative spectrum have left no doubt that the gospel Jesus preached was the gospel of the kingdom, but we need not look any further than Jesus's own words to see this. When people in Simon's hometown try to prevent Jesus from leaving them, he says, "I must proclaim the good news of the kingdom of God to the other cities also; for I was sent for this purpose" (Luke 4:43). "For Jesus," Arias asserts, "evangelization was no more and no less than announcing the reign of God."[4]

Agreement on this fact, however, has not translated through the centuries into agreement on a definition of the kingdom of God. Howard Snyder identifies eight ways in which the church has interpreted or emphasized the kingdom in history, and that is likely only the half of it.[5] According to Arias, variations of how the church has historically understood it have to do with emphasizing one aspect of the kingdom at the expense of other aspects. Reductions of the kingdom include:

1. a transcendent sphere outside the realities of this world and the struggles of history;
2. the institutional and visible kingdom of the church;
3. the apocalyptic facet of the kingdom, [that is,] a catastrophic end of this world with an imminent second coming;
4. our inner experience of salvation or the baptism of the Holy Spirit without any reference to Christ's lordship over the totality of life;
5. a historical kingdom identified with a particular scheme of revolution or social order.

"And all the time," Arias laments, "we have identified our reduction of the kingdom with the whole, at the cost of the other dimensions."[6]

Jesus has no such reductionist tendencies. He preaches that the kingdom of God drives demons away in the present (Luke 11:20), but also that we still need to pray for its future coming (Matt. 6:10). He invites individuals to enter

4. Arias, *Announcing*, xviii.
5. Howard A. Snyder, "Models of the Kingdom: Sorting Out the Practical Meaning of God's Reign," in *Mission as Transformation: A Theology of the Whole Gospel*, ed. Vinay Samuel and Chris Sugden (Oxford: Regnum, 1999), 121–31. The eight models he discusses are (1) future hope, (2) inner spiritual experience, (3) mystical communion, (4) institutional church, (5) countersystem, (6) political state, (7) Christianized culture, and (8) earthly utopia.
6. Arias, *Announcing*, 66–67.

into the kingdom, such as the repentant criminal crucified beside him at Golgotha (Luke 23:42–43), but he also threatens the status quo of the religious and political establishments (23:1–25). He preaches that the kingdom of God resides within and among us (17:21) and that it is not of this world (John 18:36), but he also preaches a kingdom with real-life implications. For example, when the disciples of John the Baptist ask on John's behalf whether Jesus is the promised Messiah, Jesus tells them, "Go and tell John what you have seen and heard: the blind receive their sight, the lame walk, the lepers are cleansed, the deaf hear, the dead are raised, the poor have good news brought to them" (Luke 7:22–23). Furthermore, Jesus describes the kingdom as gradual in growth (Mark 4:26–28), but also apocalyptic or catastrophic in its coming (Matt. 25:1–6).

In his words and deeds, Jesus does not just bear witness to one or two aspects of the kingdom; he also preaches and demonstrates the now-and-not-yet, individual/social, otherworldly/this-worldly, and eschatological/apocalyptic kingdom of God in its totality. By doing so, he brings glad tidings for the whole of the created order. He testifies to nothing less than the restoration of the *shalom* of God, to which all will have access, especially the poor, the captive, the sick, and the oppressed (Luke 4:18).

The Gospel the Apostles Preached: Jesus, Embodiment of the Kingdom

God has called the church that formed in Jesus's name to testify to that same *shalom*—the whole and reconciled gospel—by the power of the Spirit. This call has not changed for the last two thousand years. Beginning with the apostles, however, the proclamation of the gospel has had a different ring to it. Biblical scholars across the spectrum also agree that a shift occurred when the apostles began their postascension, post-Pentecost ministry. They concur for the most part that while Jesus announced that "the kingdom of God is at hand," the apostles declared, "Jesus is Lord."[7] In the succinct words of Rudolf Bultmann, "The Proclaimer became the Proclaimed."[8]

The shift itself should not surprise us, for the person of Jesus left a profound, paradigm-shifting, life-transforming impression on his followers. Though often slow to catch on to the teachings of Jesus, the disciples eventually realized that they were not just following a prophet or a wise man but rather, as Peter declared under divine inspiration, "the Messiah, the Son of the living God" (Matt. 16:16). The manner of Jesus's death and resurrection surely validated Peter's words. When the risen Jesus greeted Mary Magdalene and "the other Mary" outside the tomb three days after his crucifixion,

7. Arias, *Announcing*, 56.
8. Quoted in Arias, *Announcing*, 56.

"They came to him, took hold of his feet, and worshiped him" (Matt. 28:9). And when Thomas encountered the scarred but living Jesus, he spoke for all the disciples when he overcame his doubt and confessed, "My Lord and my God!" (John 20:28). The life, ministry, friendship, death, and resurrection of Jesus left the disciples profoundly and eternally changed. How can their proclamation to the world be anything other than "Jesus is Lord; follow him!"

Beyond their own epiphanies, however, Jesus essentially commissioned them to bear witness to him "in Jerusalem, in all Judea and Samaria, and to the ends of the earth" (Acts 1:8). And he later commissioned Paul to "bring [his] name before Gentiles and kings and before the people of Israel" (Acts 9:15). To proclaim his name throughout the known world, therefore, also constituted an act of obedience.

We cannot deny the shift from Jesus's announcement of God's reign to the apostles' proclamation of Jesus as Savior and Lord. However, for the apostles, to proclaim Jesus was to proclaim the kingdom of God. For them, the shift was no shift at all; they slowly but surely understood that in Christ, the long-awaited rule and reign of God had come.[9] They knew that "in him all the fullness of God was pleased to dwell" (Col. 1:19). Jesus personified the kingdom; he embodied it, thus making it a present reality that had the concrete power to heal bodies, drive out demons, reconcile enemies (e.g., Simon the Zealot and Matthew the tax collector[10]), and challenge religious and political power structures. When the apostles preached Jesus, therefore, they preached the good news of the reign of God; only now it had a name and a face—the name and face of Jesus.[11]

Unfortunately, as the centuries rolled on, the church began to separate the person of Jesus and the reality of the kingdom. Fast-forwarding to the twentieth century, for example, the Protestant church in North America underwent the infamous fundamentalist-modernist controversy, which, sadly, could be characterized as "the kingdom of God versus Jesus." Dallas Willard described this in a lecture wherein he said succinctly, "The liberals got the kingdom and the fundamentalists got Jesus."[12] Thus the deformed births of many, if not most, if not all, false and half gospels!

9. For more on the expectation of the kingdom, see Ronald J. Sider, *Good News and Good Works: A Theology of the Whole Gospel* (Grand Rapids: Baker, 1999), 52–54.

10. A published sermon by Gregory Boyd describes the relationship between Simon the Zealot and Matthew the tax collector as one that is only possible by the presence of the kingdom in the person of Jesus. This sermon can be found in Al Tizon, *Missional Preaching: Engage, Embrace, Transform* (Valley Forge, PA: Judson, 2012), 62.

11. Arias, *Announcing*, 58. For a more detailed discussion of this, see Lesslie Newbigin, *The Open Secret*, rev. ed. (Grand Rapids: Eerdmans, 1995), 40–55.

12. Dallas Willard, Spirituality and Ministry course, Fuller Theological Seminary, Pasadena, CA (June 2, 2003). Here I am indebted to the notes of Donn Engebretson, who was then vice president of the Evangelical Covenant Church and attended this course.

The Gospel for the Church Today: Jesus and the Biblical Kingdom

In our increasingly globalizing, diversifying, fracturing world, the church needs to recover the full message of Jesus Christ, the embodiment of the kingdom. Since the time of the apostles and until Christ returns, the God of mission has sent the church to proclaim, demonstrate, and live out this gospel throughout the whole world.

Thus far I have only implied that the gospel of the kingdom is the biblical gospel. By that I mean that among the many gospels being preached, the gospel of the kingdom alone aligns with the overall narrative of Scripture, which I assume remains the primary document of faith and practice for most of the readers of this book. Therefore, against the backdrop of false and half gospels, let me be so bold (and antipostmodern!) as to say that the gospel of the kingdom is the only true and whole gospel on the grounds of its consistency with the rest of the biblical story. While false gospels stray from the biblical narrative, half gospels leave essential parts out. The gospel of God's reign that Jesus proclaimed and embodied, on the other hand, keeps the biblical story in line and whole.

The Bible tells the story of the coming kingdom of God, and the arrival of the kingdom in Jesus Christ constitutes the crucial midway point—not the beginning—of that story.[13] Although the phrase "kingdom of God" does not appear in the Old Testament, the theme "is found in one form or another through the length and width of the Bible."[14] At the risk of oversimplification, I find the following broad outline helpful in viewing the whole of Scripture in terms of the kingdom story:[15]

1. God's rule in creation and fall (Gen. 1–11)
2. God's rule in Israel (Gen. 12–Esther)
3. God's rule through the sages and prophets (Job–Malachi)
4. God's rule in Christ (Matthew–John)
5. God's rule through a Spirit-empowered church (Acts–Jude)
6. God's rule in the new heaven and new earth (Revelation)

During God's rule in creation and fall, *shalom* existed at creation because God ruled the earth, and creation was marred because humankind succumbed to the lure of becoming ruler-gods themselves. During God's rule in Israel, we

---

13. René Padilla, *Mission between the Times*, rev. and updated ed. (Carlisle, UK: Langham, 2010), 200–201.

14. John Bright, *The Kingdom of God* (Nashville: Abingdon, 1953), 7.

15. This section is excerpted from Tizon, *Missional Preaching*, 16–18, with permission from Judson Press.

can interpret the Abrahamic, Mosaic, and Davidic covenants as God's initiatives to restore the kingdom via a particular people—namely, the Hebrews turned nation of Israel—for the sake of all peoples. Not insignificantly, the Habiru, or the Hebrews, represented an ethnically diverse group of people whom God formed into God's representative people, thus at the start laying the foundation for both the celebration of ethnic diversity and the ministry of reconciliation.[16] Through the formation of a people of God, who would live out the divine ethics of peace, mercy, justice, and righteousness on both the personal and sociopolitical levels, all the peoples of the earth would have the opportunity to see what life would be like under God's rule.

Israel, however, failed to obey this call to be light unto the nations. From early grumblings right after the miraculous exodus to the unstable period of the judges to the tragic events of the monarchy, God's people failed to stay faithful to God and to uphold justice. During God's rule through the sages and prophets, we can interpret the songs, laments, and prophecies in Israel as keeping the notion of the kingdom of God alive in the hearts and minds of God's people, despite the failures of the nation. As the sages kept them singing and reflecting deeply on true spirituality, the prophets pointed to the promise of the coming kingdom via a Messiah in the line of David, even as they pronounced judgment on Israel's unfaithfulness and injustice.

God's rule in Christ represents the crucial midway point of the kingdom story, as the birth, life, teaching, death, and resurrection of Christ, to which the four Gospels attest, began the fulfillment of the prophesied hope of the kingdom. God called Israel to embody the kingdom in its national life, but it failed miserably. In the midst of the failure, the prophets "foresaw a future day when God's Messiah would come to pour out the Spirit in a new way (Joel 2:28–29) and restore God's people as a visible community living in right relationship with God, neighbor, and earth."[17] The Christmas truth of the coming of Christ began the fulfillment of this vision. Jesus Christ, God's Messiah, embodied the reign of God in his person. Jesus incarnated the kingdom as he ministered compassion, justice, and forgiveness by word, deed, and miraculous signs, and as he taught the truths and values of the kingdom in ways the masses could access. That the conventionally excluded—the gentile, the prostitute, the sinner—had access in Christ to the things of God infuriated the establishment leaders of Jesus's day. This major bone of contention no doubt fueled their efforts to snuff him out, and they succeeded in having him condemned to crucifixion. But the Gospels

---

16. Ronald J. Sider, John M. Perkins, Wayne L. Gordon, and F. Albert Tizon, *Linking Arms, Linking Lives: How Urban-Suburban Partnerships Can Transform Communities* (Grand Rapids: Baker Books, 2008), 51.

17. Sider, *Good News*, 52.

tell us that death had no ultimate power, as God raised Jesus from the dead on the third day. The church ever since has had this good news to proclaim from the rooftops! As long as Jesus is alive, the kingdom is here.

On the strength of the kingdom's presence in Christ, God has indeed passed on the call to proclaim and embody God's reign to the ends of the earth. In God's rule through a Spirit-empowered church, God did not orphan the disciples, as the Holy Spirit empowered and resourced them to fulfill their missional call. Pentecost itself demonstrated the reconciling power of God, as both Jew and gentile heard the good news in their own tongue (Acts 2:1–12). By the power, gifts, and direction of the Spirit, God's people not only embodied the kingdom in a multiethnic community as Jew and gentile came together (itself a profound picture of kingdom reconciliation); they not only voluntarily created a common purse to ensure that no needy resided among them; they also began proactively to extend the message and values of the kingdom "in Jerusalem, in all Judea and Samaria, and to the ends of the earth" (Acts 1:8–2:42). Insofar as these epochs represent periods of time, we are here. The Spirit-empowered church today continues to reflect both the presence and future of God's reign.

Finally, in God's rule in the new heaven and new earth, we catch a glimpse of the future toward which God is working , when the cosmic struggle between good and evil will come to an end, and Jesus will arise from the ashes as Christus Victor. The healing of the nations will characterize life in the consummated kingdom—that is, the final reconciliation—because Jesus will take his rightful place as Lord of lords and King of kings. These designations often serve as metaphors today, but they will be literal in God's future! The struggles that plague creation will end, and the reign of God will prevail.

Of course, the Bible contains many more stories that provide details of the unfolding divine drama. This sprint through Scripture merely intends to identify the larger narrative of the biblical kingdom in which the gospel of God's reign in Jesus Christ finds its true home. Between the history and hope of God's reign in the Old Testament and God's future of peace, justice, and reconciled relationships, of which we catch a glimpse in the New Testament, the church today continues the apostolic mission to bear witness to the whole and reconciled gospel—the gospel of the now-and-not-yet kingdom of God in Jesus Christ—in word, deed, and life.

The Gospel of Shalom: The Reconciliation of All Things

The basic answer, therefore, to the question "What is the gospel?" boils down to "It is the good news of the kingdom." But the time has come to specify this: What exactly did Jesus and the apostles refer to when they preached the reign or kingdom of God? And furthermore, what was and is so good about it? The answers to these questions define the very message that drives the church's mission today.

At the beginning of the chapter I offered a working definition of the reign of God, which refers to the biblical vision of God's *shalom*—wholeness and fullness of life—reflected most profoundly and completely in Jesus Christ and made possible today by the ministry of the Holy Spirit. To the extent that God reigns over existence, reconciliation between God and people, between people and people, and between God, people, and creation happens. Though nothing about this definition should astonish us, it appropriately emphasizes the theme of reconciliation, which gets at the heart of the whole gospel and also paves a practical path for the church's ministry of reconciliation in today's fragmented world.

The Kingdom: Biblical Vision of God's Shalom

Reconciliation acknowledges the brokenness of the world and envisions the restoration of a fragmented, divided, and disordered creation. More fundamentally, however, it also implies that once upon a time the world was not broken. At one point in the history of the world, "God saw everything that [God] had made, and indeed, it was very good" (Gen. 1:31). In the beginning, God created *shalom*.

This Hebrew word, often translated into English as "peace," refers more to wholeness, justice, social harmony, health, well-being, and fullness of life, all of which result in peace—inner, spiritual, communal, and global. It refers to a large, complex, biblical theme that reflects the very nature of God as well as the will of God for all creation. Walter Brueggemann claims that no one biblical word captures the well-being of all of existence, but *shalom* comes close.[18] Coupled with the Greek word *eirēnē*, which refers primarily to inner and interpersonal peace, *shalom* covers the widest sense of well-being, ranging from peace with God and self, to peace among families, cultures, and nations, as well as to peace with animals and the whole created order. When I am asked to give a simple definition for *shalom*, I say it means "God's very best"—for me, for others, for all, and for all creation.

Shalom—God's very best—describes the world as God created it. "Sin" describes how the pursuit of human self-interest, depicted by the fall of Adam and Eve in Genesis 3, violated the harmony of *shalom*. The opposite of *shalom*

18. Walter Brueggemann, *Peace* (St. Louis: Chalice, 2001), 14.

is not so much conflict or war (either would be too narrow) but rather the all-pervasiveness of sin. "Sin," Randy Woodley writes, "can be defined as the absence of shalom."[19]

Sin has resulted in all manner of evil, from the inner turmoil of the human heart, to the unjust sociopolitical structures of nations, to the ugliness of war, even to the destruction of creation itself. Alienated, lonely, suicidal people; billions of poor, oppressed, and hopeless in blighted urban centers; sexism, racism, and classism; distorted sexuality that has resulted in the trafficking of millions of women and children; corruption and abuse at the hands of the rich and powerful; bloodshed and violence; environmental degradation: these horrific realities and much more characterize the handiwork of sin.

When Jesus announced that the reign of God was at hand, he essentially declared that its presence marked the eventual defeat of sin and its power. Or, said positively, he promised the restoration of *shalom*. Good news! As David Gushee asserts, "Many characteristics of a world of *shalom* are articulated by Jesus of Nazareth, under the rubric of the inaugurated kingdom of God."[20] While the garden of Eden in Genesis 2 represents *shalom* created, the new Jerusalem in Revelation 21:2—the capital of the kingdom of God—represents *shalom* that will be re-created at the end of time. Between creation and re-creation, God has called for the Spirit-empowered participation of the community of Jesus to testify to the good news of the coming *shalom* kingdom in word, deed, and life.

The Shalom Kingdom: The Reconciliation of All Things

This good news of God's *shalom* kingdom, which God is even now establishing and has invited all to enjoy, drives the whole mission of the whole church. Here I see the reconciliatory nature of the gospel most clearly, for how else will God's *shalom* kingdom be established except by putting back together what was shattered in the fall? Reconciliation defines the gospel of the *shalom* kingdom, as God promises the healing of creation by putting an end to violence, war, oppression, and injustice. God's *shalom* will be restored, and God's kingdom will be established by the divine process of the reconciliation of all things. This is the whole and reconciled gospel to which we bear witness.

19. Randy Woodley, *Shalom and the Community of Creation: An Indigenous Vision* (Grand Rapids: Eerdmans, 2012), 23.

20. David Gushee, "Shalom," in *Prophetic Evangelicals: Envisioning a Just and Peaceable Kingdom*, ed. Bruce E. Benson, Malinda E. Berry, and Peter G. Heltzel (Grand Rapids: Eerdmans, 2012), 72.

The church's message of reconciliation—the whole gospel—involves at least three dimensions: "the vertical dimension (between God and people), the horizontal dimension (between people and people), and the circular dimension (between God, people, and creation)."[21] These dimensions provide the basic framework of reconciliation as mission, so I will refer back to these frequently and expand upon them in the chapters that follow. We can make a case that these dimensions build on each other, or at least that our message begins with the good news that in Christ, God has reached out to be reconciled to people (the vertical). In Christ, God has closed the gap between God and humankind, enabling people once again to enjoy right relationship with God by the grace of God and through faith in God. Sin entered into God's *shalom* at the hands of human beings. Motivated by self-interest, Adam and Eve disobeyed the one law of God not to eat of the tree of the knowledge of good and evil (Gen. 2:15–17). This grieved and angered God, enough that God banished them from *shalom* (3:22–24). All other rifts flow out of this first rift between God and humankind. If the reconciliation of all things will happen (and it will), it necessarily begins with God's initiating move toward people to be reconciled to God's own self.

By the love of God, demonstrated most profoundly in the cross and resurrection of Christ, God has indeed taken the initiative, offering mercy and forgiveness, and thus paving the way for sinners to be reconciled to God. "Through Christ's substitutionary death 'for us' reconciliation has been achieved once for all, leading to forgiveness of sins, communion with God, and new life in God's kingdom."[22] Those who through faith receive God's gracious offer of mercy in Christ become a new creation (2 Cor. 5:17), they begin a journey of healing and transformation from the ravages of sin (Rom. 8:9–39), and they become the worshiping, missional community of the redeemed—the church (Eph. 2:19–22). The fundamentally evangelistic nature of the church's message of reconciliation should strike us here. In eternal gratitude to God for the gift of saving grace, the church joyfully, humbly, and passionately invites others to experience the forgiveness of Christ and to join the new community. The good news begins with an invitation to enter into God's love by way of repentance, confession, and commitment to Jesus, sealed in baptism.

21. Tormod Engelsviken, "Reconciliation with God—Its Meaning and Its Significance for Mission," in *Mission as Ministry of Reconciliation*, ed. Robert Schreiter and Knud Jorgensen (Oxford: Regnum, 2013), 79.
22. World Council of Churches, "Mission as Ministry of Reconciliation," May 10, 2005, https://www.oikoumene.org/en/resources/documents/other-meetings/mission-and-evangelism/preparatory-paper-10-mission-as-ministry-of-reconciliation, cited in Engelsviken, "Reconciliation with God," 85.

However, if reconciliation between people and people (the horizontal) does not follow reconciliation between God and people, we have the biblical right to question the authenticity of the vertical. "What good is it, my brothers and sisters," admonishes James, "if you say you have faith but do not have works? Can faith save you? If a brother or sister is naked and lacks daily food, and one of you says to them, 'Go in peace; keep warm and eat your fill,' and yet you do not supply their bodily needs, what is the good of that?" (James 2:14–16). The horizontal verifies the vertical.

The whole gospel testifies to God's desire to see people love other people, forgiving, serving, and enjoying one another. Neighbors loving neighbors: this is the royal law, according to James (2:8). He does not even bother to mention loving God as part of the royal law, because love of neighbor proves love of God. This is what enables Robert Moffitt to call the church's responsibility to love others, especially those in need, the "irreducible minimum." He elaborates, "The greatest commandment is to love God and to love our neighbor as ourselves; however, the Law is ultimately summarized in scripture as the love of neighbor" (see Gal. 5:14).[23]

The circular dimension of the whole gospel of reconciliation refers to how God will heal creation itself. "Reconciliation and redemption do not apply only to humans," asserts Tormod Engelsviken, "but to the whole creation, the whole of the cosmos,"[24] which the fall also effectively marred. Since sin entered the world, nothing has worked right, including the ecological system. Furthermore, in its fallenness, humanity has abused God's ecosystem, creating a great rift among humankind, creaturekind, and the earth. The relationship between these requires divine reconciliation. As Paul explains, "The creation itself will be set free from its bondage to decay and will obtain the freedom of the glory of the children of God." He longs for the reconciliation of all things: "We know that the whole creation has been groaning in labor pains until now; and not only the creation, but we ourselves" (Rom. 8:22–23). The circular dimension of reconciliation requires that the gospel, to which we bear witness in word and deed, include the good news of right relationship between humanity and the rest of the created order, fulfilling part of God's promise to mend broken creation, to reconcile all things.

This is the gospel of the *shalom* kingdom: reconciliation between God and people, between people and people, and between God, people, and creation. God calls us to preach this whole and reconciled gospel and nothing less.

23. Robert Moffitt, "Irreducible Minimum," Harvest Foundation, accessed October 25, 2017, http://www.harvestfoundation.org/harvest-basic-lessons (login required).
24. Engelsviken, "Reconciliation with God," 89.

We need to consider one more aspect of the whole gospel—namely, that the task of the reconciliation of all things belongs to God. The church announces it and models it; it doesn't bring it about. Our definition of the kingdom states that to the extent that God reigns over existence, reconciliation . . . happens. The church—a community of the broken, as we shall see in part 3—does not and cannot accomplish reconciliation; God does, though God invites us to participate. The biblical witness declares that God, who has initiated reconciliation, will ultimately finish it. Miroslav Volf explains this in terms of "non-final" and "final" levels. He writes, "[The question] is not how to achieve the final reconciliation, but what resources we need to live in peace in the absence of the final reconciliation. . . . I advocate here for a non-final reconciliation based on a vision of reconciliation that cannot be undone."[25]

Although we can enjoy knowing that the ultimate responsibility to reconcile all things rests on God, the message that we have been entrusted to proclaim requires the church's blood, sweat, and tears (*not* to be read metaphorically!) as we bear witness to God's *shalom* kingdom in Jesus Christ "in Jerusalem, in all Judea and Samaria, and to the ends of the earth."

With this understanding of the whole gospel, we are now ready to consider more deeply the role of the church, which God has formed, empowered, and commissioned to bear witness to the whole and reconciled gospel. As Emmanuel Katongole and Chris Rice write, "The vision of reconciliation . . . needs a church where real and fragile people embody the gospel."[26] In short, the church at its best makes visible the vertical, horizontal, and circular dimensions of reconciliation, made possible in Christ and by the power of the Spirit. What does this missional church look like, as it embodies and practices the whole and reconciled gospel throughout the whole world? To this question we now turn.

Discussion Questions

1. In your own words, what is the good news of the kingdom of God, and what is so good about it?
2. In what ways have you experienced God's *shalom* in your life?
3. In what ways have you seen God's *shalom* at work in the world, reconciling people to God (vertical), people to people (horizontal), and people to creation (circular)?

25. Miroslav Volf, *Exclusion and Embrace: A Theological Exploration of Identity, Otherness, and Reconciliation* (Nashville: Abingdon, 1996), 109.

26. Emmanuel Katongole and Chris Rice, *Reconciling All Things: A Christian Vision for Justice, Peace and Healing* (Downers Grove, IL: IVP Books, 2008), 109.

Part 3

Whole Church

God has entrusted the gospel of the coming kingdom to the church that Jesus built, and as such we cannot theologically separate gospel and church. Our discussion on the whole gospel in part 2, therefore, begs for a follow-up discussion on the whole church, the theme of part 3, and for that matter on the whole mission, the theme of part 4. To be sure, the intertwined nature of gospel, church, and mission—three aspects of the one reality of God's reign—makes it difficult to consider them separately. We must make the effort, however, in order to sharpen our understanding of the relationship between them, though we will unavoidably run into overlaps. Redefining holistic mission through the lens of reconciliation in a fractured world requires this kind of sharpening. Part 3 considers anew the church's identity and purpose in the world as it relates to the whole gospel of the *shalom* kingdom. What is the church, and why does it exist? Who are we as the community of God's people? What does it mean to be the whole church in the service of the whole gospel throughout the whole world?

Statistically, the whole church today means an estimated 2.3 billion professing Christians, 45,000 denominations, and 4.3 million congregations around the world.[1] These statistics make Christianity the largest religion in the world.

---

1. Todd M. Johnson, Gina A. Zurlo, Albert W. Hickman, and Peter F. Crossing, "Christianity 2015: Religious Diversity and Personal Contact," *International Bulletin of Missionary Research* 39, no. 1 (January 2015): 29. The particular number of congregations ranges wildly among sources, from 4.3 million to 40 million! I decided to go with the more conservative number, which, according to a representative of the Center for the Study of World Christianity via email, dated September 6, 2016, includes house churches and underground meetings.

Moreover, they demonstrate that Christianity is on the rise, in part because "the growth of Christianity in the Global South is now outpacing losses in the Global North."[2]

The idea of the whole church, however, means much more than what numbers might say. The global church may be growing numerically, but the fact that this has not translated into a more just and peaceable world, not even in areas where Christianity has flourished, should tell us that the church itself needs to hear the essence of the whole gospel.[3] Beyond the numbers, the idea of whole church calls for the ongoing conversion of the church to live in a manner worthy of the high call to represent the whole and reconciled gospel (Eph. 4:1–6). But it also means the lavish grace of God when the church fails to live up to that high calling (Eph. 2:4–9; 1 John 1:8–10). The church is both in the holy service of Christ and in desperate need of Christ.

These two images—a community of broken people who live on the life support of God's grace and an active, confident, missional people bearing witness to the whole gospel—do not and should not cancel each other out. I propose that the utterly human and gloriously divine sides of the church together define biblical ecclesiology. They provide a fuller picture of a church that engages the world, to employ the famous words of David Bosch, "in bold humility."[4]

Humility before Boldness

Humility necessarily comes first. Rather than understanding this virtue as a requirement of the faith, we should view it more as the only viable posture of a desperately needy people. Before we are the people of God, we are just people whose lives fall pathetically short of the glory of God. As a community of the broken, the church does not deserve the designations of holy nation, chosen race, royal priesthood, and so forth. The church is the church on a grace-alone basis (Eph. 2:8–9). In that light, what else can we be but humble?

2. Johnson et al., "Christianity 2015," 28.

3. E.g., David Zac Niringiye recounts the genocide that occurred in Rwanda in the mid-1990s, "in a country that was reckoned to have well over 95% of its eight million-strong population claiming some church affiliation." *The Church: God's Pilgrim People* (Carlisle, UK: Langham, 2014), 3.

4. David J. Bosch, *Transforming Mission: Paradigm Shifts in Theology of Mission*, 20th anniv. ed. (Maryknoll, NY: Orbis Books, 2011), 500–501. See also Willem Saayman and Klippies Kritzinger, eds., *Mission in Bold Humility: David Bosch's Work Considered* (Eugene, OR: Wipf & Stock, 2013). Although the phrase "bold humility" is found within Bosch's discussion on mission and interfaith dialogue, the editors and contributors of this Festschrift have appropriated it as an apt description of Bosch's whole approach to mission.

Ironically, however, a humble church that embraces its imperfections, inadequacies, and sins becomes the one most poised to bear witness to the good news of Jesus Christ in the world. As Bosch asserts, "Only broken [people] can lead others to the cross."[5]

I detected the existence of a significant gap between the glorious biblical theology of God's people and the real experience of church fairly early on in my Christian life. Passionate for Jesus as a new believer, I began attending a church in obedience to those who were nurturing me along in the faith. The first clue that church did not match the glory of God came as I encountered people who claimed to know the amazing, wonderful, and risen Savior but who did not seem very excited about it. The music also left much to be desired. Wanting to jump for joy with the intensity that corresponded with my newfound faith, I endured what sounded to me like funeral dirges. An incomprehensible, uninspiring speech, which someone later told me was called a sermon, followed. Then afterward the people engaged in what felt like plastic fellowship, chitchatting about meaningless things over coffee and doughnuts before driving away. I fought off moments of panic that I had made an awful decision to follow the way of Jesus!

Granted, I was an immature teenager, an adolescent in every way, who thought the counterculture of the 1960s and '70s got it right. Church felt like being in the middle of everything that era rebelled against. But I fought through these things, knowing deep down that insofar as the church represented Jesus, it represented the answer to all of life's questions. Nowadays, of course, I very much appreciate those "funeral dirges," I am now one of those boring preachers, and I no longer experience fellowship as plasticky, as I used to. So I have either joined the ranks of the "frozen chosen" just by getting older, or I have come to terms with the fact that a gap will always exist between the real and the ideal. Maybe both are true to some degree. In any case, not long after I came to faith I suspected that the community called the church will never live up to my growing understanding of abundant life under the reign of God.

This part of my own personal journey, of course, only represents the lighter side of the church not living up to the call. The heavier side includes historically colluding with colonialism, witch hunts, and fascism; it includes child abuse and subsequent cover-ups; it includes sex scandals, money scams, and unjustifiable material extravagance among high-profile Christian leaders; it includes barring from fellowship and communion "those people," whomever "those people" are at any given time; it includes being silent in the face of

5. David J. Bosch, *A Spirituality of the Road* (Eugene, OR: Wipf & Stock, 2001), 77.

injustice. For whatever else the church may have been throughout history up to the present time, it has also been undeniably a community of broken, sinful people, like all human communities.

An increasing number of churches today acknowledge and embrace this reality. If yesterday's churches tended to draw a clearer line between holy church and unholy community, the newer congregations today that have risen from the post-Christendom, postcolonial movement, are acutely aware of the brokenness that characterizes all people, and they "do church" accordingly. Ryan Bolger explains, further, that these newer types of churches "create a space where faith is not required for inclusion in the community. They offer many on-ramps to people wherever they may be on the spiritual trek. Many need a place where they can question things. These communities make no effort to determine who is in and who is out."[6]

In these posteverything "church experiments," the broken *are* the church.[7] The names of some of them reveal as much. One in particular, House for All Sinners and Saints, a congregation of the Evangelical Lutheran Church of America in Denver, Colorado, says it all. When asked whether everyone is Lutheran at HFASS, the response on its website reads, "Not even close. . . . Maybe a quarter of us identify as Lutherans; the rest are post-Evangelicals, Methodists, agnostics, Reformed, Episcopalian, and the ever-popular 'nothing.'"[8] In her book *Accidental Saints*, HFASS founder and pastor Nadia Bolz-Weber tells stories of ordinary, broken people in her congregation through whom God creatively and frequently accomplishes holy things.[9] How can this reality—God's radical, transforming grace that enables broken people to be used for divine purposes—evoke anything else but profound humility?

Boldness: Our Missional Identity

On what basis, then, can we be outwardly bold about our faith, the second half of kingdom ecclesiology? Our boldness comes from the initiating love, liberating forgiveness, and creative power of the Triune God. As we humbly submit to God's transformation, we develop the capacity to bear witness to the whole and reconciled gospel throughout the whole world. When Jesus

6. Ryan K. Bolger, conclusion to *The Gospel after Christendom*, ed. Ryan K. Bolger (Grand Rapids: Baker Academic, 2012), 354.
7. See Bolger, *Gospel after Christendom*, esp. the section "Experiments," 229–312.
8. House for All Sinners and Saints, "Who We Are," accessed October 25, 2017, http://www.houseforall.org/whoweare.
9. Nadia Bolz-Weber, *Accidental Saints: Finding God in All the Wrong People* (New York: Convergent, 2015), 193.

described his disciples as the salt of the earth and the light of the world, he meant those images to refer not to goals but to points of identity (Matt. 5:13–16). We *are* salt and light. Even as Christians today more openly embrace their common brokenness with the rest of humanity, the theological fact of the presence of the Spirit makes them a broken people *on the mend*.

Our new identity in Christ has within it the inherent properties of salt and light, or what Alan Hirsch calls "mDNA," the power of the Holy Spirit within us to change the world.[10] Despite the need to be healed and transformed themselves, the people of God qua the people of God contain within them God's desire to heal and transform the whole world. Therefore, as the broken, humble church claims its identity as God's missional people, it engages the world with the whole gospel, and it does so boldly.

Bold Humility: The Church of the Whole Gospel

The church, then, is at once broken and called. The sooner we grasp both of these sides of the nature of the church, the sooner we can "get on with it," that is, engage in mission in bold humility. These two seemingly contradictory dimensions do not cancel each other out; they in fact appear consistently throughout Scripture in its heroes. "Turns out," Michael Yaconelli explains, "that all the biblical characters were a complex mix of strengths and weaknesses. David, Abraham, Lot, Saul, Solomon, Rahab, and Sarah were God-loving, courageous, brilliant, fearless, loyal, passionate, committed holy men and women who were also murderers, adulterers and manic depressives. They were men and women who could be gentle holy defenders of the faith one minute, and insecure, mentally unstable, unbelieving, shrewd, lying, grudge-holding tyrants the next."[11] God shows mercy to undeserving sinners, and then, by the Spirit, God begins the long-term project of guiding them toward their identity as "a chosen race, a royal priesthood, a holy nation, God's own people, in order that [they] may proclaim the mighty acts of him who called [them] out of darkness into his marvelous light" (1 Pet. 2:9). From the formation of Israel out of a reluctant band of Hebrew slaves (Exod. 19:1–8) to the formation of the church out of a hodgepodge of Jewish and gentile converts (Acts 11:1–26; Eph. 2:11–22), "the Bible attests to a God who intentionally chooses and uses broken, imperfect people to accomplish God's purposes,

10. Alan Hirsch, *Forgotten Ways: Reactivating the Missional Church* (Grand Rapids: Brazos, 2006), 15–26.

11. Michael Yaconelli, *Messy Spirituality: God's Annoying Love for Imperfect People* (Grand Rapids: Zondervan, 2002), 14.

as if broken vessels themselves carry with them the message of God's saving grace."[12]

The whole church, then, does not mean perfect church; it means humble church in bold mission. It means submitting to God's work in our own lives, even as God sends us out to bear witness to the whole and reconciled gospel. Therefore, the church represents both the fruit and the instrument of the gospel, as the Spirit moves *in* and *through* it for the sake of the world. David Zac Niringiye puts it succinctly in terms of love. As both beneficiaries and instruments of the gospel, "the new community is called by love, in love, for love, and to love."[13]

Part 3 is predicated on the belief that the impact of the whole and reconciled gospel on the world depends on the wholeness of the bold and humble church. It explores what it means to be the whole church. Chapter 6 begins the discussion by asserting that "whole church" must start by considering what it means to be a whole person. For, as corporate entities, churches are at least an assembly of individuals who have submitted to God's work of transformation. In other words, the church qua church cannot move toward wholeness if its individual members are not moving toward wholeness. Chapter 7 follows the discussion on whole persons with a trinitarian look at the church as a diverse, reconciled, and reconciling community. The theological basis of the call of the church to be whole and reconciled lies in the practical mystery of the Father, Son, and Holy Spirit in perfect oneness. Chapter 8 then concludes part 3 by discussing the important relationship between worship and mission, for the effectiveness of the church's whole and reconciled mission depends on the depth of its spirituality—that is, its experience of God in its very life.

---

12. John Chung and Al Tizon, "Extending Grace and Reconciliation: From Broken Households to the Ends of the Earth," in *Honoring the Generations: Hearing with Asian North American Congregations*, ed. M. Sydney Park, Soong-Chan Rah, and Al Tizon (Valley Forge, PA: Judson, 2012), 171.

13. Niringiye, *Church*, 184.

SIX

Whole Persons

Reconciliation Beginning with Me

. . . .

You shall love your neighbor as yourself.
—Jesus (Matt. 22:39)

Palmer Theological Seminary, where I formerly taught, bears the motto "The whole gospel for the whole world through whole persons," but it did not always read that way. "Whole persons" was added later (in the early 1980s) in order to "guide students toward an awareness of their own brokenness and the need for a disciplined devotional life."[1] The motto's strength lies in the connection it makes between seeking to become persons of Christlike character and the *missio Dei*. Kudos to Palmer Seminary for thinking this connection important enough to extend its motto. Indeed, the effectiveness of the whole gospel for the whole world depends on disciples who seek to become whole persons.

During my tenure at Palmer, I attempted to make another important connection. In my introductory course on holistic ministry, I took the liberty to insert "whole church" unofficially in the motto, so it read, "The whole gospel for the whole world through whole persons and the whole church." I did not do so to campaign for yet another extension to the motto; I merely wanted to make the point to my students that the pursuit of becoming whole persons needs to be understood in the context of God's desire to form communities

---

1. Randall L. Frame, *Praise and Promise: A Pictorial History of the Eastern Baptist Theological Seminary* (Virginia Beach: Donning, 2000), 154.

of transforming people called churches, which God has called to bear witness to Christ's reconciling work in the world.

Nonetheless, the possibility of a whole and reconciled church depends on redeemed individuals, who seek in the Spirit to become whole and reconciled. Indeed, as Emmanuel Katongole and Chris Rice assert, "The journey of reconciliation begins with a transformation of the human person."[2] This chapter seeks to understand the personal transformational journey toward becoming whole and reconciled persons in Christ as an essential part of a theology of the whole church. Necessary questions emerge for this task, including basic ones, such as, What is the nature of the human person? What is the basis of human worth and well-being? And more importantly for our study, What does it mean to be a whole person in mission as part of God's call upon the whole church?

The Reconciled Self: Journey toward Wholeness

Human Nature

How we understand the nature of the human person—that is, our philosophical anthropology—informs our theology, ethics, and mission more than we might expect. It may seem as if the question "What is a human being?" invites only musings of speculative philosophers, but on the contrary, it looks for answers from all who care about the welfare of humanity.

Elsewhere I discuss the human person as a "body-soul unity" over against the more prevalent notion that the body serves as mere housing for the soul.[3] This more prevalent notion hinges on the belief that the body does not have what it takes to last, essentially because its corruptible nature cannot withstand the pure brightness of eternal glory. According to this view of the human person, we must transcend the flesh and the carnal world in which it lives if we seek to spend eternity with holy God, who is pure, flawless spirit.

Missionally speaking, therefore, to "save souls" from an irredeemable, temporal, material world becomes the primary, if not sole, definition of the church's task in the world. Those who understand the human person in this way believe that our ultimate salvation consists of someday shedding this mortal coil and transcending the material trappings of this world. As we

---

2. Emmanuel Katongole and Chris Rice, *Reconciling All Things: A Christian Vision of Justice, Peace and Healing* (Downers Grove, IL: IVP Books, 2008), 45.

3. Al Tizon, *Missional Preaching: Embrace, Engage, Transform* (Valley Forge, PA: Judson, 2012), 68–70. Parts of this section are adapted from these pages, with permission from Judson Press.

established in chapter 4, this more prevalent view of the nature of the human person bears the marks of the ancient heresy of Gnosticism, which runs contrary to the more biblically grounded truth that the human being is inseparably body and soul. "The human person," writes Joel Green, "does not consist of two (or three) parts . . . but is a living whole."[4]

Furthermore, the human being is a body-soul unity *in community with God, others, and creation.* The physical, the spiritual, and the *social* make up the human person. "Ontologically," asserts Andrea Ng'weshemi, "the human being . . . is best viewed as a living force among other forces in the universe."[5] From the story of creation onward, a biblical anthropology makes it clear that to be fully human means to be in right relationship with and fully reconciled to the Creator, fellow human beings, and the whole of the created order.

God formed Adam, breathed life into him, and set him in an ecological paradise for him to steward and enjoy (Gen. 2:7–15). As the creation story goes, Adam indeed enjoyed God's good creation, interacting with the earth and its animals, but he still felt incomplete in his humanity (Gen. 2:20). Only when God created Eve and presented her to him in Genesis 2:22–23 did the man exclaim, "At last!" as if to say, "I am now fully human." Ministers often evoke this passage at weddings, which can give the impression that singleness is something less than full humanity. This, of course, is not true; unmarried people find other means of community and can therefore experience wholeness as robustly as married people. So before the love story between Adam and Eve serves as a theology of marriage, we need to see it first as a sociology of humankind. Humans need other humans in order to be fully human.

After Adam and Eve ate of the forbidden fruit in Genesis 3, these relationships fractured. They hid from God, they blamed each other, and God eventually banished them from paradise (vv. 8–24). The rest of the biblical story can be seen as guiding broken humanity back into right relationship with God, each other, and creation as the way back to wholeness and reconciliation.[6] Indeed, the hope of the Christian is the return of Christ, when God completes the "wholeness project," wherein God's people will enjoy the direct company of God and one another in the context of a renewed heaven and a renewed earth (Rev. 21:1–22:7). The human being is a body-soul unity-in-community with God, others, and creation, and to the extent that we understand ourselves

4. Joel B. Green, *Body, Soul, and Human Life: The Nature of Humanity in the Bible* (Grand Rapids: Baker Academic, 2008), 4.

5. Andrea M. Ng'weshemi, *Rediscovering the Human: The Quest for a Christo-Theological Anthropology in Africa* (New York: Peter Lang, 2002), 14.

6. See James K. Bruckner, *Healthy Human Life: A Biblical Witness* (Eugene, OR: Cascade, 2012), 58–75, where he discusses human wholeness primarily from the book of Deuteronomy.

as such and move in the Spirit toward righting broken relationships in these three realms, we experience wholeness and reconciliation.

Human Worth

The sheer biblical fact that God, the source of life and the standard for all that we deem holy and good, created humankind makes humankind worthy of existence. This is true of all things God created, for the end of the first creation narrative says, "God saw everything that he had made, and indeed, it was very good" (Gen. 1:31).

Regarding humankind, however, the text places special emphasis on the fact that God created Adam and Eve in God's image (Gen. 1:27). Though creation itself declares the glory of God (Ps. 19:1), the creation text clearly distinguishes humankind from everything else by identifying them as being made according to the *imago Dei*.[7] But if the rest of creation also bears the divine imprint, then to distinguish humankind in this way serves not to discount God's reflection in the mirror of creation, but rather to elevate human beings over all other things created. If creation is worthy, then humanity is the worthiest of all. The *imago Dei*, intrinsic in the human person, not only makes human life valuable; it also makes it sacred. As such, it deserves to be regarded with utmost dignity, respect, and protection.

Furthermore, as David Gushee avers, "God is *equally* the Creator of *all* humans," establishing unity and equality among human variations.[8] Indeed, worthiness in God's sight applies to all human beings. Gushee insists, "No one can be excluded. From womb to tomb, from home to far away, from friend to foe, all are covered. All must be viewed with reverence and treated with respect and care."[9] For each person, regardless of developmental stage, gender, race, religion, status, power, achievement, or ability, bears the *imago Dei*.

Human uniqueness also needs to be added to our theology of worth. Lest we consider humanity too en masse and therefore too abstractly, we need to acknowledge the uniqueness of each human being. Each individual has a unique set of fingerprints, a unique face, and a unique name that identifies the individual. Each person is a product of union between a unique man and a unique woman, thus creating a unique combination of features and traits that make up that individual. And like anything rare and one of a kind, each person holds great value by virtue of that person's uniqueness. David grasped this truth and

7. For a detailed discussion on what it means for humankind to be made in the image of God, see David P. Gushee, *The Sacredness of Human Life* (Grand Rapids: Eerdmans, 2013), 39–54.

8. Gushee, *Sacredness*, 39 (italics original).

9. Gushee, *Sacredness*, 388.

celebrated it when he sang, "For it was you who formed my inward parts; you knit me together in my mother's womb. I praise you, for I am fearfully and wonderfully made" (Ps. 139:13–14). Jesus himself expressed this. Effectively employing hyperbole, he told his disciples of God's love and concern for each of them, by saying, "Even the hairs of your head are all counted" (Matt. 10:30).

Living in a hyperindividualistic culture, I more often than not emphasize the social, collective, and community aspects of humanity in an attempt to balance the scale. I will continue to do that, but I would err if I tipped the scale the other direction and neglected to recognize the great value that each individual deserves in the sight of God.

Yet another factor that establishes human worth—and perhaps most pertinent to this study—has to do with God's desire to save humanity. The Bible tells the story of God taking initiative to redeem humankind, which should convey the obvious, that God considers humankind worth saving. Add, therefore, a theology of redemption to the reasons why we should believe in the great worth of human beings.

In continuity with Abraham, Sarah, Moses, Ruth, David, Esther, and the prophets, Jesus Christ most fully expressed God's saving mission. That he took on flesh should not only dispel any notion of flesh being ultimately evil; it should also indicate the importance in the heart and mind of God to communicate the way of salvation to humanity, for what better way to communicate a message to people than to become one of them? In the flesh, Jesus taught and demonstrated the love, peace, mercy, and justice of God—all of which attest to the worth of human beings.[10] John wrote famously, "For God so loved the world that he gave his only Son" (John 3:16). Gushee adds, "And that giving culminated at the cross."[11]

Christ's death on the cross not only confirmed God's redeeming love for humanity, it also paved the way for it. On the third day, the Gospels tell us, Jesus rose again. Christ's resurrection verified the power of the cross to redeem humankind; otherwise, Christ's death would have just been another gruesome execution of a dreamer who went up against the powers and lost. But because of a rolled-away boulder, an empty tomb, and a postburial appearance to over five hundred people at one time (1 Cor. 15:3–8), the cross has since taken on a wholly different meaning. Transcending the religiopolitical execution of Jesus, the truth of the cross has become not only the ultimate symbol of God's love but also the way of salvation for a humanity worth saving. This is so because Jesus is risen!

10. Gushee, *Sacredness*, 85–94.
11. Gushee, *Sacredness*, 101.

Paul teaches that Christ's bodily resurrection serves as the firstfruits of the bodily resurrection of all (1 Cor. 15:20–23). This promise of new, abundant, gloriously embodied life under the reign of the risen Jesus constitutes the hope of the Christian. In sum, then, the *imago Dei*, human uniqueness, redemption in Christ, and the resurrection of the redeemed at the end of time together solidify the theological fact of human worth in the heart and mind of God.

Human Well-Being: The Reconciled Self

Now that we have established the nature of the human person as a body-soul unity-in-community with God, others, and creation, and that persons hold incalculable worth, we have a standard for measuring human well-being. We had to know and appreciate these first, because knowledge of God's original intent for humanity provides the standard for wellness. Moreover, it sets a clear pathway toward wholeness, as it gives a picture of humanity at its finest. We can now pose the main question of this chapter: Where do we find ourselves on the journey toward becoming a body-soul unity-in-community with God, others, and creation?

This question more than implies that in our fallenness we fall short of the standard, that God continues to transform us, that we have not yet achieved the status of whole and reconciled persons. If philosophies, religions, the social sciences, arts, and literature agree on anything, it would be our human brokenness. Christian theology describes this in terms of the fall and how sin has permeated every level of existence and has resulted in comprehensive depravity. Alienated from the Creator, humankind has forgotten the purpose of its existence. We do not know God. We dominate, enslave, and kill one another. And we degrade the earth and the animals that live on it. Fallen humanity occupies the center of the story of the world's brokenness. With Paul we lament, "Wretched man that I am! Who will rescue me from this body of death?" (Rom. 7:24).

Ironically, we take the first step toward well-being by acknowledging our brokenness. James Bruckner explains: "Created from clay and God's breath and made in God's image, human beings are constantly at risk of twisting or rationalizing the nature of their created reality." He adds, "Awareness of this factor is an important component of maintaining a healthy life."[12] Only after acknowledging our brokenness do we perceive the desperate desire to be healed, thus creating a disposition to respond to the promptings of the God who alone can heal us.

I stated earlier and repeat now that after the first two chapters of Genesis, the rest of the Bible can be seen as guiding broken humanity back into right

---

12. Bruckner, *Healthy Human Life*, 4.

relationship with God, one another, and creation as the way toward human well-being. I also stated earlier that the reconciliation of all things involves three dimensions: the vertical, between God and people; the horizontal, between people and people; and the circular, between God, people, and creation.[13] But it all begins with the self—reconciliation beginning with me. In our brokenness, we forget our uniqueness, our incalculable worth, and that God thinks each of us worth saving. Before we participate with God in "saving the world" (that is, engaging in the ministry of reconciliation), we look upward to God to heal and reconcile the broken pieces of our interior selves.

Contrary to the notion that God can be added on as the final capper toward health and wholeness, human well-being thoroughly depends on our relationship with God. As Bruckner asserts, "The so-called spiritual dimension cannot simply be pasted on like a poultice to a person's chest. By definition and in every dimension of living, the God of Scripture is witnessed as the source and goal of our individual and communal health."[14] To the extent that we learn to love God with all of our heart, soul, mind, and strength, we move toward reconciliation with God and thus move toward becoming whole persons.[15]

Our journey toward wholeness also includes horizontal reconciliation with others, with fellow human beings, even with our enemies. The vertical and the horizontal go together; they must, if we strive in the Spirit to be whole ourselves. As the Cape Town Commitment says, "Reconciliation to God is inseparable from reconciliation to one another." It goes on to say that "God's plan for the integration of the whole creation in Christ is modeled in the ethnic reconciliation of God's new humanity."[16] Peace between peoples contributes integrally to our own wholeness.

Finally, we need to be reconciled with creation if we desire to experience human well-being. In order to say this, we need to see that humanity is organically and ecologically connected to the earth and its inhabitants. The creation narrative establishes that God indeed created humankind from the same dirt as nonhuman creatures (Gen. 2:7, 19), thus establishing the organic relationship between humankind, creaturekind, and the earth. All created things come from the same material and therefore are organically connected.

13. Tormod Engelsviken, "Reconciliation with God," in *Mission as Ministry of Reconciliation*, ed. Robert Schreiter and Knud Jorgensen (Oxford: Regnum, 2013), 79.

14. Bruckner, *Healthy Human Life*, 74.

15. Bruckner asserts that "the *Shema* provides biblical description of a thriving human being" (73) and develops this compellingly in part 2 of *Healthy Human Life*, 77–153.

16. Lausanne Movement, *The Cape Town Commitment: A Confession of Faith and a Call to Action* (Peabody, MA: Hendrickson, 2011), 39.

We also see clearly the ecological connection, particularly when creation stopped responding with fruitfulness as a result of Adam and Eve's sin. "Cursed is the ground because of you," God said to Adam (Gen. 3:17). If there were no ecological relationship between humanity and the rest of creation, then humanity's actions would not have disrupted the entire ecological system. As the fall narrative goes, however, human sin affected the earth and its intricacies, thus verifying the connection. The blood of the murdered Abel, which cried out from the ground, causing fruitlessness in the land despite the toil of his murderer-brother Cain, also verifies the connection (Gen. 4:8–12). Indeed, the earth suffers because of human violence and sin (Hos. 4:1–3; Rom. 8:19–22). Organically and ecologically, humankind, creaturekind, and the earth itself are inseparably and mysteriously interrelated. Therefore, "What we do to creation and to the other creatures we do to ourselves."[17] In our disregard for the welfare of creation, we have broken relationship with the rest of the created order, and we need to be reconciled with it in order to be whole persons.

The human person is a body-soul unity-in-community with God, one another, and creation. To the extent that we experience reconciliation in these realms in the name of Jesus and by the power of the Spirit, we move toward our own wholeness and reconciliation.

Loving Our Neighbor as Ourselves: Toward a Missiological Anthropology

To understand what it means to be a whole and reconciled person requires one more important consideration—namely, the call to love ourselves. At the core of the church's mission lies the biblical mandate to love our neighbor as ourselves (Matt. 22:39; Rom. 13:9). While the weight of the Greatest Commandment rightfully leans on neighbor love—that is, on extending the compassion, justice, and truth of the gospel to others—the mandate also assumes self-love; it assumes the importance of reconciliation with the self. The consequences of the fall have wreaked havoc on everything, including the inner self, damaging our ability to love ourselves. Add to that the violence done to us by outside forces—oppression, racism, marginalization, poverty, sexual exploitation and abuse, bad parenting, dysfunctional family dynamics, toxic faith environments, and so on—and the damage to human persons hopelessly disables us from helping ourselves. We need God. As I said, the road to the reconciliation of all things in Christ "begins with me," with the self—and the Greatest Commandment, to love our neighbor, assumes and depends on this.

17. Gushee, *Sacredness*, 394.

Self-love, however, resides on an instinctual level. Instinctually, to survive, we feed and clothe our bodies, protect ourselves from harm, and desire to be treated with respect and dignity. The Greatest Commandment says to love our neighbor in the same way. But to affirm the whole gospel for the whole world as whole persons, to minister to the lost and needy out of a genuine love of self, requires going beyond assumption and instinct. To truly love our neighbor, we must ask, How well do we love ourselves? In light of the command to love our neighbor as ourselves, this becomes a missiological question.

Christians, and perhaps especially missionaries and activists, have tended to avoid talk of self-love as they equate it with self-centeredness, but these differ greatly. Self-centeredness refers to a limited, myopic vision, resulting from a preoccupation with the self, while self-love results from the ability to see ourselves (and others) as God sees us in Jesus Christ. For, as Paul wrote, "From now on . . . we regard no one from a human point of view. . . . If anyone is in Christ, there is a new creation: everything old has passed away; see, everything has become new" (2 Cor. 5:16–17). Without this Spirit-empowered ability to accept ourselves as forgiven, redeemed, and empowered—which lies in the truth of our justification in Christ (Rom. 5:1–2; Eph. 2:8–9)—the quite accurate picture of ourselves as broken, depraved, and unworthy can result not only in self-deprecation and even self-loathing, but also in missional debilitation. Left to our broken selves, we would answer God's call on our lives as Moses did: "O my Lord, please send someone else" (Exod. 4:13).

An understanding of the missional church in terms of bold humility, as we considered earlier, also applies to the human person. Our brokenness and therefore our desperate need for God should keep us humble; but central to our Christian formation is learning to see ourselves as God in Christ sees us: forgiven and changed, whole and reconciled, and equipped in the Spirit to participate in God's transforming work in the world. This is what it means to be a whole person this side of the *eschaton*. As such, we place ourselves in prime position to help others rediscover their humanity, which Ng'weshemi defines as the true meaning of the Christian mission.[18]

Self-love has at least two practical features that seemingly contradict each other: self-care and self-sacrifice.

Whole Person: Self-Care

To thrive in the grueling work of mission requires attention to ongoing healing and development of ourselves as human persons in Christ. It requires holistic

---

18. Ng'weshemi, *Rediscovering the Human*, 166–68.

self-care. Bruckner uses the Shema as a framework for understanding holistic human health. He argues that the words "heart, soul, and strength" in the command to love God "address the matrices of the human will (*levav*), the realm of embodied human relationships (*nephesh*), and the sources of human vitality (*me'od*)."[19]

I find the human development of Jesus as recorded in Luke 2:52—where we learn that he "increased in wisdom and in years, and in divine and human favor"—to be an equally compelling framework for holistic health. If we attend to the psycho-emotional (wisdom), physical (years), spiritual (divine favor), and social (human favor) aspects of ourselves, then we move toward becoming whole persons. If one accepts this, then therapy, for example, can advance us in the pursuit of wholeness, as can good nutrition, church attendance, community service, and so on. The point is, loving ourselves means striving toward holistic, healthy living in our Spirit-led quest to be reconciled to God, one another, and creation.

The call to self-care needs to be heard more than ever before, for the expectations placed on pastors and missionaries today (some self-inflicted) have reached unrealistic proportions. This has arisen at least in part from heightened awareness of the multisidedness of human need and the genuine desire to meet all needs. Trying impossibly, however, "to be all things to all people" has resulted in a disturbing rate of ministry burnout. The statistics, based on a study among church leaders in the US, include the following:

- 70 percent of clergy do not have someone whom they consider to be a close friend.
- 45 percent of pastors say that they've experienced depression or burnout to the extent that they desired a leave of absence from ministry.
- 40 percent report a serious conflict with a parishioner at least once a month.
- 80 percent of seminary graduates will leave full-time ministry within the first five years.
- Every year more than five thousand US missionaries leave their fields of service for preventable reasons such as depression, marriage and family difficulties, unresolved interpersonal conflicts with team members and nationals, and inadequate spiritual and emotional support.[20]

In the face of such statistics, the importance of the call to ministry self-care needs to be heard around the globe. In *The Spiritual Leader's Guide to*

19. Bruckner, *Healthy Human Life*, 74–75.
20. "Statistics," Alongside, accessed October 25, 2017, http://www.alongsidecares.net/what-we-do/the-need/statistics.

Self-Care, Rochelle Melander and Harold Eppley provide a useful weekly guide to help pastors, missionaries, and other spiritual leaders ensure their own welfare as they go about caring for the welfare of others. The effectiveness of this resource lies both in its holistic approach—it consists of five sections, with just as much attention given to the physical and material realms of life as to the spiritual, emotional, and relational—and in its practicality, as it guides users toward better eating habits, prayer life, conflict management, and many other daily realities of spiritual leaders.[21]

We can, of course, go overboard and view self-care as the chief end of life. Knowing the stress of ministry myself, I hesitate to put any efforts toward self-care in any sort of critical light. But it is possible to cross the line of self-care to *over*-self-care. Ironically, going overboard in the pursuit of health and wholeness can result in ill health and "unwholeness." It is ultimately not loving ourselves to love ourselves too much! I say this in light of encountering some self-care standards that seem to have taken their cue from the apostle Peter when he tried to prevent Jesus from going to Jerusalem to suffer and die (Matt. 16:22). Going to the cross was decidedly not an act of self-care for Jesus! When Peter tried to stop him, Jesus gave one of his strongest rebukes: "Get behind me, Satan!" (v. 23).

The caution regarding over-self-care, however, should not distract us from the fact that self-love requires us to care deeply for ourselves. We must attend to our overall health—psychological, emotional, physical, social, and spiritual—for the sake of our participation in God's mission.

Whole Person: Self-Sacrifice

Jesus's willingness to go to the cross points to the other side of self-love—namely, the call to self-sacrifice. Sacrifice for the sake of others says more about what it means to be a whole person than anything else, and it counters any tendency toward over-self-care. The paradoxical words of Jesus come to mind here: "Those who want to save their life will lose it, and those who lose their life for my sake will find it" (Matt. 16:25). He said this to his disciples in the context of calling them to deny themselves, to take up their cross and follow him. This should communicate to us the profound truth that self-denial or self-sacrifice is not contrary to but rather the pinnacle of self-love.

This aspect of self-love enables us to engage in God's global mission. What drives God's people to leave everything familiar, sell their possessions, and

---

21. Rochelle Melander and Harold Eppley, eds., *The Spiritual Leader's Guide to Self-Care* (Bethesda, MD: Alban Institute, 2002).

learn a new way of life, a new language, and a new way to serve and work in a cross-cultural context? What propels them to give sacrificially of their energies, resources, and time in activities that do not necessarily advance their own status? What motivates them to choose low-income professions in nonprofit or activist organizations to serve the sick, the homeless, the prisoner, and the poor? What compels them to advocate for the oppressed, the forgotten, and the marginalized? What enables God's people to love the different, even their enemies? We can credit/blame the Spirit-led love that denies the self for the sake of others. There is more, I am sure, to what we can call a missiological anthropology, but it most certainly crescendos with this truth.

Kirk Byron Jones likens self-care and self-sacrifice to the inhale-exhale motion of breathing. "Both actions are mutually dependent and essential," he writes. "If there is no inhaling, then exhaling cannot occur, and vice versa."[22] The healthy self requires the steady rhythm of breathing, inhaling for ourselves the life that nourishes and then exhaling that life for the sake of others. To the extent that we love ourselves by way of self-care and self-sacrifice, we become Spirit-enabled to love our neighbors as ourselves, which is the essence of mission.

This chapter sought to shed light on what it means to be whole and reconciled persons. The next chapter considers what it means to be the whole and reconciled church, which is at least a community of individuals who, in the Spirit, are seeking to become whole persons. But the idea of the whole and reconciled church involves more than the mere sum of redeemed individuals. The nature of the whole and reconciled church and its call to reconciliation find their theological roots in the very nature of God as Trinity. As ultimately mysterious as the Trinity may be, this topic has massive implications for the church's identity and mission in the world. To these implications we now turn.

Discussion Questions

1. What does human well-being look like? Is this a missiological question?
2. This chapter contends that we must acknowledge our brokenness before we can become a whole person. Do you agree or disagree? Why or why not?

22. Kirk Byron Jones, *Rest in the Storm: Self-Care Strategies for Clergy and Other Care-Givers* (Valley Forge, PA: Judson, 2001), 87.

3. To love our neighbor as ourselves assumes that we indeed love ourselves. In our pursuit of self-love (reconciliation beginning with me), what is the difference between selflessness and selfishness?

4. Self-love has two faces: self-care and self-sacrifice. Why are they both important?

5. Do you lean more toward the inhale of self-care or the exhale of self-sacrifice?

SEVEN

Church of the Trinity

Community, Diversity, and Reconciliation

. . . .

Go therefore and make disciples of all nations,
baptizing them in the name of the Father and of
the Son and of the Holy Spirit.
—Jesus (Matt. 28:19)

Being as Mission

Several years ago, I led a group from our former church in Philadelphia on a two-week trip to India. The day before we left, we thought it fitting to share a meal together at an Indian restaurant as a precommencement activity for the journey. On arrival, we began to help the waiters rearrange the furniture to accommodate our nine-person team—three Asian Americans, five African Americans (two of whom were children), and one Euro-American. A handful of equally colorful family members accompanied us, making the group a total of fifteen people, give or take a few. I noticed two women staring at us from a nearby booth. They were probably annoyed, I thought, as our motley crew just took over the small restaurant.

"I hope we're not being too noisy," I initiated. My words startled them as they realized they were staring at us.

"Not at all, and sorry for staring," one of them replied. "But if you don't mind me asking . . ." She made a sweeping gesture with her arm in the direction of our group, and then blurted, "What is this?"

Not exactly sure what she was referring to, I took a guess and said, "We're from a church up the road, and we're headed off to India tomorrow to support a ministry to needy children. Thought we'd give our taste buds a head start."

"Amazing," one of them said. Their eyes continued to survey us. Then a few seconds later, "I didn't know churches like this existed."

"Churches like what?"

"Churches that . . ." she had difficulty finding the words, "well, where different kinds of people go." I had obviously grown accustomed enough to the multiethnic nature of our faith community that I no longer gave it a second thought. Those women, however, beheld us with second, third, and fourth thoughts. They could not help but marvel at the diversity of our group, perhaps something they had never seen before, at least when it came to church.

"It's beautiful," one of them said finally. To be honest, until that comment, I was uncertain whether they thought negatively or positively about us. Relieved, I began to share with them conversationally how diversity reflects the creativity of God and how unity amid diversity reflects the will of God. They agreed. I told them about our church and then invited them to come and join us on a Sunday morning sometime.

When they left, I remarked to the group, not scheduled to leave until the next morning, that our mission had already begun. Just by *being* God's diverse people, I told them, we bore witness to the gospel of God's multicolored, reconciling kingdom to a couple of women.

Beyond the church being merely the sum of "whole persons," the idea of "whole church" includes the call to represent diverse human community at peace with itself as a result of faith in Christ. This kind of community, which we demonstrated in the restaurant, struck those two women profoundly. They saw the possibility of a reconciled, intercultural community of faith in a world replete with injustice, racism, genocide, war, and threats of war. As I have reflected on that incident over the last several years, those two women have become representative of the world's hunger for genuine hope, and God has called the whole and reconciled church to offer "the feast of the world's redemption"[1]— the hope found in the indiscriminate love of the Father, the radical forgiveness of the crucified and risen Son, and the powerful creativity of the Holy Spirit.

Beyond Belief: Practicing the Trinity

The church proves faithful to this call and moves toward wholeness when it demonstrates community, diversity, and reconciliation in the world, and

---

1. This powerful descriptor of Holy Communion comes from John Koenig, *The Feast of the World's Redemption* (Harrisburg, PA: Trinity Press International, 2000).

I intend in this chapter to establish that the very nature of God as Trinity provides the basis for these realities. Or we can say it the other way: by these realities, the people of God live out their mission to bear the image of the Triune God in the world. Far from being a mere doctrine to which the church must give absolute assent (lest it be deemed heretical), the idea of God as Father, Son, and Holy Spirit has practical implications for the church-in-mission.

John Franke recounts a discussion he had with a group of young students wherein he pushed them to articulate the practical significance of the Trinity. When they could not come up with a satisfactory answer—thus demonstrating the disturbing chasm between what we believe and how we live—Franke challenged their posture of holding themselves and others absolutely accountable to a doctrine "that otherwise made no difference in their lives except that they believed it."[2]

With Franke and others, I assert that the doctrine of the Trinity has crucial practical implications; it is not a "useless essential." On the contrary, the trinitarian nature of God lays the foundation not only for the church's self-understanding but also for its mission in the world. Now by this I do not mean to say that we cannot be the church and that we cannot engage in mission if we do not understand the Trinity. Talk about setting ourselves up for failure! For indeed the Trinity ultimately represents the mystery that surrounds the wholly Other.

From the start the contentious historical development of the doctrine attests to the impossibility of understanding God fully. Stanley Grenz confirms that "the quest to find a means to bring together the confession of Jesus and the experience of the Holy Spirit with the heritage of belief in one God repeatedly enveloped the church in controversy."[3] The eventual tripartite formulation of God by the Cappadocian fathers in the fourth century sought to avoid ways of thinking that the early church found incompatible with the then-300-year-old tradition surrounding Jesus.[4] Tritheism (three gods), modalism (one God in three different forms), and subordinationism (the Father as supreme over "the lesser gods" of the Son and the Spirit) represented the main heresies.[5] For the next 1700 years and counting, the doctrine of the Trinity—three distinct,

2. John R. Franke, *Manifold Witness: The Plurality of Truth* (Nashville: Abingdon, 2009), 54.

3. Stanley J. Grenz, *Theology for the Community of God* (Grand Rapids: Eerdmans, 1994), 56.

4. Grenz, *Theology for the Community of God*, 60. See also Roderick T. Leupp, *Knowing the Name of God: A Trinitarian Tapestry of Grace, Faith & Community* (Downers Grove, IL: InterVarsity, 1996), 73–83.

5. Leonardo Boff, *Trinity and Society* (Maryknoll, NY: Orbis Books, 1988), 46–50.

interdependent personalities of Father, Son, and Holy Spirit making up the essence of the One God—has been the litmus test for orthodox Christian faith.

Even so, the Trinity falls short of fully explaining God and therefore speaks ultimately of mystery. The egg, water, and three-leaf clover analogies simply do not satisfy. They may even bear marks of ancient heresies. The doctrine of the Trinity attempts to systematize our understanding of God, but in the end, it refers to a Reality that goes light-years beyond human comprehension. The created cannot fully understand the heart, mind, and activities of their Creator. The doctrine of the Trinity ultimately points to mystery, forcing us to think paradoxically about truth, as we hold in creative tension both the Oneness and the Threeness of God. It forces us to worship the One God, even as we bow the knee to God the Father, God the Son, and God the Holy Spirit.

Nonetheless, as ultimately mysterious as the Trinity may be, we do know something about God. After all, as Richard Rohr remarks about mystery, "[It] isn't something you *cannot* understand—it is something you can *endlessly understand*!"[6] Mystery means never knowing completely, and thus discovering and learning continuously. We know that although the word "Trinity" does not appear in the Bible, the witness of Scripture testifies to one God, and yet refers to the Father, the Son, and the Holy Spirit as God (John 20:17, 28; Acts 5:3–4, to cite a few). We also know that the Triune God has called out and formed a people from among many peoples and has sent them out beyond themselves for the sake of the world (Gen. 12:1–3; Matt. 28:18–20; Acts 1:8). As David Bosch penned regarding the *missio Dei*, "God the Father sending the Son, and God the Father and God the Son sending the Spirit was expanded to include yet another movement: Father, Son, and Holy Spirit sending the church into the world."[7]

This movement requires a closer look. How does the nature of God as Trinity give shape to the church and its mission? In exploring this question, at least three (of course!) practical commitments come to the fore that define the church of the Trinity: community, diversity, and reconciliation. By these three practical commitments, the church moves toward wholeness as it embodies the wholeness of God.

Plurality of God: A Call to Community

Affirming the Trinity essentially means believing at the core that plurality fundamentally describes the nature of God. God qua God constitutes a

---

6. Richard Rohr, *The Divine Dance: The Trinity and Your Transformation* (New Kensington, PA: Whitaker House, 2016), 27 (italics original).

7. David J. Bosch, *Transforming Mission: Paradigm Shifts in Theology of Mission*, 20th anniv. ed. (Maryknoll, NY: Orbis Books, 2011), 399.

community—three distinct, interdependent, harmonious personalities interacting with one another. If nothing else, this belief in the plurality of God should dispel the notion that loneliness motivated God to create humankind. God was not lonely, for within God's very self, three persons have been and will always be eternally interactive, social, and relational, independent of anything created. "In the beginning was the Relationship," Rohr declares.[8] And as an extension of that relationship, God made humankind, as an integral part of the larger project of creation, to participate with God in the enjoyment of life.[9]

Franke celebrates a relatively recent shift among theologians that emphasizes relationality as "the most helpful way to understand the Trinity." This, he writes, offers "an alternative to the metaphysics of substance that dominated theological reflection on the Trinity throughout much of church history."[10] Whereas grappling with the threeness of God ontologically has been the cause of endless church conflicts, understanding the Trinity relationally not only results in less tension among theologians, it also provides the basis for Christian ethics and mission.

Of course, the relational turn of which Franke speaks is not new but, rather, represents a resurgence of ancient ways of thinking about the Trinity. In trying to grasp the interrelatedness of God, theologians of the past, such as Gregory of Nazianzus in the fourth century and John of Damascus in the seventh,[11] employed the idea of perichoresis, which generally means deep, harmonious, and loving interpenetration.[12] In theology, it refers to an interrelatedness so deep, harmonious, and loving between Father, Son, and Holy Spirit that we cannot but accept the three as mutually, creatively, and equally one. God is not just a plurality, as if the Trinity were merely a mathematical fact. God is, rather, an integrated social plurality, a harmonious dance, a loving community, a perfect unity, who together said at creation, "Let us make humankind in our image" (Gen. 1:26). Insofar as human beings, therefore, demonstrate harmonious community with one another, they bear the image of the Triune God.

---

8. Rohr, *Divine Dance*, 30.

9. Franke, *Manifold Witness*, 59–60.

10. Franke, *Manifold Witness*, 57. See also Franke's chapter "Good News for All People," particularly 62–65, in *Revisioning, Renewing, Rediscovering the Triune Center*, ed. Derek J. Tidball, Brian S. Harris, and Jason S. Sexton (Eugene, OR: Cascade, 2014), where he goes into more detail about "the relational turn" in understanding the Trinity.

11. Tarmo Toon, *Classical Trinitarian Theology: A Textbook* (New York: T&T Clark, 2007), 41.

12. Catherine LaCugna, *God for Us: The Trinity and Christian Life* (New York: Harper-Collins, 1991), 271.

The Bible, however, from Genesis 3 on, tells the story of brokenness, alienation, fragmentation, and violence between human beings. It tells of humanity's tragic missteps in the divine-human dance, but also of how God, the essence of perichoretic community, set in motion a plan to bring us back in step. Roderick Leupp identifies one of the distinctions of Christianity among the world's religions as "God's relentless search for community among those whom [God] created."[13] In this light, we can understand God's promise in Genesis 12 to form a great nation as the beginning of the missional call for the redeemed to model the restoration of genuine human community. In continuity with the call of Genesis 12, the church moves toward wholeness when its members intentionally commit to becoming a Christ-centered, Spirit-empowered community, wherein they embody righteousness, compassion, love, justice, and peace—*shalom*—as a model for the whole world.

Though the gathering of the redeemed in Christ defines the church, the experience of genuine community does not come automatically. It does not just happen. We must be intentional about building and practicing community. For in our fallenness, we default *against* community. Without the power of the Spirit operating in our lives, we seek independence over interdependence, individual advancement over the common good, and competition over co-operation. I remind us of our fallenness simply to say that if a church does not intentionally embrace its identity as the church of the Trinity, then it will by default inevitably experience life like all other human institutions, marked by strife, division, and conflict. God calls the church to defy this fate and instead to model transformed life under the reign of the Triune God. This will take intentionality in the Spirit and a practical commitment to be Christ's representative community for the sake of all communities.

Distinctions of God: A Call to Diversity

A church moving toward wholeness strives to be a community, but what kind of community? The kind characterized by justice, peace, equality, and unity in the context of human diversity. The previous section discussed community in contrast to individualism; this section lifts up diverse human community in contrast to communities of human sameness.

Whereas the plurality of God has an inherent call to genuine community, the fact that three distinct persons make up the one God contains an inherent call to diversity. The doctrine of the Trinity provides the theological basis for

13. Leupp, *Knowing the Name of God*, 29.

this as well, as it accentuates the distinctions of God. Franke explains, "The Father is not the Son or the Spirit; the Son is not the Father or the Spirit; and the Spirit is not the Father or the Son. This means that in the life of God is the experience of that which is different, other, not the same."[14]

Considering God's diversity should begin with gender. Let me say it directly: Both masculinity and femininity define the core of God; both fatherly and motherly qualities flow from the nature of God. Though such statements likely raise a few evangelical eyebrows, they should not be controversial. The God who created humankind in the divine image created us both male and female (Gen. 1:27). It makes no sense, therefore, to believe in the sole masculinity of God when humankind, created in God's image, is both male and female. In this light, the burden of proof lies on those who believe that God is all male!

That being said, Bible scholars and theologians differ on how they negotiate the masculine and feminine aspects of God, attesting to the complexity of even thinking about God in terms of gender. Hannah Bacon explains that "some have set about trying to redeem the traditional language; some have sought to recover female imagery for God within the corpus of scripture; others have presented the Holy Spirit as the feminine dimension of God; and others still have tried to rename the whole Trinitarian reality, either through the use of explicitly female metaphors or through desexing or depersonalizing the Trinity."[15]

I find most compelling the argument that the Holy Spirit represents the feminine dimension of the Trinity.[16] Many biblical linguists have pointed out that the Hebrew, Aramaic, and Syriac words for "spirit" are either feminine or neuter. Moreover, many of them have made crucial connections between the Spirit and wisdom (*sophia*), and between the Spirit and the maternal understanding of the divine in Hebrew literature. But perhaps the ethical angle provides the strongest argument for this view: it matters ethically how we think and talk about God. Feminist and womanist scholars, such as Elizabeth Johnson and Karen Baker-Fletcher, have rightly pointed out that all-male conceptions of the Triune God have created, promoted, and reinforced sexist,

14. Franke, "Good News for All People," 64–65.

15. Hannah Bacon, "*Thinking* the Trinity as Resource for Feminist Theology Today?," *Crosscurrents* 62, no. 4 (December 2012): 447. In her listing, she footnotes resources for each of the approaches in case researchers care to delve deeper in any one or all of them.

16. For more on this, see Maria Pilar Aquino, *Our Cry for Life: Feminist Theology from Latin America* (Maryknoll, NY: Orbis Books, 1993); Yves Congar, *I Believe in the Holy Spirit* (New York: Seabury, 1983); Johannes van Oort, "The Holy Spirit as Feminine: Early Christian Testimonies and Their Interpretation," *HTS Teologiese Studies/Theological Studies* 72, no. 1 (2016), http://dx.doi.org/ 10.4102/hts.v72i1.3225.

patriarchal systems that have proved oppressive to women throughout time and all over the world.[17]

Recognizing the diversity of God begins with acknowledging both the masculinity and femininity of God, which is why I not only use the feminine pronoun for the Holy Spirit but also avoid the masculine pronoun for God as much as possible throughout this book. But more importantly, acknowledging God's masculine and feminine dimensions lays the foundation for our understanding and appreciation of God's diversity at the core. In their beautiful, masculine-feminine distinctiveness, the three persons of the Trinity constitute a perichoretic unity so complete that they are one. The Trinity defines a perfect unity-amid-diversity. To the extent that the church strives to model the same, it reflects the image of the Triune God in the world.

Practicing unity-amid-diversity, of course, poses formidable challenges. If striving for human community takes great effort, striving for *diverse* human community takes even greater effort. Unity-amid-diversity differs radically from uniformity. A uniform church forms around sameness of culture, class, perspective, and so on, which falls short of reflecting the image of God, whose very distinctions defy uniformity. We must remember that the doctrine of the Trinity does not refer to three different forms of the same God but to three distinct and different persons in perfect perichoretic harmony.

A church that desires to reflect the image of the Triune God, therefore, does not strive for uniformity, which *avoids* and even resists diversity; it commits itself, rather, to Trinity-based unity, which *welcomes* diversity. Just as genuine community does not just happen in church life, practicing unity-amid-diversity also requires intentionality. It requires a practical commitment, and a church that moves toward wholeness takes this commitment seriously. Focusing on ethnic and cultural diversity, I think of two areas of church practice.

Intercultural Koinonia

To affirm diversity requires God's people to work toward intercultural koinonia—that is, genuine fellowship across cultures rooted in Christ himself, whose earthly lineage was also profoundly multiethnic.[18] After establishing the

---

17. Elizabeth A. Johnson, *She Who Is: The Mystery of God in Feminist Theological Discourse*, 25th anniv. ed. (New York: Herder & Herder, 2017); Karen Baker-Fletcher, *Dancing with God: The Trinity from a Womanist Perspective* (St. Louis: Chalice, 2006).

18. I have chosen the word "intercultural" over "multicultural" or "cross-cultural," to avoid the subtle pitfalls of the latter two. At best, they convey a neutral relationship between two cultures; at worst, a default colonial relationship of dominance and subservience. "Intercultural,"

multicultural and multiracial ancestry of Jesus, Curtiss DeYoung describes him as an "Afro-Asiatic Jew."[19]

The missionary work of the first disciples of the multiethnic Jesus in fact resulted in an intercultural movement. As they proclaimed the gospel throughout the Mediterranean, walls between Jew and gentile worlds began to break down dramatically (Acts 10:44–48; 11:19–26; 15:1–35; Rom. 11:7–24). And lest we think Jew and gentile represented only two people groups, David Rhoads reminds us that neither was monolithic: "Judaism itself was multiform in that era of history—both in Palestine with its various sectarian groups and among the communities of Jews dispersed throughout the Roman Empire and throughout the Parthian Empire to the east." As for gentiles, he reminds us that the word "literally means nations. Across the ancient Mediterranean world, there was an incredible array of local ethnic communities, subcultures and language groups within the aegis of the Roman Empire."[20] Indeed, the gospel ministry of the early church resulted in the coming together of many cultures—intercultural koinonia—which reflected the very nature of the Triune God as a unity-amid-diversity.

I have intentionally chosen the word koinonia over "church" because I do not want to convey that the call to practice diversity limits itself only to faith communities physically located in overtly diverse contexts. On the contrary, because diversity finds its roots in the very nature of God as Trinity, the call to intercultural koinonia applies to all God's people for all time and for all places. This, of course, begs the question, "How then would churches in monocultural contexts practice diversity?"

First, contexts that look the same on the surface may not be as monocultural as they appear. Practicing diversity then likely means becoming more aware of "invisible people," that is, those disenfranchised, neglected, and/or even harassed based on difference. Most supposedly monocultural communities have such invisible people. Migrant workers in rural farm towns in the US, members of a minority tribe in a majority-tribe village in Congo, eunuchs in India, street kids in Brazil, and Syrian refugees in Sweden immediately come to mind. As churches become more aware of and begin ministering to such populations in what only look like monocultural contexts, they practice the diversity reflective of the Triune God.

---

on the other hand, conveys the idea that transformation happens to all involved—nationals and missionaries, as well as the communities in which they serve together—in the gospel encounter.

19. Curtiss P. DeYoung, *Coming Together in the 21st Century: The Bible's Message in an Age of Diversity* (Valley Forge, PA: Judson, 2009), 53–54.

20. David Rhoads, quoted in Curtiss P. DeYoung, Michael O. Emerson, George Yancey, and Karen Chai Kim, eds. *United by Faith: The Multiracial Congregation as an Answer to the Problem of Race* (Oxford: Oxford University Press, 2003), 26.

These churches also practice diversity when they intentionally develop a global perspective among their members by inviting guest preachers from other cultures, lifting up missionary stories and updates, facilitating short-term vision (mission) trips, and partnering with other churches whose members are made up of a culture different from their own.[21] This list merely samples diversity-affirming activities; the possibilities have no end for churches that seek to bear the diverse image of the Triune God in the world.

However, the phenomenon of intercultural churches represents the most visible form of intercultural koinonia. So wherever possible, the church should intentionally strive in the Spirit toward intercultural church formation. The authors of the significant volume *United by Faith* would heartily agree and would add that the intercultural congregation (they use the term "multiracial") is an important, visible gospel answer to the problem of racism. Therefore, their call to North American Christians to make the twenty-first century "the century of multiracial congregations" is a challenge for all Christians everywhere since racism, ethnocentrism, and nationalism represent a global problem.[22]

In the last book of the Bible, we catch a glimpse of the end of time, when a community of redeemed people from every tribe, tongue, and nation will be worshiping God before the throne (Rev. 7:9). Peace and harmony between these different peoples will characterize this new community, as they will experience no more mourning, crying, or pain (Rev. 21:4). The tree of life that produces leaves for the healing of the nations in Revelation 22:2 implies that much of the mourning, crying, and pain experienced by people throughout time has had to do with strife between nations. The new creation in the Triune God promises international healing and therefore an end to mass suffering.

I believe that these glimpses of God's future serve as more than a teaser, more than a mere preview of things to come for which we simply and passively wait. They also provide the end goal toward which the church in mission should strive and move today. Central to what it means to pray as Jesus instructed, "Your kingdom come. Your will be done, on earth as it is in heaven" (Matt. 6:10), is to commit in the here and now, irrespective of location and context, to the intercultural koinonia that characterizes the future of the Triune God.

---

21. See John Perkins, Ronald J. Sider, Wayne Gordon, and F. Albert Tizon, *Linking Arms, Linking Lives: How Urban-Suburban Partnerships Can Transform Communities* (Grand Rapids: Baker Books, 2008).

22. DeYoung et al., *United by Faith*, 2. The generally accepted definition of a multiracial church, as one in which "no one racial group accounts for 80 percent or more of the membership," originated from DeYoung and colleagues in this work (3). Based on this 20 percent threshold of multiethnicity, the 2010 national survey of The Faith Communities Today reports that 14 percent of congregations in the US would be considered multiracial. "FACT 2010," Faith Communities Today, http://faithcommunitiestoday.org/fact-2010.

Intercultural Koinonia Planting

Trinity-based intercultural koinonia has practical missional implications as well. If we understand the mission of the church as proactively extending the blessings of kingdom life to the ends of the earth, then we should strive to plant seeds of intercultural koinonia throughout the whole world.

In light of this conviction I take serious issue with the well-known Homogeneous Unit Principle (HUP), a missiological church growth theory that, though it enjoyed its heyday in the 1970s and '80s, still holds sway in many churches and church-planting organizations. HUP argues that doing evangelism and church planting among people of the same culture is more effective. To that, I say, of course! Missionaries prefer to plant and grow monocultural churches over intercultural ones precisely because it is faster and easier, and it has a much greater potential to grow in numbers. In the words of HUP's innovator, Donald McGavran, people "like to become Christians without crossing racial, linguistic or class barriers."[23]

To be sure, church planting faces enough challenges even among same-culture people, and even more among people of different socioeconomic, racial, and cultural backgrounds. Proponents of the intercultural church movement have never denied the hardships and challenges of negotiating difference.[24] But a monocultural church—the logical result of applying the HUP theory—falls glaringly short of the call to serve as a signpost of the intercultural koinonia to come. As Efrem Smith writes bluntly, "It may be easier to plant, grow, and sustain a homogeneous church in Black or White [or Brown], but it's unbiblical."[25]

To be fair, HUP mission theorists do not advocate for permanently homogeneous churches; they are not ultimately segregationists or anti-intercultural (or at least I have never met any HUP advocates who are). Those who plant churches according to HUP principles hope these churches eventually flourish into their intercultural potential. The Pasadena Statement, a document signed by both champions and critics of HUP in a consultation convened in 1978, still provides the definitive word. It states, "All of us are agreed that in many situations a homogeneous unit church can be a legitimate and authentic church. Yet we are also all agreed that it can never be complete in itself."[26] Though I have serious doubts that a homogeneously planted church will one day just automatically desire to become intercultural (which is why I remain critical

23. Donald McGavran, cited in "The Pasadena Statement," in *Making Christ Known*, ed. John Stott (Grand Rapids: Eerdmans, 1996), 62.

24. See DeYoung et al., *United by Faith*, 170–79.

25. Efrem Smith, *The Post-Black and Post-White Church: Becoming the Beloved Community in a Multi-Ethnic World* (San Francisco: Jossey-Bass, 2012), 6.

26. "Pasadena Statement," in Stott, *Making Christ Known*, 64.

of HUP as a missiological approach), both champions and critics of HUP can agree that insofar as the church in mission moves toward God's intercultural future, it reflects the coming kingdom in a faithful way.

To commit to interculturality from the outset provides the better alternative; that way, the very core—the DNA—of that church includes God's intended diversity. If we plant an intercultural seed, there is a better chance that an intercultural tree will sprout and grow. This approach entails a commitment to diversity in the leadership, worship, dress, and language from the beginning of the church plant. Growth may be slower and challenges harder, but the result will be a tree that powerfully confronts the sexism, racism, classism, and other injustices of our broken, divided, fractured world. By virtue of being an intercultural tree, it will produce leaves "for the healing of the nations" (Rev. 22:2).

Love of God: A Call to Reconciliation

Emphasis on the plurality of God calls for genuine community, and the distinctions of God call for diversity, but it is the love generated by the interior life of God that calls for reconciliation among broken peoples in a broken world. In the extended allegory *The Shack*, we encounter this redeeming intratrinitarian love.[27] For all the literary license that author William Paul Young took in writing this splendid novel, he accurately captures the truth of the love between Father, Son, and Holy Spirit; when humanity (personified by the protagonist Mack) encounters them (that is, the Triune God), it experiences healing and becomes whole.

The deep, self-giving, "self-donating,"[28] mutually benefiting nature of the relationship between the three distinct persons of the Trinity not only makes possible our understanding of God's oneness (unity-amid-diversity) but also defines the very essence of love. The perichoretic unity between Father, Son, and Holy Spirit is not bound *by* love; it *is* love. Love is not some kind of abstract, supreme force in the universe to which even God submits; rather, God's perfect triunity provides the standard of love from which all other loves—self, marital, familial, ecclesial, and social—flow. John captured this profound

---

27. Wm. Paul Young, *The Shack* (Los Angeles: Windblown, 2007). One must read the whole book to fully enjoy it, but I encountered the redeeming intratrinitarian love most poignantly when Mack meets the three persons for the first time on 80–87.

28. Miroslav Volf, "'The Trinity Is Our Social Program': The Doctrine of the Trinity and the Shape of Social Engagement," *Modern Theology* 14, no. 3 (July 1998): 412–17. Volf uses the interesting term "self-donation" to convey the idea of the circular giving and receiving between the three persons of the Trinity. For a helpful interpretation of Volf's concept of divine self-donation, see Corneliu Constantineanu, "Exclusion and Embrace: Reconciliation in the Works of Miroslav Volf," *Kairos—Evangelical Journal of Theology* 7, no. 1 (2013): 49–51.

truth irreducibly when he admonished God's people to "love one another . . . for God is love" (1 John 4:7–8). Therefore, people loving one another across differences bear the image of the Triune God like nothing else.[29]

Of course, we know of this amazing love most profoundly through God's self-revelation in Jesus Christ. According to John 3:16–17, God so loved the world that the Father sent the Son not to condemn the world but to save it. The coming/sending of Jesus therefore constituted an act of love, of God extending God's own self into the world to bring prodigal humanity back into genuine community.

Whereas the incarnation demonstrated God's initiative to extend trinitarian love toward a lost people, the crucifixion revealed God's purging of sin in order to restore human community through the sacrificial love of the Son. The resurrection sealed the deal, so to speak, demonstrating the power of love in the Holy Spirit to overcome every obstacle, even death (Rom. 8:11), to become all that God has called us to be. In each of these salvific events, all three persons of the Godhead were wholly involved. As Leupp points out regarding the cross, for example, "We meet not one-third of the Trinity, not Jesus Christ acting alone, but the fullness of God."[30]

In the incarnation, crucifixion, and resurrection of Christ, we encounter the Triune God as the great Reconciler. Those who respond to the beckoning of the Father, through Jesus Christ and the power of the Holy Spirit, constitute together the church, the reconciled and reconciling community of God, in the world.

Reconciled and Reconciling

What does it mean for the church of the Trinity to be both reconciled and reconciling?

It means, first of all, to be reconciled to God. The truth of our salvation in Christ and the personal relationship that forms from it constitute the soul of the Christian faith, and any understanding of reconciliation that does not include the vertical dimension misses the mark. Indeed, as the Cape Town Commitment plainly states, "Human beings are lost. The underlying human predicament remains as the Bible describes it: we stand under the just judgment of God in our sin and rebellion, and without Christ we are without hope."[31]

---

29. In *The Shack*, the three persons are depicted as an African American woman (Father), a Middle Eastern man (Son), and an Asian American woman (Spirit), thus accentuating that the unity and love enjoyed by the three are amid diversity and difference.

30. Leupp, *Knowing the Name of God*, 114.

31. Lausanne Movement, *The Cape Town Commitment: A Confession of Faith and a Call to Action* (Peabody, MA: Hendrickson, 2011), 7.

This vertical dimension of reconciliation—our personal salvation—comes as a gift: it is offered freely by God, who is rich in mercy, and it is not earned by our good works (Eph. 2:4–9). Furthermore, God has offered it while our backs are turned to God. As Paul celebrated, "While we were still weak, at the right time Christ died for the ungodly. . . . God proves his love for us in that while we still were sinners Christ died for us. . . . While we were enemies, we were reconciled to God through the death of his Son" (Rom. 5:6, 8, 10). The repetition of this truth, said three different ways over just five verses, speaks to its significance. The God of love, by the miracle of grace through Jesus Christ, has initiated reconciliation with humanity. Personal salvation—reconciliation with God—results from simply accepting this gift, and then working it out in our lives and in our service under the creative leadership of the Holy Spirit.

Herein lies the nature of the evangelistic mandate: Our experience of reconciliation with God compels us by love to proclaim the good news of reconciliation to others. The vertically reconciled become a horizontally reconciling force in the world. As we have been made new in Christ, so we go forth as Christ's ambassadors throughout the world with the message: "Be reconciled to God" (2 Cor. 5:20). The whole church of the Trinity lives out its own vertical reconciliation by intentionally practicing evangelism in the best sense of that word. Far from being the formulaic, manipulative, pressurized practice that we have made it to be, authentic evangelism is an act of love, inviting people to experience God's lavishness (Luke 15:20–24), to get in step with the trinitarian dance by way of repentance and confession, and to begin moving toward newness of life, found only in Christ (2 Cor. 5:17). To be a reconciled and reconciling church means, first of all, to live fully into the ministry of evangelism.

The church, however, distorts the call to be reconcilers if it focuses solely on the vertical. To be reconciled also means to be reconciled to one another across differences. Those who have been vertically reconciled to God are now also called to be horizontally reconciled with one another. In the same letter to the Ephesians where Paul celebrates the grace of God through which we are saved, he also celebrates in the very same chapter how in Christ the dividing wall between Jew and gentile has come crashing down (Eph. 2:14). He encourages the believers in Ephesus with the truth that in Christ one new humanity is being created, wiping out the hostility between clashing cultures and reconciling to each other those "who were far off [gentiles]" and "those who were near [Jews]" (v. 17). In Paul's theology, God has called Jewish and gentile believers to forge an intercultural community together in the name of Jesus and by the power of the Holy Spirit, and thus provide a model of the new humanity. In Christ, "the whole structure is joined together and grows into a holy temple in the Lord; in whom you [gentiles] also are built together [with Jews] spiritually into a dwelling place for God" (vv. 21–22).

The call to be reconciled, therefore, needs to go as wide as it goes high. Although the same grace that saves us vertically enables us to be reconciled horizontally, the ministry of reconciliation also takes great intentionality. Whereas intercultural koinonia emphasizes the importance of diversity, the practical commitment to the ministry of horizontal reconciliation describes what it takes to achieve it. Without this commitment, diversity goes only skin-deep. As people come to faith in Christ, gender, racial, cultural, and socioeconomic tensions do not automatically go away, so it is not enough to simply gather diverse peoples to form multiethnic churches.

Grace Ji-Sun Kim and Jann Aldredge-Clanton, in their volume *Intercultural Ministry*, differentiate between diversity and interculturality: "People within diverse churches . . . may exist side by side, but they do not come together to learn from one another and to engage one another in mutual relationships. They do nothing to change the power imbalances that persist when one culture remains dominant. They may be diverse, but they are not intercultural."[32] Interculturality requires a commitment to reconciliation, for only through courage to confront the oppressions of our time (sexism, racism, classism, and more) can we enjoy fellowship based on equality, respect, and trust—that is, intercultural koinonia. Without a commitment to horizontal reconciliation, diversity becomes but a token sideshow.

The Evangelical Covenant Church in North America (ECC), to which I belong, exemplifies this commitment to the hard work of reconciliation. This can be seen most strikingly in its Invitation to Racial Righteousness initiatives. One of these initiatives is called Sankofa, "an intentional, cross-racial prayer journey that seeks to assist disciples of Christ on their move toward a righteous response to the social ills related to racism."[33] During a four-day bus ride, Sankofa transports a diverse group of participants to key sites that have come to define the civil rights movement in the US. While Sankofa focuses on the black-white divide in the US, the Journey to Mosaic uses the same approach to heighten awareness of other cultural injustices endured, for example, by Native or First Nations peoples in the Pacific Northwest or the Hispanic peoples in the Pacific Southwest sectors of the US.

---

32. Grace Ji-Sun Kim and Jann Aldredge-Clanton, introduction to *Intercultural Ministry: Hope for a Changing World*, ed. Grace Ji-Sun Kim and Jann Aldredge-Clanton (Valley Forge, PA: Judson, 2017), x.

33. "A Journey toward Racial Righteousness," Evangelical Covenant Church, accessed October 25, 2017, http://www.covchurch.org/justice/racial-righteousness/sankofa.

The effectiveness of both Sankofa and Journey to Mosaic lies in the conviction that the road to racial righteousness must run through, not around, the difficult histories of slavery, genocide, and the marginalization of whole peoples as part of the fuller history of the US. Genuine reconciliation between black, white, and brown people requires this kind of confrontation of past evils, not only to provide opportunity for repentance and confession but also to heighten awareness of ongoing racism today and to challenge it whenever and wherever it rears its hideous head. As overseer of ECC's global mission efforts, I am personally gratified that we require our missionaries to experience Sankofa or Journey to Mosaic, attesting to the denomination's commitment to racial righteousness and reconciliation on both the local and global levels.

These efforts describe but one denomination's acknowledgment and practice of the hard work of reconciliation. Many other examples exist. The second half of a volume titled *Mission as Ministry of Reconciliation*, for instance, has compiled inspiring stories of Christians from around the world who have defied the dividing walls of politics and culture and, by doing so, have engaged faithfully and courageously in the ministry of reconciliation, often at the risk of their own lives.[34]

The Great World House: The Beloved Community in Global Perspective

To be reconciled to God and to one another across the divides places the church in prime position to be a reconciling force in the world, both vertically and horizontally. The image of "the beloved community" immediately comes to mind here, for contrary to the notion that it describes only the church, the beloved community ultimately points to the image of the whole world enjoying God's peace, justice, and love. At its best, the whole and reconciled church models the beloved community to bear witness to the love of the Triune God for all.

Coined by the founder of the Fellowship of Reconciliation, Josiah Royce, but popularized and deepened by the great civil rights leader and gospel minister Dr. Martin Luther King Jr., the phrase "the beloved community" does not just represent wishful, utopian thinking.[35] It refers, rather, to the very call of the whole and reconciled church to model the beloved community for the

---

34. Robert Schreiter and Knud Jorgensen, eds., *Mission as Ministry of Reconciliation* (Oxford: Regnum, 2013), 173–318.

35. "The King Philosophy: The Beloved Community," The King Center, accessed October 25, 2017, http://www.thekingcenter.org/king-philosophy#sub4.

rest of the world, and not just model it but extend it proactively so that the whole world has access to it and becomes a part of it.

Although the civil rights movement in the US provided the context of King's work, the vision of the beloved community transcends the black-white divide in North America. However, in my search for works that have sought to understand King from a global perspective, I have only found a few titles. In *Toward the Beloved Community*, Lewis Baldwin applies King's social vision to address apartheid in South Africa.[36] In the more recent *The Great World House*, Hak Joon Lee develops a global ethic based on King's body of work.[37] I hope these volumes, which are few and far between, spur on more research to develop King's social theology in global perspective, for indeed, King's vision of an intercultural community of faith, hope, peace, justice, and love reflects God's vision for the whole world. What, for example, would a missiology of the beloved community look like? While missiologists such as Orlando Costas, Melba Maggay, Jayakumar Christian, Bryant Myers, and others have incorporated the transformation of socioeconomic structures in their writings, a constructive study specifically focusing on King's beloved community model would make a significant contribution to a socioethically informed missiology.

The "great world house," this equally potent but lesser-known descriptor also found in King's writings, would lend itself well to that endeavor as it captures the global extension of the beloved community. In the final chapter of his last book, *Where Do We Go from Here?*, King "proposes his vision for the world—the great world house where the whole of humanity lives as a single family in God."[38]

In this vision—a vision of nothing less than the kingdom of God—the church of the Trinity, the great world house in microcosm, serves as a vanguard of that kingdom. As such, it not only models belovedness in its life together; it also embraces the ambitious task of proactively working toward global reconciliation as a crucial dimension of the church's mission in the world, even as it affirms in humility and faith that the responsibility "to reconcile all things" ultimately belongs to God.

Community, diversity, and reconciliation: these characterize the whole and reconciled church, the church of the Trinity, a people who not only have experienced the love of the Father, Son, and Holy Spirit both vertically and

---

36. Lewis V. Baldwin, *Toward the Beloved Community: Martin Luther King Jr. and South Africa* (Cleveland: Pilgrim, 1995).

37. Hak Joon Lee, *The Great World House: Martin Luther King, Jr. and Global Ethics* (Cleveland: Pilgrim, 2011).

38. Lee, *Great World House*, xi–xii.

horizontally but are also compelled by that love to extend it worldwide in mission.

One more aspect of the whole and reconciled church needs attention: its practice of spirituality. Without an adequate understanding of how spirituality relates to mission and vice versa, the church would be in danger of becoming just another humanitarian organization that attempts to do good in the world. Of course, we should not minimize the value of humanitarian organizations; they do wonderful and difficult work. But the church is about that and more. Or more accurately, the church can be effectively humanitarian only by virtue of its relationship with God. The authenticity of the church's mission in the world depends on its understanding of spirituality and the practice of worship that flows from it. To these important aspects of the whole and reconciled church we now turn.

Discussion Questions

1. Given that the Trinity is a practical doctrine, in what ways is God's three-in-one nature operative in the world?
2. Share a time in your life when you have experienced genuine community.
3. In what ways have you pursued or desired to pursue diversity?
4. The image of the "great world house," where community, diversity, and reconciliation define existence, is God's big vision. What is the role of the church in realizing this vision?

EIGHT

Spirituality of Mission

The Church in the Power of the Spirit

. . . .

As they spent much time together in the temple,
they broke bread, . . . praising God and having the goodwill
of all the people. And day by day the Lord added to their
number those who were being saved.
—Acts 2:46–47

Several years ago I participated in a mission conference in a large church in Anyang City, South Korea. One could sense the life that pulsated in and beyond the walls of that church. It took up several city blocks, and though the modern architecture did not evoke the wow of centuries-old cathedrals, it held a certain magnificence. The life that emanated from that place, however, did not come from the structure per se. Perhaps I was merely projecting, but the life I sensed seemed to stem from its people, who knew their purpose and who lived it out together in unity. And the city seemed responsive as the church, one of the pastors told us, has steadily grown in numbers since its inception. Though numerical growth does not always indicate success in the kingdom sense, success in this church appeared to correspond directly with the church's outreach efforts.

During a break, one of the pastors took a group of us on a tour of the facility. Alongside the large, spacious room where we gathered for the plenary sessions, our tour guide showed us the classrooms, the offices, the beautiful sanctuary, and other parts of the building, periodically stopping with commentary at portraits of previous pastors or a piece of artwork. Then his face brightened, as if he had saved the best for last, and he guided us down to the basement of the church. What we saw when we arrived, I am convinced, revealed the secret to the church's vibrant, missional life: people praying for the world. The pastor explained that the church's prayer ministry is 24-7; church members form a tag team to intercede for the needs of the church, the city, the country, and the world, around the clock, seven days a week. That church in Anyang City never stops praying! It seemed fitting that the basement served as the location of this ministry, thus vividly symbolizing prayer as the foundation of the church. At that moment I realized that I was not just projecting this vision; the vibrant mission I intuited throughout the week in this church radiated from the prayer life of its people.

Finally, for our understanding of what it means to be the whole and reconciled church, we need to consider the spirituality and worship practices of the people of God. For the church's missional activity in the world depends on the church's own experience with its Savior and Lord. The Greatest Commandment demonstrates this simple logic, as love for neighbor flows out of love for God. "You shall love the Lord your God with all your heart, and with all your soul, and with all your mind," Jesus taught. "This is the greatest and first commandment. And a second is like it: You shall love your neighbor as yourself" (Matt. 22:37–39). Simply put, love for neighbor—the mission of the church—flows out of the church's love for God, its spirituality. This chapter explores the nature of spirituality, more specifically a spirituality of mission, in our quest to understand what it means to be the whole and reconciled church.

What is a spirituality of mission, and what does it look like? How, if at all, should this kind of spirituality shape the church's practice of worship? And how should worship shape the church's practice of mission? These are crucial questions that the church too often leaves unasked. In many congregations across the globe, sadly, worship and mission operate in separate spheres, often "without the possibility of cross-fertilization and without the question of their unity being raised at all."[1] And yet the health and relevance of churches depend on the interrelatedness between spirituality, worship, and mission.

A Spirituality of Mission

I define spirituality of mission as the *Holy Spirit at work in our hearts and in the world; it is the power that enables the church both to experience God and*

---

1. J. G. Davies, quoted in Al Tizon, *Missional Preaching: Engage, Embrace, Transform* (Valley Forge, PA: Judson, 2012), 24.

to engage in the mission of God; it serves as the basis of holistic transforma-
tion; and it conveys the joy that sustains us in the suffering of mission. Four
main ideas provide the substance of this definition.

Spirituality Is Pneumatology Is Missiology

First, spirituality is the necessary outcome of a proper pneumatology. Christian spirituality assumes the centrality of Christ; as Daniel Groody writes, "[It]
involves living out what Jesus most valued."[2] But, strangely, it does not often
recognize the significance of the person of the Holy Spirit. I say "strangely"
because the very word "spirituality" should make it obvious in the Christian
sense that it has everything to do with the person of the Holy Spirit, core
member of the Trinity, and her life-giving, creative, nurturing, and powerful
ministry in the world.

This person-al nature of Christian spirituality distinguishes it from generic,
impersonal, ethereal definitions that more often than not come to mean nothing because they attempt to include everything. *Spirituality for Dummies*,
for example, describes it as "beyond all religions yet containing all religions,
beyond all science yet containing all science, beyond all philosophy yet containing all philosophies."[3] Such an all-inclusive description may satisfy at
some level, but not in the concrete reality of our lives.

By way of contrast, Christian spirituality has historical, biblical roots,
based on the beauty of our "Father's world,"[4] the death and resurrection of
Jesus, and the powerful, creative ministry of the Holy Spirit. As a spirituality
of the Trinity, it contains the substance from which people in the real world
can draw real hope and purpose. Christian spirituality means full engagement
with the person of the Holy Spirit, who advances the mission of Jesus and
the kingdom in, through, and beyond the church.

The Spirit represents the active, missional dimension of the Trinity, the
creative energy source of God's transformative work. In this sense spirituality is pneumatology is missiology. "The Spirit of the Lord is upon me," Jesus
announced, "because he has anointed me to bring good news to the poor"
(Luke 4:18). Furthermore, this work of the Spirit weaves in and out of both
the interior and the exterior, the personal and the social, in our hearts and in

2. Daniel G. Groody, *Globalization, Spirituality, and Justice* (Maryknoll, NY: Orbis Books, 2007), 240.

3. Sharon Janis, "Exploring the Meaning of Spirituality," Dummies, accessed October 25, 2017, http://www.dummies.com/religion/spirituality/exploring-the-meaning-of-spirituality.

4. Maltbie Babcock's hymn "This Is My Father's World" comes to mind here. See http://www .hymnary.org/text/this_is_my_fathers_world_and_to_my.

the world. Spirituality of mission means holistic transformation. I will say more about this later. Suffice it to say here that when the Holy Spirit blows through a house, people are changed (Acts 2:1–4), and when she travels beyond the church, the world falls under loving and holy conviction (John 16:8–11). The work of the Spirit in our hearts and in the world constitutes the core of a Christian spirituality of mission.

Spirit Baptism: Power for Personal Life and Global Mission

Spirituality of mission has to do with the Holy Spirit, but specifically with the *power* of the Holy Spirit. This power enables us to experience God in profoundly personal ways (in our hearts) and to engage in God's mission (in the world). This power, the *dynamis* of God, is the meaning behind what we encounter in the book of Acts as the baptism in the Holy Spirit (Acts 1:5). J. Rodman Williams says it plainly: "The power of God—transcendent power—is the purpose of the gift of the Holy Spirit."[5] Spirit baptism refers to the experience of being fully immersed in that power.

Though Pentecostal/charismatic scholars have dominated the literature around this biblical experience—and naturally so, given that it underscores their tradition—they do not have proprietary rights to it. On the contrary, Spirit baptism—full immersion into the creative power of God—belongs to the whole church and its witness throughout the whole world. As Tony Campolo makes clear, "All of us who are 'born again,' . . . not just those who call themselves Pentecostals, . . . should be able to have something to say about being invaded by the Spirit and being made into the new persons that God wants us to be."[6]

Spirit baptism means "primarily . . . power for witness," writes Williams. "Though the immediate response of the disciples to the gift of the Spirit will be the praise of God directed upward, the purpose of that gift will be the service of humanity and therefore directed outward."[7] I ultimately agree with this. However, we would be remiss if we jumped too quickly to affirming the outward at the expense of celebrating the upward. For the move of the church outward in mission flows out of the upward experience of the whole and reconciled church in worship.

5. J. Rodman Williams, "Baptism in the Holy Spirit," in *International Dictionary of Pentecostal and Charismatic Movements*, rev. ed., ed. Stanley M. Burgess and Eduard M. Van Der Maas (Grand Rapids: Zondervan, 2002), 359.

6. Tony Campolo, "Romans 8—The Pentecostal Movement," in *Following Fire: How the Spirit Leads Us to Fight Injustice*, ed. Cheryl Catford (Springvale, Australia: UNOH, 2008), 73.

7. Williams, "Baptism," 359.

Before those "dunked in the Spirit" began turning the world upside down in the New Testament, they themselves were being turned upside down in their innermost being. They experienced God so profoundly that their own languages could not contain their praise; so they worshiped "in other languages, as the Spirit gave them ability" (Acts 2:4, 11; see 1 Cor. 14:2). The power of God through an encounter with the Spirit surged through them, and as a result they experienced transcendence like never before.

Intellectual assent to God, adherence to a set of doctrines, and ritual practices of church tradition have their place in the Christian community, but without personal experience in Christ through prayer, song, Scripture reading, and, for some, ecstatic praise in other tongues, we would most probably encounter a church that lacks vibrancy, exuberance, healthy fellowship, and/ or passion for mission. It should be the plea, therefore, of every Christian and every church to be baptized in and to be regularly filled with the Holy Spirit.

The baptism in the Holy Spirit authenticates the gospel of Christ and his kingdom in the lives of the faithful. By this I refer to the Spirit's work in enabling us to go beyond a cerebral, doctrinal assent to the faith and to make it experientially and personally true. "I know that I know," not just because of intellectual persuasion, a creed, and/or a tradition handed down by previous generations, but because "I spoke to God today, and God spoke to me."

However, when believers stop at this juncture, when we see personal experience/relationship as the end goal of Spirit baptism and not as the means of releasing us to serve the lost and needy in Jesus's name, then we tragically short-circuit the full voltage of the power generated by Spirit baptism. Speaking specifically of their Pentecostal tradition, Julie and Wonsuk Ma write candidly, "It is . . . honest to recognize that Pentecostalism has revealed the shadow side of power orientation."[8] When people seek after the experience itself (not unlike Simon the magician in Acts 8:18–19) and/or when alleged miracle workers perform signs and wonders without any theological or institutional accountability, then the weird, the excessive, and the ridiculous create the sideshow that the world rightly dismisses and mocks, thus marring the church's witness to Christ around the globe.

We must grasp and grasp firmly that the same power enabling us to experience God in intensely personal ways also energizes us to be Christ's witnesses "in Jerusalem, in all Judea and Samaria, and to the ends of the earth" (Acts 1:8). The power of Spirit baptism does not just refer to personal experience; it also and primarily refers to empowerment for witness. A heart touched by

---

8. Julie Ma and Wonsuk Ma, *Mission in the Spirit: Towards a Pentecostal/Charismatic Missiology* (Eugene, OR: Wipf & Stock, 2010), 39.

the Spirit of our missional God ultimately propels us to engage in mission with bold humility throughout the world. The Spirit does not stop at simply blessing believers with personal experiences but necessarily graduates them into a passion to change the world in Jesus's name. The book of Acts records the acts of people who themselves experienced God deeply and profoundly and, by virtue of that, were driven by the singular vision of global transformation in the name of Jesus. A Christian spirituality of mission awakens both the mystic and the missionary in us, as the Holy Spirit works in our hearts and in the world, empowering followers of Jesus to participate relationally with God in the transformation of the world.

The Wholly Spirit

Another dimension of a spirituality of mission has to do with sharing the blessings of life under the reign of God with the rest of the world. Kingdom blessings were always and ultimately meant for the whole world, not just for those within the faith community. The Lord promised Abraham and Sarah that through them a great nation would emerge, not just to bless their own family but to bless all the families of the earth (Gen. 12:3).

What does it mean to be blessed? The answer to this question points to another core aspect of a spirituality of mission—namely, that it serves as the basis of the full range of kingdom blessings, resulting in holistic transformation. At the risk of being slightly (or *very*) corny, the Holy Spirit is the Wholly Spirit! If we grasp nothing else from the pages of this book, let it be the truth that the gospel of the kingdom of God, as Christ preached and modeled it, refers to the total redemption of creation and everyone in it; that it bears the message of salvation, from soul to society; that it means the reconciliation of all things.

The possibility of becoming whole and reconciled with God, one another, and all of creation in Christ constitutes what is so irresistibly good about the good news. The gospel is good, precisely because it announces God's mercy, love, peace, righteousness, and justice for all who believe in faith—not just one or two of those things but all those things. The Spirit commissions the called and empowered, the whole and reconciled church, to extend this comprehensive goodness—what Lisa Sharon Harper celebrates as "the very good gospel"—to the uttermost parts of the earth.[9]

Far from the idea that personal piety, the building up of the church, and a smattering of conversions constitute the chief end of the Spirit's work,

---

9. Lisa Sharon Harper, *The Very Good Gospel: How Everything Wrong Can Be Made Right* (Colorado Springs: Waterbrook, 2016).

Charles Ringma reminds us that "the Spirit generates the impulses of integral and holistic mission. There is nothing skimpy or limiting that the Spirit seeks to do. Persons are made whole in Christ, communities are built or restored, the spiritual as well as the economic dimensions of life are addressed, and the work of justice is carried forward."[10] By the power of the Holy Spirit, we bear witness to the very good gospel of holistic transformation in Jesus Christ.

It makes no sense to limit God's agenda, for we would be hard pressed to think of anything that the Creator God does not seek to save. If in the beginning God deemed all of creation not just good but *very* good (Gen. 1:31), then it stands to reason that God's plan of redemption includes all that sin contaminated. God seeks to reconcile *all* things. How then can God's missional agenda of transformation be anything less than everything?[11] A Christian spirituality of mission celebrates the Spirit's work in and through the whole and reconciled church to proclaim the whole and reconciled gospel for the whole world.

In their work *The God of Intimacy and Action*, Tony Campolo and Mary Albert Darling make the crucial connection between spirituality (or their preferred term, "mysticism") and holistic ministry. Through the lens of mystics, ancient and contemporary, they drive home the point that "God-ordained spirituality . . . must involve a commitment to intimacy with Christ that results in evangelism and justice work—that is, if we want to strive for what Jesus lived, died, and rose again for."[12] Concerning evangelism, they state, "Those who are empowered by the Holy Spirit often report . . . an irresistible urge to tell the salvation story so that people will commit to live it."[13] Their observation supports the biblical pattern, as Peter, for example, after the Holy Spirit fell on him in Acts 2, preached a powerful sermon that resulted in three thousand conversions (vv. 14–41).

Elsewhere in a short reflection, I lament the propensity of an increasing number of Christian social activists who have abandoned the practice of evangelism, some inadvertently but others intentionally. In this meditation I recount God's invasion into my own life, because of those who dared to share the good news with me during my time of adolescent rebellion. In light of my own experience, how can I not also be the bearer of good news to other rebels? How can I possibly not believe that the transformation of the world

---

10. Charles Ringma, "God's Spirit and the Poor," in Catford, *Following Fire*, 55.

11. I argue similarly in my *Missional Preaching*, 6–7.

12. Tony Campolo and Mary Albert Darling, *The God of Intimacy and Action: Reconnecting Ancient Spiritual Practices, Evangelism and Justice* (San Francisco: Jossey-Bass, 2007), 207.

13. Campolo and Darling, *God of Intimacy and Action*, 28.

also includes the transformation of the heart?[14] Indeed, our own experience with God results in a passion for authentic, love-based evangelism.

For works of compassion and justice, Campolo and Darling assert that "it is the Holy Spirit who creates in us an awareness and a sensitivity to what victims of injustices must endure, as well as a deep commitment to set things right for them."[15] The Spirit enables us to see with Christ's eyes those whom society at large does not readily see. Indeed, "invisible people" exist in every society. The lepers we encounter in the Gospels come to mind, as do carriers of HIV/AIDS today. As we draw nearer to Jesus, who himself was empowered by the Spirit to proclaim good news to the poor (Luke 4:18), we catch searing glimpses of how God sees the world, and then the Spirit releases us to do justice and love mercy among the poor, oppressed, and marginalized.

Champions of compassion and justice do not just see the invisible in society; the Spirit also enables them to encounter Jesus himself in and through them. Jesus said to the compassionate that when they feed the hungry, give water to the thirsty, welcome the stranger, clothe the naked, nurse the sick, and visit the prisoner, they do these things to him (Matt. 25:34–36). Those who engage in compassion and justice ministries position themselves to see Jesus, who evidently lives in and among the disinherited. Epiphany!

A spirituality of mission serves as the basis of holistic transformation in the world, as it binds together love for God and love for neighbor, or in practical terms, evangelism and justice. As we draw closer in our intimacy with God, our mission to "the least, the lost, and the last" comes into sharper focus.

Joy: Toward a Missiology of Suffering

Finally, "spirituality of mission" refers to joy that comes through suffering—not suffering per se, as if suffering in and of itself has virtue, but suffering when we live out the values of the kingdom of God (2 Thess. 1:5). In God's upside-down kingdom, blood, sweat, and tears for the sake of others result not in despair but in supernatural joy.

We have seen that a spirituality of mission means power for divine encounter as well as for holistic witness. But at the end of the day, a spirituality of mission offers joy. Contrary to the notion that joy means being happy or having an unrelentingly cheerful disposition, joy refers to a powerful confidence in God's eventual victory over hatred, injustice, evil, and death.

14. I say more about this in a short article, "When in Doubt Reminisce," Evangelicals for Social Action, March 6, 2015, http://www.evangelicalsforsocialaction.org/evangelism-posts/when-in-doubt-reminisce.

15. Campolo and Darling, God of Intimacy and Action, 40.

Contentment flows from this confidence, a steadiness that keeps one active and hopeful in spite of wars and rumors of wars, poverty, catastrophe, and other global realities that can fill us with despair. Confidence, contentment, and courage to serve others even in the face of great odds—these characterize joy. And it comes when, in faith and action, we embrace the promise that one day God will say "Enough!" and will then proceed to consummate what Christ set in motion at the cross and empty tomb—the reconciliation of all things.

Yet why does this joy have to come through suffering? Does living out the gospel today inevitably lead to suffering? The short answer is yes: "If any want to become my followers," Jesus says plainly, "let them deny themselves and take up their cross daily and follow me" (Luke 9:23). The call to bear the cross daily—that is, to carry a burden, to take on pain, to suffer—refers to the cost of living out the good news of God's kingdom amid other kingdoms that do not want to hear it. As Jonathan R. Wilson explains, "When the church is empowered to live by the kingdom of God in a world that is in rebellion against that kingdom, suffering is the consequence of faithful witness."[16] When we share the good news to the disinherited, we offer hope and courage to victims of the system—that is, the world—and thus undermine the ways of the world. Therefore, those who benefit most from those ways lash out, persecute, maim, and kill anyone who threatens the status quo.

As part of my ministry, I oversee missionaries and their work with partners around the globe. This requires extensive travel in order to see firsthand God's people across cultures working together for the sake of the gospel. Nothing inspires me more than to see these ordinary people achieving extraordinary feats in the Spirit. I return home each time with my heart beating with gratitude, as well as my mind spinning with ideas and strategies to change the world. I also return home with a reminder of an obvious truth that I often take for granted—namely, that mission work is hard.

Missionaries and their national partners around the world have set aside normal life pursuits and have committed themselves to care for the sick and malnourished, empower the poor through community development, participate in dangerous peacemaking, give voice to the voiceless, cultivate disciples, plant and pastor churches, and develop future leaders. In short, they have sacrificed their own personal ambitions in order to give hope to others in the name of Jesus. As Dietrich Bonhoeffer famously said, "When Christ

16. Jonathan R. Wilson, *Why Church Matters: Worship, Ministry and Mission in Practice* (Grand Rapids: Brazos, 2006), 137.

calls [us], he bids [us] come and die."[17] Missionaries and their partners have operationalized this call. In many contexts, the faithful live under constant threat of harassment, imprisonment, and death. Contrary to the notion that martyrdom belongs to a bygone era, the death toll of Christians today because of their faith is on the rise.[18]

In addition to these overt acts of persecution, missionaries and their partners also endure more mundane challenges. I know, for example, the difficulty that missionaries face while living in cultures wholly different from their own, and I know the difficulty of nationals hosting culturally challenged, fumbling, and sometimes insensitive missionaries in order to achieve effective partnerships. Not to mention the daily endurance necessary to handle varying degrees of corruption, inefficiency, and unreliable running water, electricity, and internet connection, among others. Life and mission are not for the faint of heart! In my mind, these realities of sacrificial, selfless, intercultural mission add up to lives that are nothing short of heroic. At their own expense, these heroes enter the fray of mission with a Spirit-inspired sense of call to bear witness to the whole and reconciled gospel among the lost, poor, oppressed, and marginalized.

This "missiology of suffering" ironically results in the deepest of joys for these unsung heroes. The same Spirit who inspires people to a life of missional suffering also gifts them with unspeakable joy. The Spirit has various "middle names," such as Paraclete, Advocate, Comforter (John 14:16, 26; 15:26; 16:7), that describe her as walking alongside the faithful, defending, protecting, comforting, and giving peace and encouragement. Joy sustains them in the hard, grueling work of mission. Nehemiah knew of this joy, as he declares in the middle of the hard, conflicted work of rebuilding the walls of Jerusalem, "The joy of the LORD is your strength" (Neh. 8:10).

This joy does not come from trying to secure, protect, and enrich our own lives; it comes rather by giving our lives away in the service of others. In one of my favorite allegories, penned by Leo Tolstoy, an angel named Michael finally grasps the lesson that he was sent down to learn. After years of living among humans and waiting for God to teach him, Michael declares, in the story's climax, "I know now that people only *seem* to live when they care only for themselves, and that it is by love for others that they really live."[19] Joy, the

17. Dietrich Bonhoeffer, *The Cost of Discipleship*, rev. ed. (New York: Macmillan, 1963), 99.
18. The number of Christian martyrs today is disputed and depends on how one counts. Regardless of which statistic one prefers, the number is astounding. Yes, it still happens today, and it happens intensely. For more on different ways to interpret the number of Christian martyrs today, see Ruth Alexander, "Are There Really 100,000 New Christian Martyrs Every Year?," BBC, November 12, 2013, http://www.bbc.com/news/magazine-24864587.
19. Leo Tolstoy, *What Men Live By* (White Plains, NY: Peter Pauper, n.d.), 58.

joy of the Lord, comes through missional suffering. The Holy Spirit inspires us to live a life of mission, a life of suffering for the sake of the gospel, and as our great reward this side of heaven, we receive the gift of deep and abiding joy for the flourishing of our souls.

Whole Church Worship: Spirituality of Mission in Practice

Although spirituality manifests one way or another in all that a church does, it expresses itself most overtly in the church's practice of worship. For example, the beautifully ornate and highly formalized worship of so-called high churches speaks to people's underlying sense of reverence for God, while the simple, exuberant, spontaneous worship of so-called low or free churches celebrates people's sense of access to God.

Many types of spiritualities, and therefore kinds of worship, abound. Differences in theology, form, musical style, level of formality, and so on run deep enough that periodically churches find themselves amid what in the last thirty years has been called "the worship wars."[20] These differences manifest among and within congregations because of the differences in the way people relate to God—that is, in the different spiritualities that have formed among and within them. I argue that the church moves most directly toward wholeness when it worships God according to a spirituality *of mission*. A church that defines, plans, orders, and conducts its service of worship by way of this kind of spirituality moves toward its true missional identity as the whole and reconciled church.

"Worship" in general refers to our response to who God is and what God has done (and is doing). In the specific congregational sense (in contrast to the all-of-life sense of Rom. 12), worship involves, according to Clayton Schmit, "the full complex of activities (song, prayer, praise, lament, proclamation, silence, offerings, meditation, fellowship, announcements, and so on) that make up our public adoration of God." Worship informed by a spirituality of mission has another crucial layer, which Schmit describes as "those actions that relate to the work of Christian discipleship in the world."[21] These two parts together make up what can be called missional worship. A church that practices missional worship bears several distinct marks.

---

20. For more on the worship wars, as well as a theology to overcome them, see Thomas G. Long, *Beyond the Worship Wars: Building Vital and Faithful Worship* (Lanham, MD: Rowman & Littlefield, 2014).

21. Clayton J. Schmit, *Sent and Gathered: A Worship Manual for the Missional Church* (Grand Rapids: Baker Academic, 2009), 29.

Holistic Worship: Adoring the God of Everything

First, missional worship bears the mark of the whole and reconciled gospel, the gospel of the kingdom. Missional worship is holistic worship. It leads people to adore not just the God of social justice and peace, not just the God of personal salvation and piety, but the God of all these things, of everything. In a missional holistic worship service, people encounter the God who cares about their inner life, their families, their neighborhoods, their cities, their nation, and indeed the whole world.

They encounter the God who at once affirms and transforms them as well as the world around them. As God's people engage in missional holistic worship, the vision of God's kingdom comes into sharper focus, while lesser visions blur. Missional holistic worship causes people to see that the vision of the American or global dream—or whatever one calls the all-consuming pursuit of wealth, fame, getting ahead, establishing security for ourselves and our loved ones, and other personal gains—is not big enough. In missional holistic worship, the Spirit of the whole and reconciled gospel possesses us, and as a result our ambition to prosper personally is eclipsed by the desire for God's kingdom to come in fullness so that all may prosper.

To be transformed in this way by missional holistic worship calls for no small paradigm shift, for to care primarily about our own welfare has been humanity's default since Cain infamously retorted, "Am I my brother's keeper?" (Gen. 4:9). Holistic worship kills our old, selfish nature and allows our missional identity in Christ to come alive. This in part is what Mark Labberton means when he beckons the church to engage in dangerous worship. "Worship," he writes, "turns out to be the dangerous act of waking up to God and to the purposes of God in the world, and then living lives that actually show it."[22] He describes how he prepared himself for Sunday worship when he served as the senior pastor at First Presbyterian Church in Berkeley, California. As a regular practice, Labberton read the weekly email update from a missionary family serving at-risk children in Cambodia before Sunday service, because, he writes, "I want[ed] . . . to lead our worship services . . . with my heart freshly reminded of the realities of suffering in the world, the urgency of hearing and living out the hope of the gospel, and the joyous and costly call to sacrificial living in the name of Christ."[23]

---

22. Mark Labberton, *The Dangerous Act of Worship: Living God's Call to Justice* (Downers Grove, IL: IVP Books, 2007), 13.
    23. Labberton, *Dangerous Act*, 33–34.

Intercultural Worship: Adoring the God of the Nations

Missional worship also bears the mark of the global character of God, which corresponds to the intercultural koinonia discussed in chapter 7. Intercultural worship celebrates who God is and what God has done (and is doing) in the powerful creativity of the Holy Spirit in the context of diverse cultures. To worship God interculturally, therefore, demonstrates the lordship of Christ over all cultures.

Authentic worship, however, also reflects (or should reflect) the cultural context of the worshipers. For example, when worshipers use indigenous musical instruments, or when a church in a rice-eating culture uses rice instead of bread for communion, or when worshipers use their mother tongue to sing, recite, pray, and preach, they worship in and through their respective contextual particularities. These contextual ways of worship pave the way for authentic encounters with God; without them, worship can devolve into transcendent irrelevance.[24]

However, if worship properly focuses on the God whom we encounter in the Scriptures, then we ultimately bow down to the one who transcends—but certainly does not bypass—the particularities of culture. As Charles Farhadian asserts, "Culture itself, given by God, can serve as a conduit for meaningful worship, but only when it is secondary to the recognition of God as Creator, the source of diversity."[25] Intercultural missional worship aspires to reflect the global character of the Triune God, even as it takes seriously the values and forms of particular cultures.

In intercultural missional worship, God's people adore the God of the nations as a foretaste of the worship service to come, as in Revelation 7, when a great multitude from every nation, tribe, and people will gather to worship God in their respective languages (v. 9). I am strongly critical of the lone presence of the US flag in church sanctuaries, the locus of community worship, because it conveys parochialism and breeds exceptionalism, which can fuel the pathos of Christian America (see chap. 2). But if it hangs among many flags in the sanctuary, then it says something different; it says that the God to whom we bow the knee transcends red, white, and blue; it says that when we worship Jesus, we celebrate the Triune God of all nations.

24. See "Nairobi Statement on Worship and Culture," particularly section 3, found in the appendix of *Christian Worship Worldwide: Expanding Horizons, Deepening Practices*, ed. Charles E. Farhadian (Grand Rapids: Eerdmans, 2007), 285–90.

25. Charles E. Farhadian, "Beyond Lambs and Logos: Christianity, Cultures, and Worship Worldwide," in Farhadian, *Christian Worship Worldwide*, 8.

Sandra Van Opstal says plainly, "Intentional multiethnic worship provides great challenges."[26] We must not understate this fact. Indeed, intercultural worship has larger, more complex obstacles to overcome than same-culture worship. Some of these obstacles include ignorance of other cultures, preference for one's own culture, fear of the different, and grave concern that certain practices different from one's own are somehow sacrilegious. Intercultural worship requires intentionality, determination, and creativity. There is more than one way to do it. Van Opstal outlines four models of intercultural worship—acknowledgment, blended, fusion, and collaborative rotation—and she gives practical guidelines for churches that are growing in their awareness of God's beautifully diverse world.[27]

Beyond intentionality, determination, and creativity in planning, whole and reconciled churches recognize the need for the ministry of reconciliation to be operative throughout the week if intercultural worship on Sunday is to have any credibility. In other words, authentic worship requires intercultural koinonia, which includes the practical commitment to reconciliation (see chap. 7). As the church affirms the power of the gospel to break down ethnic and racial walls, it cannot gloss over the possible injustices that exist between different tribes and peoples represented in the congregation. The church needs to acknowledge and deal with these injustices—which is the hard work of reconciliation—if it seeks to practice diverse worship with integrity. This is not to say that churches should cease trying to practice intercultural worship when racial tensions arise; on the contrary, "Worship is the power that opens us up to the possibility of reconciliation."[28] We would do well, therefore, to think of the relationship between intercultural worship and the ministry of reconciliation as interdependent and symbiotic—intercultural worship enabling the ministry of reconciliation, and reconciliation making way for authentic intercultural worship.

Sending Worship: Adoring the God of Action

Last, missional worship bears the mark of a sent people—people activated by the Spirit to do justice, love mercy, and walk humbly in their everyday lives. Missional worship produces doers of the Word, as God's people adore the God of action, week in and week out. Just as faith without works is dead, according to James 2, so too worship without mission is meaningless.

26. Sandra Van Opstal, *The Next Worship: Glorifying God in a Diverse World* (Downers Grove, IL: IVP Books, 2016), 27.
27. Van Opstal, *Next Worship*, 101–8.
28. Brenda Salter McNeil and Rick Richardson, quoted in Van Opstal, *Next Worship*, 62.

Furthermore, it angers God. "I hate, I despise your festivals," the Lord famously said to a people who neglected and even oppressed the poor by their business dealings. "I take no delight in your solemn assemblies. . . . But let justice roll down like waters, and righteousness like an ever-flowing stream" (Amos 5:21, 24). Missional worship is sending worship; it sends God's people out into the world in power and love.

And then when they gather again, they testify to the marvelous ways in which God has moved in people's hearts, neighborhoods, nations, and the world. These sorts of testimonies evoke worship, which in turn energizes people when they are sent out again. And so goes the worship-mission cycle of healthy, growing, exciting discipleship in the community of faith.

Of course, I am describing the ideal. When things do not go so well in the world, when our missional efforts do not seem to make any difference, and when God seems silent and uninvolved, then I hope that the regathering times will be characterized by honesty, tears, and lament. The point is, the whole and reconciled church understands the seamlessness of worship and mission, two acts flowing from the same life of the community of disciples. If we call the gathering of God's people on Sunday morning "liturgy," then Ion Bria has rightly called the church's mission in the world Monday through Saturday as "the liturgy after the liturgy."[29] After all, "liturgy" comes from the Greek *leitourgos*, meaning public worship—or simply, God's people sharing the life found in Christ with all peoples.[30]

A Missional Worship Service

How would this missional theology of worship—holistic, intercultural, and active—inform the various elements of a service of worship? Diversity, first of all, would characterize the leadership, as women and men, black, white, and brown, and young and old facilitate the service. Song leaders would choose (or write) hymns and songs not only according to the theme of the day but more fundamentally in step with the God who loves all the cultures of the world. This could mean songs sung in different languages and instruments used from different parts of the world. Prayers of the people would not be limited to the needs of the body but extended to include the community and the world. Confession would plead for God's mercy, not only on us because we have lied or lusted or drunk a little too much, but also because we have

29. Ion Bria, *The Liturgy after the Liturgy: Mission and Witness from an Orthodox Perspective* (Geneva, Switzerland: WCC, 1996), 20.

30. Shane Claiborne, Jonathan Wilson-Hartgrove, and Enuma Okoro, *Common Prayer: A Liturgy for Ordinary Radicals* (Grand Rapids: Zondervan, 2010), 10.

neglected to love our neighbors as ourselves and have participated in unjust economic and racist structures. Announcements would not only inform people of the date of the next congregational meeting or potluck; they would also give opportunities to serve the community and the world. The preaching would draw out the missional dimension of the Scriptures; whether the text is a ceremonial cleansing passage from Leviticus or the Great Commission of Matthew 28, the preacher would call the congregation to live lives of faithful action.[31] Communion would invoke remembrance of Christ's loving sacrifice not just for those present but for the whole world, especially the broken and the persecuted. And the benediction would not simply mark the end of the service; it more importantly would remind people of God's invitation to participate in God's redeeming acts in their everyday lives as well as in their intentional commitment to the whole gospel for the sake of the whole world. From beginning to end of a service of worship, the people would have lifted up the God, yes, who has shown mercy on them, but who has also called them to do the same in Jerusalem, Judea and Samaria, and the ends of the earth.

What would happen if people experienced a worship service like this every Sunday, a service informed by a robust spirituality of mission? The church would not only rediscover the power (and danger!) of corporate worship; it would also open itself up to the missional energy of the Holy Spirit to "go therefore and make disciples of all nations, baptizing them in the name of the Father and of the Son and of the Holy Spirit, and teaching them to obey everything that I have commanded you" (Matt. 28:19–20). The whole and reconciled church would be poised and empowered to engage in whole and reconciled mission, the subject of the next and final section of this book.

Discussion Questions

1. In what ways is it detrimental to the life of the church when spirituality and mission fail to interact, as they often do?

2. Recall a time when you have experienced a genuine move of the Spirit in your own life or community.

3. How does your church's worship inspire and motivate its members to live a life of mission?

---

31. I go into more detail regarding the missional nature of the whole Bible in *Missional Preaching*, 12–23.

Part 4

Whole Mission

The threads of mission have weaved in and out of this study, but in this final part we focus on the threads themselves. With a better understanding of the whole gospel and the whole church in the context of the whole world, we can now ask in a much more informed way, "What is the whole mission?" If we fail to ask it, then all we have discussed thus far will amount to little. For the threads of mission do not simply provide decorative embroidery; they make up the very fabric of the church. Without the threads of mission, the church falls apart at the seams!

To be sure, better time-tested metaphors exist, such as Emil Brunner's burning fire analogy. "The church exists by mission," Brunner wrote famously and brilliantly, "as fire exists by burning."[1] The thought of a church that does not actively engage in mission should tax the brain as much as trying to think of fire that does not burn. Regardless of which metaphor, we have come to the crux of the matter: what it means for the whole church, stewards of the whole gospel, to be engaged in God's whole mission throughout the whole world.

Making Kingdom Disciples: The Vocation of the Church

Part 4 seeks to understand the whole mission of the church in a fractured and fracturing world. As we shall see, it will involve reinforcing the relationship between evangelism and social justice as well as establishing peacemaking as central to any missional paradigm that claims to be holistic.

1. Emil Brunner, *The Word and the World* (New York: Charles Scribner's Sons, 1931), 108.

Before discussing these missional aspects, however, we need to consider the driver that governs them. As a missiologist, I am quite aware of the complex history of the church's wrestling to understand its mission in the world. Craig Ott reminds us, "The ways in which the church has historically defined its mission have evolved dramatically."[2] However, at the risk of oversimplifying this complex history, I believe that, with a proper understanding of biblical discipleship, the call on the church to make disciples of all nations is central to the various proposals. Such a statement may simply expose my evangelical bias; on the other hand, it may overtly state what all churches desire as a result of their mission efforts. For what church would not want any and all, including its members, to experience, enjoy, and be changed by the manifold blessings of the kingdom of God?

Twentieth-century mission history shows that the deemphasis on making disciples was due, at least in part, to a rejection of narrow evangelical/fundamentalist definitions of discipleship that made evangelism the primary, if not the sole, missionary task of the church. In continuity with evangelical pioneers of holistic mission, I reject this narrow view while still maintaining that disciplemaking provides the ultimate motivation for the church's mission in the world.

In a moment I will give a fuller definition of discipleship, thereby giving us an idea of what exactly we are supposed to be making. For now, we need only to grasp that disciplemaking is not just another item to add to the list of missionary activities; it refers, rather, to the inspiration behind those activities. It refers to the ultimate motivation of the church to engage the nations with the gospel. As disciples, we preach and teach the story, love mercy, do justice, and engage in peacemaking to bear witness to the whole gospel, *in order to make more disciples* who do the same. That the whole world and everyone in it would know the *shalom* of God in Jesus Christ drives the mission of the whole and reconciled church.

Discipleship is, after all (or before all), the central idea of the Matthean Great Commission, Jesus's clearest call and instruction to his disciples as to what to do next. Depending on the angle of the teacher or preacher, the Great Commission has inspired global mission, evangelism, and/or Christian education. It has also launched theological discussions on the Trinity, ecclesiology, baptism, and/or the authority of Christ. None of these are wrong unless it prevents us from seeing *mathēteuein*, disciplemaking, as the essence of the parting words of Jesus. If, for example, we interpret "Go" as the imperative

---

2. Craig Ott, introduction to *The Mission of the Church: Five Views in Conversation*, ed. Craig Ott (Grand Rapids: Baker Academic, 2016), x.

of the Great Commission, coupled with a narrow view of disciplemaking as evangelism, then the church goes wayward as it defines the whole mission as sending evangelist-missionaries to make converts of the nations. Read that way—as I argue in chapter 9—the Great Commission is not so great. In all of its kingdom implications, disciplemaking constitutes, in the words of David Bosch, "the heart of the commissioning"[3] in the call on the church to live out the Great Commission among the nations.

Congregations lose their way when they go deaf to this call. They lose their way when seeking to become more faithful disciples of Christ is no longer the main purpose of the church, when the primary reason for the church's existence is something less than encountering the living God in Jesus Christ (worship) and being steadily but radically changed by it both individually and collectively. Dying churches and defeated Christians can indeed be traced to what Dallas Willard calls "the Great Omission," the neglect of genuine discipleship as taught in the New Testament.[4] Many churches unfortunately are guilty of the Great Omission, and consequently, says Willard, "we can be 'Christians' forever and never become disciples."[5]

Similarly, congregations lose their way when making disciples of Christ is no longer the impetus for mission. "Jesus told us explicitly what to do," Willard asserts. "He told us, as disciples, to make disciples."[6] To safeguard against the view that disciplemaking is just one more missionary activity and emphasize that it is instead the ultimate motivation for all missionary activities, I find it helpful to describe disciplemaking as the vocation of the church. The tasks of evangelism, compassion, justice, and peacemaking—the mission of the church—flesh out this vocation in the world. The global church engages in mission to live out the Great Commission, which is to make and deepen kingdom disciples of, among, and throughout all the nations of the world.

I make this assertion knowing full well that the application of the Great Commission in the colonial period all too often brought great damage to the world—in the name of Christ, no less. The Christendom church "made disciples of all nations" by way of paternalism, conquest, and ethnocide (see chaps. 2 and 3). In this way we can speak of "victims of the Great Commission." And insofar as this legacy remains operative in mission circles today through a lingering belief in cultural, economic, and/or educational

---

3. David J. Bosch, *Transforming Mission: Paradigm Shifts in Theology of Mission*, 20th anniv. ed. (Maryknoll, NY: Orbis Books, 2011), 74.

4. Dallas Willard, *The Great Omission: Reclaiming Jesus' Essential Teachings on Discipleship* (New York: HarperCollins, 2006), ix–xii.

5. Willard, *Great Omission*, xi.

6. Willard, *Great Omission*, xii.

superiority, the application of the Great Commission needs to be challenged and interrogated.[7] In the words of Richard Twiss, it also needs to be rescued "from the cowboys, or Western cultural captivity,"[8] if there is to be any possibility of formulating a postcolonial missiology—that is, what whole and reconciled mission looks like in the twenty-first century. To the extent that the church can rescue or redeem the Great Commission from the colonial curse, it can live out its true biblical vocation to make disciples throughout the whole world—not as a community of completed disciples who are simply adding to their ranks, but as "a people on the way,"[9] a people who are still being molded into mature disciples themselves. When the people of God think of themselves this way, humility marks the missional practice of the whole and reconciled church among the nations.

What Is Discipleship?

"The word 'disciple' occurs 269 times in the New Testament," leading Willard to conclude that "the NT is a book about disciples, by disciples, and for disciples of Jesus Christ."[10] But anyone who has ever asked a group of Christians to define "discipleship" or "disciple" can verify the alarmingly different understandings that exist among them. Dick Lucco, a senior leader in the Evangelical Covenant Church, recounted a time when he gathered a group of denominational staff to define "discipleship." Thinking this was going to be a relatively easy task, he proceeded to facilitate the process and realized early on that it was going to be a long day![11]

If the principal vocation of the church as a community of disciples is disciplemaking, as I argue, then it behooves us to have a working definition and a compelling enough picture of what a disciple looks like. Despite my own research verifying the range of understandings concerning discipleship, I offer this broad definition, which represents a composite of what I believe to be its key elements: *Discipleship means following Jesus Christ in love, worship, and community while submitting to the lifelong, Spirit-empowered process of*

7. I recommend beginning with Mitzi Smith and Jayachitra Lalitha, eds., *Teaching All Nations: Interrogating the Matthean Great Commission* (Minneapolis: Fortress, 2014).
8. Richard Twiss, *Rescuing the Gospel from the Cowboys: A Native American Expression of the Jesus Way* (Downers Grove, IL: InterVarsity, 2015), 31.
9. This descriptor of the church comes from David Ng, who edited a volume by this title: *People on the Way: Asian North Americans Discovering Christ, Culture, and Community* (Valley Forge, PA: Judson, 1996), xvii–xix.
10. Willard, *Great Omission*, 3.
11. Email conversation, March 17, 2017.

*learning the ways of the kingdom of God in all areas of life and in all arenas
of life, even unto death.* This definition easily breaks into three key phrases.

Following Jesus . . .

Following Jesus in love, worship, and community leads the way. Discipleship means following a person; "it is determined by the relation to Christ
himself, not by conformity to an impersonal ordinance."[12] A learned scholar
of theology who has with sophistication mastered the creeds and doctrines of
the church does not provide the ultimate picture of biblical discipleship; on
the other hand, an awestruck lover of God, a worshiper whose life has been
radically transformed, does.[13]

Discipleship, moreover, means following the person of Jesus in community with others. As Katie Rawson notes, "Jesus made disciples through
communities." She mentions "the inner circle of Peter, James and John; the
twelve apostles; the women who followed him; and the seventy he sent out
to preach the kingdom" as exemplifying Jesus's community-based approach
to making disciples.[14] We do not and cannot walk the discipleship journey
alone; we walk it together in community in accordance with the image of
the Triune God. The picture of "me and Jesus" falls woefully short of the
portrayal of discipleship in the New Testament. We become disciples as we
make disciples and thus together create communities of disciples who bear
witness to the reign of God in the world. Willard captures this beautifully
when he writes, "Once we who are disciples have assisted others with becoming disciples, . . . we can gather them, in ordinary life situations, under the
supernatural Trinitarian Presence, forming a new kind of social unit never
before seen on earth."[15]

Submitting to the Lifelong Spirit-Empowered Process . . .

I remember, when I first came to faith in Christ, being led by an older
Christian to go through a workbook on basic Christianity. When I completed
it—which took about five hours over a span of four weeks total—I turned to
the page that invited my signature. I remember signing it and feeling as though
I had just completed the discipleship journey and had become a certified

12. Bosch, *Transforming Mission*, 68.
13. Al Tizon, "The Graduate," *Covenant Quarterly* 74, no. 3–4 (August–November 2016):
55–56.
14. Katie J. Rawson, *Crossing Cultures with Jesus: Sharing Good News with Sensitivity and
Grace* (Downers Grove, IL: IVP Books, 2015), 171.
15. Willard, *Great Omission*, xii.

disciple of Christ. The "CONGRATULATIONS" (yes, in caps) below my signature reinforced my elation.

I am not just a little embarrassed about this today. I do not want to dismiss that exercise entirely, because it did introduce me to then-alien concepts of the faith such as the Trinity, baptism, new life in Christ, and so on. What mortifies me today is the memory of feeling that I had achieved full-on Christian discipleship by going through a series of lessons, as if there were nothing more to learn. For, as I have gone further along on the faith journey, I see that we are at best disciples in progress, forever students of the Jesus school of radical discipleship. Discipleship is a lifelong process.

As an integral part of this lifelong process, we learn to depend on the Holy Spirit and not ultimately on our intellect, our might, or our wealth. Discipleship means being formed by the Spirit to be like Jesus, who transcended the religiosity of his day. Without the Spirit, discipleship devolves into rote worship, doctrinaire legalism, irrelevant theology, lifeless catechism, manipulative evangelism, and unwhole mission. Furthermore, it can devolve into dangerous mission. I am convinced that the church's collusion with empires in the colonization of the world, for example, resulted from the church engaging in "missions" without the Holy Spirit. I cannot improve on Jeffrey Greenman's description of spiritual formation as "our continuing response to the reality of God's grace, shaping us into the likeness of Christ, through the work of the Holy Spirit, in the community of faith, for the sake of the world."[16]

Learning the Ways of the Kingdom . . .

Discipleship means following, submitting, and lastly *learning the ways of the kingdom of God in all areas of life and in all arenas of life even unto death.* As we discussed earlier, in chapter 5, "the reign of God" or "the kingdom of God" refers to the biblical vision of God's *shalom*—peace, justice, mercy, love, and fullness of life—reflected most profoundly and completely in Jesus Christ and made possible today by the ministry of the Holy Spirit. Discipleship means reorienting our whole beings according to this vision as we learn to reject love of money, sex, power, and other lesser gods that once ruled our lives. It means taking off vice and putting on purity; taking off greed and putting on generosity; taking off prejudice—racial, cultural, or otherwise—and putting on equality; taking off living for self and putting on living for others. Learning the ways of the kingdom of God means unlearning the ways of the kingdoms of this world.

16. Jeffrey P. Greenman, "Spiritual Formation in Theological Perspective," in *Life in the Spirit: Spiritual Formation in Theological Perspective*, ed. Jeffrey P. Greenman and George Kalantzis (Downers Grove, IL: IVP Academic, 2010), 24.

If the all-areas-of-life part of the definition orients us to the personal aspects of the discipleship journey, then the all-arenas-of-life part compels us to confess Christ's lordship in the social, cultural, economic, and political spheres. Discipleship means living fundamentally different from prevailing culture, not bowing down to the emperor—that is, nationalism and living according to the imperial agenda—but instead pledging full-on, uncompromising allegiance to the kingdom of God. This is *radical* discipleship, not in the sense of freakish extremism or violent fanaticism, but in the sense of returning to the New Testament root of what it means to follow Jesus.[17] Lee Camp says it plainly: "The gospel demands radical discipleship."[18] In the New Testament, there is no other kind.

Radical discipleship means joyful obedience to the ways of the kingdom in every aspect of our personal and social lives, from relationships to work to the very ambitions and goals that define us—this, in contrast to sectioning off our faith as only one part of our lives, which does not necessarily impact the other parts. As "Sunday Christians," we can affirm belief in Jesus as our highest priority but continue to conduct business as usual Monday through Saturday even if business means taking advantage of the poor. We can sing "I Surrender All" but continue to amass great wealth and live in luxury while the global majority lives in desperate poverty. We can say our prayers for peace but continue to hate our enemies and justify war against them. We can claim Jesus as Lord of all but continue to view people of other races and ethnicities as inferior. We can commit to God's global mission but continue to support policies that keep out immigrants and refugees in the name of protecting national interests.

Camp rightly blames the spirit of Christendom for this kind of sectioning off. He argues that in a Constantinian world, "discipleship gets castrated. . . . 'Following Jesus' becomes something one does on Sundays and in one's quiet time in order to 'go to heaven,' but the way of Christ has no place in the real world."[19] The way of Christendom is not the way of biblical faith, as we established in chapter 2. Therefore, disciples of the Christ of Christendom have a different agenda than disciples of the Christ of the New Testament.

The following list needs more developing, but I see at least seven areas that need cultivation in the life of a disciple. The lifelong, Spirit-empowered process of learning the ways of the kingdom of God requires the ongoing formation of (1) a devotional life of worship, (2) a wise life of Bible study and

---

17. Lee Camp, *Mere Discipleship: Radical Christianity in a Rebellious World*, 2nd ed. (Grand Rapids: Brazos, 2008), 28–29.

18. Camp, *Mere Discipleship*, 28.

19. Camp, *Mere Discipleship*, 35.

obedience, (3) an interdependent life in Spirit-filled community, (4) an ethical life of personal and social holiness, (5) a peculiar life of contrast and distinction, (6) a missional life of local and global witness, and (7) a reproductive life of mentoring or making disciples (both in the qualitative and quantitative sense). Discipleship is radical because it demands obedience in all areas of our lives and in all arenas of life—personal, social, cultural, economic, and political.

It is also radical because it may cost us our very lives. Refusing to bow down to the idols of Mammon, cultural superiority, political power, and nationalism has gotten people killed. Dietrich Bonhoeffer's classic work *The Cost of Discipleship* endures because it attests to the gospel truth that following Jesus leads to the cross. As Bonhoeffer wrote, "Discipleship means adherence to the person of Jesus, and therefore submission to the law of Christ which is the law of the cross."[20] *The Cost of Discipleship* also endures because of its credibility: the author wrote it on the way toward his own martyrdom. With Bonhoeffer on the "Who's Who" of those who have suffered intensely and/or died for the faith in the not-too-distant past are Corrie ten Boom and her family in World War II Holland, Watchman Nee in China, Óscar Romero in El Salvador, and Janani Luwum in Uganda. But these better-known figures only represent millions of Christian disciples all over the world, yesterday and today, whose commitment to Jesus bears the marks of suffering, sacrifice, and death.[21] At the time of this writing, for example, over forty Egyptian Christians were killed in several bombings while worshiping God together on Palm Sunday.[22] These martyrs—historical and contemporary—reflect true discipleship, which bears the cross and thus demands commitment unto death.

Discipleship means following Jesus Christ in love, worship, and community while submitting to the lifelong, Spirit-empowered process of learning the ways of the kingdom of God in all areas of life and in all arenas of life, even unto death. The vocation of the church is to make these kinds of disciples among the nations in humility, even as members of the church continue their own discipleship journey. Disciplemaking constitutes the heart and soul of the Great Commission and provides the impetus for the church's whole mission throughout the whole world.

20. Dietrich Bonhoeffer, *The Cost of Discipleship*, rev. ed. (New York: Macmillan, 1963), 96.
21. William D. Taylor, Antonia van der Meer, and Reg Reimer, eds., *Sorrow & Blood: Christian Mission in Contexts of Suffering, Persecution, and Martyrdom* (Pasadena, CA: William Carey, 2012), 137–314, includes case studies of persecuted and martyred Christians all over the world.
22. Makarios Nassar, Omar Medhat, and Molly Hennessy-Fiske, "Egypt Plunged into State of Emergency as Palm Sunday Church Bombings Kill at Least 44," *Los Angeles Times*, April 9, 2017, http://www.latimes.com/world/la-fg-cairo-church-bombing-20170409-story.html.

A fresh understanding of the whole mission to make disciples requires reviewing and reaffirming the integral relationship between evangelism and social justice, which is the goal of chapter 9. The greatness of the Great Commission depends on how well we grasp this crucial relationship. Chapters 10 and 11 develop the ministry of reconciliation as mission. The fragmentation of the world has never been more acute. It has, therefore, become necessary to redefine holistic mission in terms of "putting the world back together" in Jesus's name and by the power of the Spirit. The church as reconciler: this is what God is calling the whole church to become more than ever, as it seeks in the Spirit to fulfill the fullness of the Great Commission in our broken world.

NINE

Word and Deed

The Greatness of the Great Commission

. . . .

What good is it, my brothers and sisters, if you say
you have faith but do not have works?
—James 2:14

Reality Check

What does the faith require: to believe correctly or to do correctly? Is the
gospel fundamentally good news or good works? Should the church's mission
be about evangelism or social concern? These questions burned with perfect
sense in religion classes across the North American theological landscape.
As eager young ministerial students in the early 1980s, we entered the fray
of the fundamentalist-modernist, personal-versus-social gospel debate, as
if the salvation of humankind depended on it. Some toed the hard line that
evangelism must persevere as the only legitimate mission of the church as they
argued, "What good is it if we feed and clothe their bodies, but their souls end
up in hell for eternity?" Others showed sympathy toward the radical claims of
liberation theology, the then-new movement that had taken the global church
by storm, insisting that faith without works, particularly among the poor, is
dead. And in between the two poles, others offered nuanced alternatives, lean-
ing one way or the other on the continuum. We debated, argued, clarified, and
prioritized the church's mission. It all seemed crucial and relevant at the time.

And then I began working among the poor in real life.

From suburban classrooms in the US to an urban squatter community in the Philippines, I attempted to practice what I thought I had worked out in my studies. Piloting a local, church-based, community development approach, I began to work with a small congregation located right up against one of Manila's main garbage dumps, called Payatas. Church members resided in the community and therefore suffered the same hardships and celebrated the same joys as the rest. A strong sense of family, vibrant faith, weddings and baptisms, yet also unemployment, a lack of clean water, no nearby health services, dwellings made of scrap wood and rusty corrugated tin, the unnecessary deaths of their children, domestic abuse, drugs, depression, family dysfunctions, the powerlessness of cultural religion, and so on: these realities of life in a squatter community bound them together. What does the faith require in this context: right thinking or right doing? Does the gospel demand word or deed? Should the church practice evangelism or compassion and justice? The answer is yes!

It was not that those classroom debates had no value; I continue to this day, in fact, to credit those debates with setting the course of my life and ministry. But as Caloy, Jean, Belen, Butz, Pael, Florencio, Nenette, their children, and many others in that first community where I served allowed me entry into their lives, a different set of questions began to emerge. How can the gospel I share with my mouth gain credibility with the unemployed, the sick, the hungry? How can I, as an outsider, help with resources, to which I have access as a Westerner, without fostering dependence? How can I communicate the truth of God's love cross-culturally, that is, with my improving but still limited Tagalog? What can I learn from my new friends, who according to every standard I know are desperately poor but who have such strong, joyful faith in God? How is God converting not only them but also me in this process wherein God is obviously at work?

Reality changed the questions.

It put the evangelism-versus-social concern debate in proper perspective. Missiologists from the non-Western world have rightly pointed out that the debate has largely been "a Western hang-up."[1] Non-Western thinking in general tends to be more naturally holistic, so to understand mission holistically should not have posed a theological problem to the non-Western church. However, although we cannot wholly blame the North American missionary enterprise, it did its significant part in diffusing the fundamentalist-modernist controversy throughout the whole world. Consequently, it has

---

1. Brian Woolnough, "Good News to the Poor," in *Holistic Mission: God's Plan for God's People*, ed. Brian Woolnough and Wonsuk Ma (Oxford: Regnum, 2010), 5.

not been uncommon even today to encounter non-Western church leaders espousing either an individualistic, evangelism-only approach to ministry at the expense of social justice, or a social gospel–only approach at the expense of evangelism.

Gratefully, after seventy-five-plus years of an overly emphasized debate, and despite the unfortunate diffusion of an alien controversy throughout the world, the global church has experienced a laudable degree of what David Bosch describes as "a convergence of convictions."[2] Half gospels still exist, as we saw in chapter 4, but the call to bear witness to the gospel in both word and deed has, for the most part, come to define the church's essential mission across the conservative-liberal divide. The Cape Town Commitment, for example, states, "We commit ourselves to the integral and dynamic exercise of all dimensions of mission to which God calls [the] Church," followed by two bullets that flesh this out:

- God commands us to make known to all nations the truth of God's revelation and the gospel of God's saving grace through Jesus Christ, calling all people to repentance, faith, baptism, and obedient discipleship.
- God commands us to reflect [God's] own character through compassionate care for the needy, and to demonstrate the values and the power of the kingdom of God in striving for justice and peace and in caring for God's creation.[3]

The Whole Commission

Such articulations of the church's mission bode well for a church that desires to engage in genuine, biblical disciplemaking among the nations, for the Great Commission calls the church to baptize and teach all nations *everything* Jesus commanded. Precisely because the Great Commission during the colonial period did not include a commitment to justice and peace—that is, it did not teach "everything Jesus commanded"—the church ended up colluding with the violent colonization of the world. As Mitzi Smith disturbingly points out in the context of colonized Africa, "Many missionaries, in collusion with European colonizers, separated the physical, unjust, inhumane treatment and oppression of Africans and slaves from the saving of their souls."

2. David J. Bosch, *Transforming Mission: Paradigm Shifts in Theology of Mission*, 20th anniv. ed. (Maryknoll, NY: Orbis Books, 2011), 418.
3. Lausanne Movement, *The Cape Town Commitment: A Confession of Faith and a Call to Action* (Peabody, MA: Hendrickson, 2011), 21.

Referring specifically to the tragic misinterpretation of the Great Commission in which social justice had no place, she continues her strong critique and writes, "Teaching and baptizing black souls trumped the liberating of black bodies from the shackles of their white oppressors."[4]

This undeniable history screams for the necessity of a post-Christendom, postcolonial missiology, in which reconciliation holds the center. The church must recover the wholeness of the Great Commission; it must once again hear the call "to share the good news of Jesus Christ which involves a passion to challenge those things that deny life in its fullness—things based on power and hierarchy such as race, class and gender."[5] The whole mission necessitates a reaffirmation of the commitment to both word and deed, articulation and incarnation, evangelism and social justice; it requires the church to keep intact what Orlando Costas called "the integrity of mission."[6] It also requires a reaffirmation of the truth that the Great Commission demands holistic or integral mission. The greatness of the Great Commission hinges on the church embracing the wholeness of the gospel. The Great Commission is the Whole Commission.

A History of Whole

The road toward establishing—or rather, reestablishing—the integrity of mission among evangelicals has a history, and we would do well to review it to help prevent future attempts to divorce word from deed, and deed from word. Or to say it more positively, to learn from that history and to build on it.

Holistic Mission

History verifies that at key times in the last century the missiological use of "whole" provided a way for church leaders to circumnavigate the turbulent waters of the fundamentalist-modernist debate in North America. As these "circumnavigators" sought to challenge shortsighted theologies and imbalanced missiologies, they found something in the idea of wholeness that helped them challenge "unwhole" notions of gospel, church, and mission on both sides of the debate.

4. Mitzi J. Smith, "'Knowing More than Is Good for One': A Womanist Interrogation of the Matthean Great Commission," in *Teaching All Nations: Interrogating the Matthean Great Commission*, ed. Mitzi J. Smith and Jayachitra Lalitha (Minneapolis: Fortress, 2014), 128–29.
5. Esther Mombo, "From Fourfold Mission to Holistic Mission: Towards Edinburgh 2010," in Woolnough and Ma, *Holistic Mission*, 43.
6. Orlando Costas, *The Integrity of Mission* (San Francisco: HarperCollins, 1979).

Palmer (formerly Eastern Baptist) Theological Seminary, where I taught for almost a decade, can boast of being one of the earliest institutions to use the language of "whole" in this way. Its original insignia included the phrase "the whole gospel for the whole world," which has remained the basis of the seminary's motto to this day.[7] The seminary came into being in 1925 because the founders wanted to establish a school that went against the strong winds of theological liberalism while avoiding the counterwinds of ultraconservatism. Amid the now-infamous fundamentalist-modernist controversy, Palmer Seminary's founders envisioned a "conservative, yet progressive" brand of theological education as they attempted to forge a third way.[8] The motto strove (and strives) to convey what we today would call a biblically faithful, centrist theology.

Integral to the fundamentalist-modernist controversy was the battle over the nature of the church's mission: Did God task the church with evangelism or social concern? As modernists promoted the social gospel increasingly at the expense of evangelism, fundamentalists essentially retreated from social involvement altogether—what has been described as "the Great Reversal"—for fear of being associated with a movement they believed had betrayed historic Christian faith.[9] With the modernists doing social action on one side and the fundamentalists doing evangelism on the other, Palmer's motto, "The whole gospel for the whole world," not only safeguarded against theological extremism (whether to the left or the right) but also affirmed a "both-and" (i.e., holistic) approach to the church's mission of world evangelization and social justice.

In my research of "whole" in mission archives, I discovered a short-lived ecumenical organization that was established immediately after World War I called the Interchurch World Movement (IWM), whose motto read, "The giving of the whole gospel to the whole world by the whole church."[10] IWM's vision served as the precursor for the ecumenical brand of missiology that the

7. Randall Frame, *Praise and Promise: A Pictorial History of Eastern Baptist Theological Seminary* (Virginia Beach: Donning, 2000), 44. Frame writes, "Neither the seminary publications nor the board minutes provide specific details of its origin." Written in Greek on the insignia (some scholars say erroneously!), "The whole gospel for the whole world" was the seminary's motto until the mid-1980s, when it was expanded to read, "The whole gospel to the whole world through whole persons" (154).

8. Frame, *Praise and Promise*, 14–15.

9. David O. Moberg, *The Great Reversal: Evangelism versus Social Concern* (Philadelphia: Lippincott, 1972), 303–4. Credit for the term should ultimately go to historian Timothy L. Smith, as Moberg himself acknowledges (11, 30). Moberg, however, expands on the phenomenon from a sociological perspective and deserves the credit for popularizing it.

10. William M. King, "Interchurch World Movement," in *The Encyclopedia of Protestantism*, vol. 2, *D–K*, ed. Hans J. Hillerbrand (New York: Routledge, 2004), 953.

World Council of Churches (WCC) eventually came to represent as it sought to unify churches amid the rubble of World War I. In the early 1950s, the WCC resumed the use of "whole" terminology in the spirit of IWM, employing it to keep the efforts of church unity and world mission inseparably together.[11]

Then, in 1961, WCC general secretary W. A. Visser 't Hooft used "whole" terminology that went beyond the bridging of unity and mission and made an enduring purpose statement—not for the WCC, however, but inadvertently and ironically for the evangelical missionary movement. He wrote, "The command to witness . . . is a commission given to the whole church to take the whole gospel to the whole world."[12] Coincidentally, in that same year, Billy Graham preached in chapel at Palmer Seminary, where he certainly encountered its motto.[13] Given Graham's astute knowledge of issues surrounding mission at that time, he almost certainly knew of Visser 't Hooft's compelling words. It would be safe to say that "whole" language affected Graham significantly, for during his plenary address at the 1974 International Congress on World Evangelization in Lausanne, Switzerland, he boldly claimed that "the whole Church must be mobilized to bring the whole Gospel to the whole world."[14]

Coming from Visser 't Hooft it was one thing, but coming from Graham quite another for evangelicals during a time when evangelical-ecumenical relations were tense. Validated by Graham, evangelicals claimed "whole" language as their own. "The whole church taking the whole gospel to the whole world" became (and continues to be) the inspiration for evangelical holistic mission.[15]

11. In a document published in *The Ecumenical Review* in 1951 titled "The Calling of the Church to Mission and to Unity," the Central Committee sought to set the record straight in defining "ecumenical" and wrote, "It is important to insist that this word . . . is properly used to describe everything that relates to the whole task of the whole Church to bring the Gospel to the whole world" (*Ecumenical Review* 4, no. 1 [October 1951]: 68). This statement wanted to make clear that "ecumenical" meant more than striving for church unity for unity's sake; it must refer to all that the church does in the world. Missiologist J. C. Hoekendijk picked up on this idea in his article "The Church in Missionary Thinking" in 1952 and used it to strengthen his argument that the church exists insofar as it is bringing the gospel to the whole world; otherwise what we call "the church" is really not the church (*International Review of Mission* 41, no. 3 [July 1952]: 336).

12. W. A. Visser 't Hooft, cited in Christopher J. H. Wright, "The Whole Church Taking the Whole Gospel to the Whole World: The Vision of Lausanne," *Encounter: Journal for Pentecostal Ministry* 7 (Summer 2010): 4.

13. Frame, *Praise and Promise*, 93–94.

14. Billy Graham, "Why Lausanne?," in *Let the Earth Hear His Voice*, ed. J. D. Douglas (Minneapolis: World Wide Publications, 1975), 31.

15. Theology Working Group, "The Whole Church Taking the Whole Gospel to the Whole World," Lausanne Movement, June 1, 2010, http://www.lausanne.org/en/documents/all/twg/1177-twg-three-wholes.html.

Although the statement still reflected the assumption that missionaries "take" or "bring" the gospel anywhere—as if God were not already present and at work in these places—the statement did well to open the hearts and minds of evangelicals to social ministries as part of the task of world evangelization.

Mission as Transformation

How "whole" language specifically developed in North America, of course, does not tell the full story of holistic mission among evangelicals worldwide. Other terms were adopted and developed in various parts of the world to convey a reawakening of the evangelical social conscience since Lausanne. Elsewhere, for example, I chronicle how progressive evangelicals, mostly from the majority world, adopted the term "transformation" in the 1980s as an alternative to "community or international development," which more than a few postcolonial scholars critiqued as inherently paternalistic. "Transformation" also provided an alternative to "liberation," which many commentators deemed hopelessly Marxist in its orientation.[16]

More positively, these progressive or radical evangelicals employed the term "transformation" to convey "a change from a condition of human existence contrary to God's purposes to one in which people are able to enjoy fullness of life in harmony with God."[17] Institutions such as the Oxford Centre for Mission Studies and the International Fellowship for Mission as Transformation (INFEMIT) continue today to make the most of the language of transformation.

Integral Mission

"Integral mission" also emerged in the late 1960s and '70s. Its roots can be traced to the Latin American Theological Fraternity (LATF), whose founders formed it in 1970 with the vision of doing theology contextually and holistically over against the assumed dominant role that the North American evangelical missionary enterprise had played.

Convinced of the inadequacy of simply applying North American fundamentalist theology to their contexts, Latin American theologians, such as C. René Padilla, Catherine Feser Padilla, José Míguez Bonino, Emilio A. Nuñez, Samuel Escobar, and Orlando Costas formed LATF to do theology

16. See Al Tizon, *Transformation after Lausanne: Radical Evangelical Mission in Global-Local Perspective* (Eugene, OR: Wipf & Stock, 2008), esp. 65–70.
17. "Wheaton '83: Statement on Transformation," in *The Church in Response to Human Need*, ed. Vinay Samuel and Chris Sugden (Grand Rapids: Eerdmans, 1987), 257.

with a Latin American face. This meant a commitment to forging a missiology that sought to integrate evangelism, discipleship, compassion, and
social justice to address relevant issues specific to their contexts as the faithful
call of the church-in-mission.[18] LATF leaders began to use *misión integral*,
or "integral mission," to describe this type of theology of mission, which
developed more in revolutionary soil and less in the academy. In the words
of Ruth Padilla DeBorst, it "was honed not in an academic ivory tower, but
in urgent dialogue with their context. Theirs was a radical evangelical missiology rooted in Scripture and wrought in the fire of their clamoring social,
political, and economic reality."[19]

Beyond LATF's continuing usage of "integral mission," the Micah Network—a growing global movement of holistic organizations and practitioners
that began in 1999, particularly to take on global poverty head-on—also
makes the most of the term.[20] More recently the Lausanne Movement has also
begun to replace "holistic mission" with "integral mission" in its literature.[21]

Word, Deed, and Sign

In the early to mid-1990s, scholars and missionaries from the Pentecostal/
charismatic tradition began to espouse a whole-mission orientation based on
a theology of the kingdom of God.[22] A kingdom theology of the whole gospel
aligned well with other holistic mission scholars; Pentecostals and charismatics added their emphasis on the power of the Holy Spirit, not only resting on

18. See the special issue of the *Journal of Latin American Theology: Christian Reflections
from the Latino South* 4, no. 2 (2009), where Daniel Salinas provides theological and missiological sketches of five founders of LATF. For a brief historical rendering of the integral mission
movement, see also Ann C. Borquist, "Beyond Our Four Walls: Developing a Common Understanding of the Critical Factors and Best Practices for Engaging in Integral Mission for Churches
of the National Baptist Convention of Brazil" (DMin diss., Palmer Theological Seminary, King
of Prussia, PA, 2014), esp. 55–81.

19. Ruth Padilla DeBorst, "An Integral Transformational Approach: Being, Doing, and Saying," in *The Mission of the Church: Five Views in Conversation*, ed. Craig Ott (Grand Rapids:
Baker Academic, 2016), 45.

20. "Integral Mission," Micah Network, accessed October 25, 2017, http://www.micahnet
work.org/integral-mission.

21. This language shift has been relatively recent. See, e.g., Lausanne's feature of an article
penned by C. René Padilla in 2004 ("Holistic Mission," Lausanne Movement, 2004, https://www
.lausanne.org/wp-content/uploads/2007/06/LOP33_IG4.pdf); and then in 2013, Lausanne published a brief definition of "integral mission" with Ravi Jayakaran featured as the catalyst for
integral (or holistic) mission ("Integral Mission," Lausanne Movement, April 12, 2013, https://
www.lausanne.org/networks/issues/poverty-and-wealth).

22. See Murray A. Dempster, Byron D. Klaus, and Douglas Petersen, eds., *Called &
Empowered: Global Mission in Pentecostal Perspective* (Peabody, MA: Hendrickson, 1991),
especially section 1.

Jesus himself but also resting on the church ever since, to bear witness to the kingdom "in word, deed, and *sign*."[23] Other phrases began to emerge that reflected this renewed sense of the Spirit's work in holistic mission, such as "word, work, and wonder" and "word, kingdom, and Spirit."[24]

Notable socially informed Pentecostal missiologists include Peter Kuzmic, Douglas Petersen, Joseph Suico, Julie Ma, Wonsuk Ma, Eldin Villafane, Heidi Baker, Joshua Banda, and Joel Tejedo. These urged (and continue to urge) their rank and file to see the supernatural power of the Holy Spirit as producing not only "a passion for souls" but also a desire to see the hungry fed, the sick healed, the oppressed set free, and communities transformed. They do not, however, limit their message to fellow Pentecostals; the whole church needed (and needs) to hear anew the powerful, creative role that the Holy Spirit plays in bearing witness to the full implications of the now-and-not-yet kingdom of God. Today networks such as Pentecostals and Charismatics for Peace and Justice (PCPJ) continue the scholarly exploration and missional practice of Spirit empowerment for holistic missional engagement.[25]

One Movement

By way of summary, "whole" emerged out of the fundamentalist-modernist controversy mainly in North America and was later adopted by evangelicals worldwide through Lausanne to urge the church to affirm both evangelism and social concern in its missionary practice. "Transformation" emerged from radical evangelicals, primarily from the majority world, who sought to avoid the pitfalls of "development" and "liberation" language and to affirm a more biblically rooted theology of mission. "Integral mission" grew out of the efforts of Latin American evangelical theologians, who courageously challenged Western missionary dominance and who sought to forge a contextual theology that addressed the comprehensive needs of their particular communities. And a missiology of "word, deed, and sign" developed among Pentecostals and charismatics around the world, emphasizing the creative power of the Spirit in both evangelism and social justice.

Far from being separate, however, these movements brought together—in gatherings and in publications—many of the same people. One can surely argue that these discernible global stirrings constituted a single movement of the Spirit, taking on different names as it manifested in different parts of the

---

23. Peter Kuzmic, "Pentecostals Respond to Marxism," in Dempster, Klaus, and Petersen, *Called & Empowered*, 160.

24. See Tizon, *Transformation after Lausanne*, 94–97.

25. Pentecostals and Charismatics for Peace and Justice, https://pcpj.org.

world. Their different but overlapping histories notwithstanding, at the end of the day, "whole," "transformation," "integral," "signs and wonders"—and their variations: holistic (or wholistic) mission, transformational development, *misión integral*, power evangelism, and so on—have come from a deep, common desire of informed and passionate evangelicals around the world to convey the width and breadth of the gospel, and therefore the width and breadth of the church's mission.

Fortunately for the whole church, only an ash heap remains of this battle, as few today would deny that evangelism and social justice go hand in hand and that contextualization is key in understanding and practicing gospel, church, and mission around the world. Theologians and missiologists such as John Stott, Orlando Costas, Kwame Bediako, Ronald Sider, René Padilla, Peter Kuzmic, John Perkins, Melba Maggay, Vinay Samuel, JoAnn Lyon, David Gitari, Samuel Escobar, Miriam Adeney, and many more fought the battles that needed to be fought over the last sixty years, and in the words of one of them, "We won!"[26]

Onward, Word and Deed

The future of mission depends on building on this historic victory. Evangelism and social justice flow from the same gospel, the gospel of God's reign in Jesus Christ, the whole and reconciled gospel. And to the extent that the church bears witness to this gospel by way of proclamation and demonstration, it maintains the integrity of the Christian mission to make kingdom disciples among the nations.

Rehearsing this history helps to prevent future generations from fighting the same battles; yet some may argue that it was unnecessary since Millennial and Generation Z Christians have already fully embraced social justice as integral to God's mission. Elsewhere I asserted that the evangelical inheritors of the whole mission generally "view the evangelism vs. social concern issue as a curious debate of a less enlightened time."[27]

But has their passion for social justice now overshadowed the ministry of evangelism? Holistic mission veterans Ronald Sider, Philip Olson, and Heidi Unruh define evangelism as "sharing Jesus' gospel by word and deed

26. Ron Sider said this to me in an informal conversation several years ago. If he gloated over it in good fun at the time, he said as much in a more serious (and kinder!) way in the foreword to my *Transformation after Lausanne*, xiii.
27. Al Tizon, "Evangelism and Social Responsibility: The Making of a Transformational Vision," in *The Lausanne Movement: A Range of Perspectives*, ed. Margunn Serigstad Dahle, Lars Dahle, and Knud Jorgensen (Oxford: Regnum, 2014), 170.

with non-Christians with the intention and hope that they will embrace the message and repent, accept and follow Christ, and join a Christian church community for ongoing discipleship."[28] How does evangelism in this sense fare today? "By almost any metric," Thom Rainer laments, "the churches in our nation are much less evangelistic today than they were in the recent past." Concerning his denomination (Southern Baptist), he continues, "We are reaching non-Christians only half as effectively as we were 50 years ago (. . . [measuring] membership to annual baptisms)."[29]

A recent Barna study concurs with Rainer's overall assessment that the practice and/or effectiveness of evangelism has declined sharply, except, surprisingly, among Millennials. In contrast to older generations, faith-sharing practices among Millennials increased from 56 percent in 2010 to 65 percent in 2013. But lest we become too hopeful about this, Barna Group president David Kinnaman writes, "One way to understand this trend is that there are proportionally fewer born again and evangelical Christians among Millennials than is true among older generations." Most Millennials are in fact leaving the church. "So part of the explanation," he continues, "may be that those who remain committed to these theological perspectives are all the more motivated to make a 'case' for their faith among their peers."[30] Nevertheless, this statistical fact, which demonstrates that the "social justice generation" also cares about evangelism, should encourage us.

In contrast, the decline of evangelism in the overall church in North America in particular, and the Western world in general, should concern us. I cannot overemphasize the importance of rehearsing "the history of whole," for unwholeness is unwholeness no matter which part one emphasizes at the expense of the other. In 1974 Ron Sider founded an organization that sought to restore the social dimension of the gospel on the evangelical mission agenda, naming it overtly "Evangelicals for Social Action." I surmise that if he were to start an organization today, given that evangelism now seems to be the endangered species in evangelical churches and organizations, he would name it "Evangelicals for Evangelism"! Dichotomous, imbalanced thinking is dichotomous, imbalanced thinking no matter which way the lopsidedness leans.

28. Ronald J. Sider, Philip N. Olson, and Heidi Rolland Unruh, *Churches That Make a Difference: Reaching Your Community with Good News and Good Works* (Grand Rapids: Baker Books, 2002), 64.
29. Thom Rainer, "Fifteen Reasons Our Churches Are Less Evangelistic Today," February 23, 2015, Thom S. Rainer, http://thomrainer.com/2015/02/fifteen-reasons-churches-less-evangelistic-today.
30. "Is Evangelism Going Out of Style?," Barna, December 17, 2013, https://www.barna.com/research/is-evangelism-going-out-of-style.

Whole mission means keen awareness of imbalance, overemphasis, and unwholeness, with the intent to correct it. It means affirming the fullness of the gospel, which affects every area of our lives and every arena of life. It means equal commitment to the ministries of evangelism and social justice. It means "refusing to understand evangelization without liberation, a change of heart without a change of structures, vertical reconciliation without horizontal reconciliation, and church planting without community building."[31]

The Greatness of the Great Commission

The necessity of this holistic orientation to gospel, church, and mission is crucial for a faithful rendering of the Great Commission. Without it, I argue, the Great Commission is not very great. In fact, without the whole mission of God in view, the Great Commission has proved to be evil since it has "provided scriptural rationale for the invasion, colonization, and biased teaching of others while compartmentalizing, totally ignoring, or devaluing the humanity and justice rights of others."[32]

Smith questions the very labeling of Matthew 28:18–20 as the Great Commission, because the label "has had the impact of delimiting and orientating how readers should understand the passage and the entire Gospel of Matthew,"[33] not to mention the entire missional message of the Bible. Contrary to popular belief, "the Great Commission" is not a biblical phrase. It originated with Justinian Von Welz in the seventeenth century and was popularized by the famous missionary Hudson Taylor of the China Inland Mission in the latter part of the nineteenth century.[34] The "iconic labeling," as Smith calls it, evidently caught on so thoroughly that it has been confused with Scripture itself, "as if written by the very finger of God."[35]

Smith opts to do away with the iconic label so we can interpret the passage anew through a different lens. While this approach has merit, I propose a different one: keep the label—for Jesus's words recorded in Matthew 28 deserve the label of "great"—but not at the expense of other Bible "greats." I state clearly in the introduction to part 4 my conviction that global disciplemaking defines the church's fundamental vocation, even as we ourselves continue our own discipleship journey. If the label "Great Commission" helps the church

31. Tizon, *Transformation after Lausanne*, 6.
32. Smith and Lalitha, introduction to *Teaching All Nations*, 4.
33. Smith and Lalitha, *Teaching All Nations*, 127.
34. Robbie F. Castleman, "The Last Word: The Great Commission Ecclesiology," *Themelios* 32, no. 3 (May 2007): 68.
35. Smith and Lalitha, *Teaching All Nations*, 135.

understand and practice its disciplemaking vocation, then it serves an important purpose. Instead of trying to remove the Great Commission tattoo from the body of Christ, I propose that we identify other "greats" in the Bible to fill in, deepen, beautify, and complete it.

The Great Mission Statement

For example, we can easily call the words of Jesus in Luke 4:18–19 "the Great Mission Statement." "The Spirit of the Lord is upon me," he declares, "because he has anointed me to bring good news to the poor. He has sent me to proclaim release to the captives and recovery of sight to the blind, to let the oppressed go free, to proclaim the year of the Lord's favor."

As the Great Mission Statement launched the preaching ministry of Jesus, the Great Commission concluded it. Like bookends, these two Bible greats depend on each other to uphold the teachings of Jesus in between. If there were no Great Mission Statement—if Jesus did not proclaim good news to the poor, set prisoners free, heal the sick, and champion justice and peace—then the Great Commission would have nothing good to offer to the nations. For what would be so great about a commission that sends people out to make more disciples who also *do not* proclaim good news to the poor, *do not* set prisoners free, *do not* heal the sick, and *do not* champion justice and peace?

Indeed, the greatness of the Great Commission depends on a church claiming the Great Mission Statement as its own. What would happen if churches took the words of Jesus in this passage and simply adopted them for their own respective mission statements? Whether they use the exact wording or not, to the extent that they reflect the Great Mission Statement in their life and practice in the world, they uphold the greatness of the Great Commission.

The Great Sermon

Between these two great bookends lies the greatest sermon ever preached, recorded in Matthew 5–7. The church knows it better as the Sermon on the Mount, but we can easily call it the Great Sermon. "Blessed are the poor in spirit," Jesus begins, "for theirs is the kingdom of heaven" (v. 3). "Blessed are the meek, for they will inherit the earth" (v. 5). "Blessed are you when people revile you and persecute you and utter all kinds of evil against you falsely on my account" (v. 11). The Beatitudes and the narrative that follows have been the basis of Christian ethics and worldview for the last two thousand years.

This sermon has encouraged and challenged Christians and non-Christians alike. In response to the Palm Sunday bombings of churches in April 2017, which killed forty-five worshiping Christians, the Egyptian Bible Society distributed thirty thousand Arabic-English copies of the Sermon on the Mount titled "Words That Changed the World." Distributed during the peace rally of Pope Francis, the Great Sermon not only comforted traumatized Christians; it not only urged them not to retaliate; it also encouraged all to see Jesus Christ and his teachings as the source of world peace.[36]

The Great Sermon instructs us on how to live the right-side-up values of the kingdom of God in an upside-down world. Jesus demonstrated holy audacity as he called the poor, the sad, and the persecuted the blessed ones; as he taught that our righteousness must exceed the piety of the religious leaders; as he exhorted his listeners not to worry about material things but to seek God's kingdom first. The Great Sermon best captures what discipleship calls us to learn and unlearn. From all accounts, it reads like a revolutionary manifesto for what John Stott calls the Christian counterculture, as it calls followers of Jesus—kingdom disciples—to be people of justice, peace, and love in a world of injustice, violence, and hatred.[37]

At its best, the Great Commission seeks to make disciples who embody this holy revolutionary spirit among the nations. For what would God have sent the church to proclaim and model throughout the world via the Great Commission if not the justice, peace, and love of the Great Sermon? The greatness of the Great Commission to make kingdom disciples of all nations hinges on whether the church preaches and practices the Great Sermon in the world.

The Great Sacrifice

What we can call the Great Sacrifice—the suffering, death, and resurrection of Christ—constitutes another "great" that provides the substance of the Great Commission. If the two previous greats emphasize the peace and justice side of the gospel, then this one emphasizes the atoning work of the gospel. At the center of the greatness of the Great Commission lies the church's message of Jesus Christ's atonement for the sins of the world and rising again to become the hope of the world. The Great Sacrifice defines our proclamation of forgiveness and hope in terms of Jesus, Savior of the world.

36. See Stan Friedman, "Partnership Enables Bible Society Outreach in Egypt," *Covenant Companion*, May 23, 2017, http://covenantcompanion.com/2017/05/23/partnership-enables -bible-society-outreach-in-egypt.

37. John Stott, *Christian Counter-Culture: The Message of the Sermon on the Mount* (Downers Grove, IL: InterVarsity, 1978). For a more recent treatment of and practical guide to Stott's teaching on the Sermon on the Mount, see John Stott with Dale Larsen and Sandy Larsen, *A Deeper Look at the Sermon on the Mount: Living Out the Way of Jesus* (Downers Grove, IL: InterVarsity, 2013).

Without this kind of specificity, we reduce the Great Commission to a mere humanitarian mission in which the church serves alongside the Red Cross, United Nations, Peace Corps, and other international relief, development, and peacekeeping organizations. Although that would not be all bad, the Great Commission would fall short of serving as the vehicle of biblical disciplemaking, which also takes seriously the healing and transformation of the human heart. The church preaches nothing less than the Great Sacrifice, the crucified and risen Jesus—and thus makes disciples of *Jesus*. Not just disciples of humanitarian moral goodness or of generic peace and justice, but disciples of Jesus, the Lord of true justice and true peace. Without this kind of specificity, without proclaiming Jesus, the Great Commission might do good but not necessarily be all that great—that is, no different from other relief and development efforts. The Great Commission derives its greatness from the clear conviction of the hope found in the crucified and risen Jesus.

The Great Reconciliation

The vision of Revelation 7, what we could easily call the Great Reconciliation, identifies yet another "great" that substantiates the Great Commission. In it the seer catches a glimpse of a future worship service that includes countless people from all tribes and nations (v. 9). We see them there poised for worship because the one standing before them—the Christ of the Great Sacrifice—put an end to persecution, hunger, natural disasters, mourning, tears, and death (vv. 14–17).

The presence of all tribes and nations in this vision gives a compelling picture of the Great Reconciliation to come. If we view the church's mission today as reflecting in our words, deeds, and lives the future of God, then the Great Reconciliation provides indispensable dimensions of mission—namely, intercultural understanding, peacemaking, and reconciliation between divided peoples. Paul certainly understood that the ministry of the gospel involved breaking down dividing walls and becoming an intercultural fellowship in Christ. He reminded the Ephesian believers, for example, that Christ was their peace, who "has made [Jew and gentile] into one and has broken down the dividing wall, that is, the hostility between us, . . . that he might create in himself one new humanity in place of the two" (Eph. 2:14–15). Paul and those who followed suit in the ministry of reconciliation and intercultural church over the last two millennia have borne witness to the Great Reconciliation to come.

This is not to say that our efforts at reconciliation will bring about the Great Reconciliation; they merely reflect what God will do in God's due time, as we discussed in chapter 5. As a signpost of the finale to come—the reconciliation of all things—God calls and empowers the church today to engage in the ministry of nonfinal reconciliation between nations, cultures, and peoples. If the Great Commission does not include this dimension as a part of its mission, if it does not find its inspiration in the all-tribes-and-nations future of God in Revelation 7, then, I contend, the church jeopardizes the greatness of the Great Commission.

If we had endless time and space, we could also certainly discuss the Greatest Commandment of Mark 12:28–30 and the Great Appeal of Romans 12:1–2. We could have also drawn from the Old Testament to talk about the Great Nation of Genesis 12:1–3, the Great New Creation of Isaiah 65, and the Great Requirement of Micah 6:8. There are too many "greats" in the biblical story to discuss them all. I contend that these "greats"—the ones discussed and the ones only honorably mentioned—constitute the spirit of what Jesus meant when, as part of the Great Commission, he called his followers to teach the nations *everything* he had commanded. The link between these greats and global disciplemaking lies at the heart of practicing the whole mission of God in the world.

We have one more task to accomplish: to understand and practice God's whole mission in terms of the ministry of reconciliation, the subject of the last two chapters. As a signpost of the Great Reconciliation to come, God calls the church to be reconciled together in Christ and to become together a reconciling agent in the world—the church as reconciler. For if we neglect to address the unprecedented fragmentation, division, and conflict between cultures and nations today, how can we possibly claim to be practicing the Whole Commission? To be holistic means taking part in God's mission to "put the world back together again."

Discussion Questions

1. In today's church, how would you assess the balance between evangelism and social justice? And in your own church?
2. What is the relationship between holistic mission and disciplemaking?
3. In what way does the Great Commission depend on other "greats" in Scripture discussed in this chapter? What other "greats" would you add to the discussion?

TEN

Reconciliation and the Great Commission

Peacemaking as Mission, Part 1

. . . .

Blessed are the peacemakers, for they will
be called children of God.
—Jesus (Matt. 5:9)

Peacemakers often die for the cause. On July 1, 2016, near Mandera, Kenya, several suspected members of extremist group al-Shabaab ambushed a bus, firing into it and killing six people, including Reverend John Njaramba Kiruga, head of the Evangelical Covenant Church of Kenya.[1] Ironically for Kiruga, it occurred while he was traveling from town to town and facilitating peace seminars between Christians and Muslims. Just a few days earlier, Kiruga emailed David Husby, director of Covenant World Relief (CWR), updating him on a peace mission that CWR was supporting. He wrote, "[I'm] at Garrisa, . . . heading to Mandera tomorrow. Pray for us. Pray for Kenya. Political temperatures are

1. This account, including quotes, is based on several articles, which slightly differ in detail: "Bus Ambush in Northern Kenya Kills Six," Deutsche Welle, July 1, 2016, http://www.dw.com /en/bus-ambush-in-northern-kenya-kills-six/a-19370980; Stan Friedman, "Kenya Church Moderator Led Peacemaking Seminar Prior to Death," *Covenant Companion*, July 3, 2016, http:// covenantcompanion.com/2016/07/03/kenyan-church-moderator-led-peacemaking-seminar -prior-to-death; John Kiruga, with introduction by David Husby, "Peace at Any Cost," *Covenant Companion*, November 21, 2016, http://covenantcompanion.com/2016/11/21/peace-at-any-cost.

high. . . . Mandera is not that safe, but we must preach peace at all cost." Husby laments that for Kiruga, "the cost of preaching peace was his life."

Some may deem foolish Kiruga's choice of going to places located near the Somali border, where just a year earlier al-Shabaab took 700 students hostage, eventually killing 148 of them because of their Christian faith. Dangerous, to be sure, but foolish? Just as it is the sick and not the healthy who need a physician (Matt. 9:12; Mark 2:17; Luke 5:32), it is places of violence and not enclaves of safety that need a peacemaker. Kiruga—denominational leader, evangelist, and pastor—did right in going courageously where bullets flew and blood flowed, even though that decision proved fatal. "We must preach peace at all cost" were essentially his last words, and they need to be heard today more than ever before.

Kiruga did not always think this way. His earlier views of Muslims included the belief that God did not love them. Prejudice formed in his heart, and Kiruga's conversion to Christ did not immediately change this. For him, the combination of zealous faith and a one-dimensional view of Islam meant only one kind of legitimate interaction with Muslims: evangelism through traditional apologetics and secret meetings, for Christians needed to save Muslims, plain and simple.

Kiruga reported several success stories in winning Muslims to Christ. But as these new converts experienced heavy persecution from their families and communities, he began to realize the complexity of Muslim evangelism. A deep, underlying distrust between Christians and Muslims exposed the inadequacy of his methods. "That's when God revealed to me," he shared, "that we needed to move beyond debates and arguments. We had to start preaching the gospel of peace."

This revelation of the need to preach Christ's peace resulted, for Kiruga, in a more relational approach, one that involved ministering with and among Muslims to better their communities. He began to minister in this way among the isolated, dispossessed Muslim community of the Waata people. Such an approach contrasted sharply with the aggressive evangelistic methods of many churches (including Kiruga's), which only exacerbated the Christian-Muslim tension, thus hindering the spread of the gospel.

And what is the gospel anyway but the gospel of peace? "The ministry we are given in this world is to reconcile," Kiruga taught toward the end of his life, "mending ways where relationships have been broken." Kiruga went from engaging Muslims in contentious apologetics to loving them and becoming a peacemaker among them in the name of Christ, the Prince of Peace. "Peace at all cost" lies at the center of the legacy of John Njaramba Kiruga. Insofar as the church in Kenya (and beyond) takes his words seriously, it honors his life, translates his violent death into meaningful martyrdom, and advances the crucial ministry of reconciliation in a fractured world. "Blessed are the peacemakers, for they will be called children of God" (Matt. 5:9).

Whole Mission: Reconciliation and Disciplemaking

Kiruga's testimony is but one of many that have been given by Christian peacemakers throughout the ages who have grasped the indispensability of the ministry of reconciliation, which must significantly inform our understanding and practice of holistic mission in the world. The basic premise of this book is that holistic mission can no longer be just about bringing evangelism and social concern back together. Besides, history has shown, as we saw in chapter 9, that the valiant efforts to integrate them have succeeded for the most part, even though half gospels still exist.

As holistic mission goes beyond the integration of word and deed, it beckons us to take part in a different kind of integration—namely, the mending of cultural, tribal, and national brokenness, reconciling enemies among the nations as integral to the Great Commission. Peacemaking is not the whole of disciplemaking, but without it, the church is not making disciples of Christ. Peacemaking is disciplemaking is mission.

As we discussed in chapter 9, the greatness of the Matthean Great Commission involves affirming other "greats," one of those being the Great Reconciliation of Revelation 7. The greatness of the Great Commission relies on the church's witness to the power of the gospel to overcome human divisions. These next two chapters focus on this aspect of the Great Commission, which is specifically and typically what we would call the ministry of reconciliation, but which I choose to call "peacemaking as mission."

I do this to avoid the potential confusion between the specific ministry of reconciliation, which calls us to address human divisions, and "the reconciliation of all things," which, to state the obvious, includes *all things*—that is, more than just rifts between people and people. The reconciliation of all things is the whole mission of God, involving the three dimensions of the vertical (reconciliation with God), the horizontal (reconciliation between humans), and the circular (reconciliation with the physical and spiritual cosmos or the universe).[2]

These last two chapters focus on the horizontal, or the social meaning of biblical reconciliation, which has everything to do with peacemaking

---

2. Tormod Engelsviken, "Reconciliation with God," in *Mission as Ministry of Reconciliation*, ed. Robert Schreiter and Knud Jorgensen (Oxford: Regnum, 2014), 79.

as mission.[3] As the hemorrhaging of the world worsens, the whole and reconciled church, now more than ever before, needs to demonstrate the power of the gospel to break dividing walls and to make peace. It needs to show that reconciliation between peoples is possible in Christ, that the power of the whole gospel transforms our reality, that the whole gospel works! Peacemaking cannot lie on the periphery of mission; both biblical theology and the fractured state of our world demand that it be front and center in our understanding and practice of Christian witness in the world. As the document "Reconciliation as the Mission of God" states, "The work of becoming peacemakers between divided peoples is not secondary or optional, but is central to the Christian mission along with planting churches and making disciples."[4]

Church as Evangelist, Peacemaker, and Steward

The vertical, horizontal, and circular dimensions, or "'triple reconciliation' for individual persons, society and creation," point to the main objects of God's whole mission and therefore the church's whole mission.[5] As we established in chapter 9, the Great Commission is the Whole Commission, the participation of the global church in God's project to reconcile all things in Christ. Missionally speaking, these dimensions express themselves in the ministries of (1) evangelism, facilitating reconciliation between God and people; (2) peacemaking, between people and people; and (3) stewardship, between God, people, and creation. The church as evangelist, peacemaker, and steward: these describe the whole and reconciled church engaged in the Whole Commission. Essential, then, to establishing the horizontal dimension of peacemaking is first to see it as integral to the other two dimensions of the Whole Commission, to understand peacemaking in the larger context of reconciliation and discipleship.

3. For an excellent treatment of the social meaning of biblical reconciliation, see Corneliu Constantineanu, *The Social Significance of Reconciliation in Paul's Theology* (London: T&T Clark, 2010), or the more abbreviated, Constantineanu, "Reconciliation as a Missiological Category for Social Engagement," in *Bible and Mission: A Conversation between Biblical Studies and Missiology*, ed. Rollin G. Grams, I. Howard Marshall, Peter F. Penner, and Robin Routledge (Schwarzenfeld, Germany: Neufeld-Verlag, 2008), 132–59.

4. Reconciliation Network, "Reconciliation as the Mission of God: Christian Witness in a World of Destructive Conflicts," January 2005, https://divinity.duke.edu/sites/divinity.duke.edu/files/documents/cfr/reconciliaton-as-the-mission-of-god.pdf, 17.

5. Chris Rice, "Cape Town 2010: Reconciliation, Discipleship, Mission, and the Renewal of the Church in the 21st Century," in Schreiter and Jorgensen, *Mission as Ministry of Reconciliation*, 58–59.

Vertical Reconciliation: Evangelism in the Whole Commission

Authentic evangelism seeks reconciliation between people and God. "The basic human predicament," writes Engelsviken, "is alienation . . . from God, [and] the cause of this alienation is . . . sin."[6] Sin is a disposition that runs contrary to the holiness of God, elevates the self, and leads to disobedience, that is, behavior and acts that have disrupted the harmony of the universe—*shalom*—since the fall. "The relationships between God and humanity, God and creation, and humanity and creation, were all fractured" as a consequence of sin.[7] Sin's tentacles have reached and affected the cosmos, but its origin lies within the human heart. Therefore, insofar as evangelism addresses the heart, by way of the good news of God's radical forgiveness in Jesus Christ, it goes to the root of the world's problems. For the sake of both sin-soaked and sin-ravaged human beings, the church as evangelist testifies to the opportunity for all to reset in Christ, to be "born again," to experience heart transformation that leads to fullness of life, and then to become part of the healing and not the wounding of nations. The message of the church to the world (and to itself), therefore, is "On behalf of Christ, be reconciled to God" (2 Cor. 5:20).

Many Christians, myself included, have developed somewhat of an allergy to evangelistic programs, formulas, gimmicks, and "perfect witnessing tools." But we must be careful not to equate the methods we devise with the beautiful, holy call to share Jesus with others. The famous conversation between evangelist D. L. Moody and a cynical woman comes to mind. As the story goes, after the evangelist preached one night, the woman criticized him, saying, "I don't like the way you do evangelism." He then asked her how she did it, to which she replied, "I don't do it," eliciting Moody's famous retort, "Then I like my way of doing it better than your way of not doing it."[8]

As "allergic" or jaded as we may become to evangelistic methods that fall short of representing God's amazing love, we cannot abandon the holy task. The good news of Christ is too good not to share, compelling us to be relentless in our desire to match our methods with the nature of the gospel as invitation. At the risk of oversimplifying the matter, I argue that at least recovering the art of genuine conversation, which includes honing our listening skills as well as our talking skills, starts us off on the right foot.

6. Engelsviken, "Reconciliation with God," 81.
7. Nnamdi Emanuel Omeire and John Corrie, "Sin/the Fall," in *Dictionary of Mission Theology: Evangelical Foundations*, ed. John Corrie (Downers Grove, IL: InterVarsity, 2007), 362.
8. Quoted in Ed Stetzer, "Where Have All the Evangelism Conferences Gone?," *Christianity Today*, January 6, 2016, http://www.christianitytoday.com/edstetzer/2016/january/where-have-all-evangelism-conferences-gone.html.

The point is, without evangelism—the vertical dimension of reconciliation—the Great Commission would amount to international humanitarian aid and development work with a cross on top. It might do good in the world but would fall short of "great" if it did not address the depravity, alienation, selfishness, and despair—the sin root of the human heart. The church as evangelist announces the good news that God so loves human beings that "while we still were sinners Christ died for us" (Rom. 5:8; cf. John 3:16). The church as evangelist proclaims to us that we can be reconciled to God, and when we respond in faith, "there is a new creation: everything old has passed away; see, everything has become new!" (2 Cor. 5:17). The ministry of evangelism is indispensable to the church's Great Commission as it guides any and all to follow Jesus and to flourish to fullness of life as a result, even as the church itself continues its own journey of becoming disciples.

However, as indispensable as evangelism may be to the Great Commission, it does not constitute the whole of it or the core of it. Contrary to conventional belief, world evangelization does not define the central thrust of Matthew 28:18–20; that honor belongs to disciplemaking among the nations. Evangelism plays a crucial initiating role in that, but making kingdom disciples constitutes the heart of the commission. As Bob Moffitt asserts, "Disciplemaking, not evangelism, is the end-goal, the ultimate purpose of the Great Commission." In fact, he exhorts controversially, an overemphasis on evangelism can lead to disobedience.

By that he means that if the church believes it has completed its task by increasing the head count of the church, then it does not go on to make disciples and thus fails to fulfill or obey the Great Commission. "Treating evangelism as the goal rather than the first step of our task can lead to the sin of disobedience," he writes. "It keeps us from accomplishing the primary task Jesus gave us, i.e., discipleship." I stress the radical discipleship of the kingdom of God that we established in the introduction to part 4, which includes commitments to compassion, justice, peace, and love. As Moffitt writes, "The Great Commandment and the Great Commission are not in conflict."[9] In fact, as I have stressed, the Great Commission depends wholly on other Bible greats, including the Greatest Commandment.

Still, if the church does not serve the world as evangelist—even as it acknowledges its own need for ongoing conversion—then it falls short of practicing the whole and reconciled gospel. To describe evangelism as essential but not central may sound like doublespeak. I argue that, on the contrary, it

9. Bob Moffitt, *Could Evangelism Lead to Sin?* (Tempe, AZ: Harvest Foundation, 2017), 29–30.

speaks to a holistic understanding of the Matthean text that indispensably includes evangelism but calls for more. Evangelism is essential but not the whole of the church's mission.

Horizontal Reconciliation: Peacemaking in the Whole Commission

The horizontal dimension of reconciliation—peacemaking as mission—will get more attention in the chapter that follows. However, we also need to discuss it here because peacemaking needs to be viewed within the larger context of global disciplemaking. Along with the vertical and circular dimensions, the church as peacemaker does its integral part in fulfilling the Whole Commission.

John Kiruga's testimony points to the crucial connection between peacemaking and disciplemaking. Kiruga was an evangelist and pastor at the core. His desire to see people flourish under the lordship of Christ drove his practice of peace with and among his Muslim neighbors. He taught us by example that the practice of the Great Commission must include peacemaking since it creates real space for the kingdom of God's love, justice, and forgiveness to manifest itself, and thus enables all people to respond to God's invitation to enjoy abundant life in Jesus Christ. He realized that not making space for the kingdom of God by way of the gospel of peace thwarted the work of disciplemaking.

As part of Kiruga's ongoing conversion, he came to this realization later in his ministry. It did not come immediately or automatically. Vertical reconciliation may initiate or catalyze horizontal reconciliation, but nothing about that transition happens automatically. In fact, part of the stain on the church's criminal record has been its participation in human-rights atrocities during colonial times, precisely because the colonial view of the Great Commission elevated evangelism over justice.[10]

But lest we think that the misguided prioritizing of evangelism over justice speaks only of the colonial past, horizontal sin committed by vertically reconciled Christians continues to this day. I know of a mission agency based in the southern United States, for example, that has separate trainings for its white and black missionary personnel. It justifies this practice by appealing to contextualization: the geographical location still practices racial segregation, the agency rationalizes, and so segregated training will be our practice too. A major denomination has two annual meetings: one for its white churches

---

10. Beatrice Okyere-Manu, "Colonial Mission and the Great Commission in Africa," in *Teaching All Nations: Interrogating the Matthean Great Commission*, ed. Mitzi J. Smith and Jayachitra Lalitha (Minneapolis: Fortress, 2014), 15–31, esp. 29–31.

and the other for its nonwhite (predominantly black) churches. I know this to be true because I spoke at both just a few months apart. The history of a seminary with which I was once affiliated includes a shameful time in the not-too-distant past when it prohibited African Americans from using the school's swimming pool. Obviously, then, based on these kinds of examples, vertical reconciliation does not automatically lead to horizontal reconciliation.

I mention these institutional examples to demonstrate the deep embed-dedness of prejudice, so much so that it often seeps, unchallenged, into our very structures and policies. We would be remiss, however, not to mention the hard, overt cases of human-to-human brokenness manifested in racism, sexism, classism, tribalism, Islamophobia, homophobia, and so on. And let it be crystal clear that I am talking about just the sins in the church![11] Therefore when we repent and submit to the Spirit's work of personal and structural transformation among God's people, we initiate the journey toward becoming a peacemaking church, which is essential for a people who desire to live out the Whole Commission.

To be true to God's whole mission, the vertical must lead to the horizontal. But the horizontal must also not forget or neglect the vertical. Just like evangelism needs peacemaking in the Whole Commission, peacemaking needs evangelism. As Engelsviken reminds us, "A mission that speaks and acts with regard to reconciliation between humans, but fails to proclaim reconciliation with God is a truncated mission that will never accomplish God's ultimate purpose: the salvation of all into [God's] present and coming kingdom."[12] The whole and reconciled church serves the world in gospel faithfulness when it does so as both evangelist and peacemaker. But there is still more.

Circular Reconciliation: Stewardship in the Whole Commission

The Whole Commission also and finally mandates the church to engage in mission as steward, the circular dimension of God's reconciliation project. "Circular" describes this dimension well in that it conveys the divine process going full circle, from reconciliation between God and people, to reconciliation between people and people, and now, to reconciliation between God, people, and creation.

Furthermore, when we say "circular," the round physical earth comes to mind, which is apt since this dimension of reconciliation encompasses the redemption of land, sea, and stars—heaven and earth—and all their

---

11. See Mae Elise Cannon, Lisa Sharon Harper, Troy Jackson, and Soong-Chan Rah, *Forgive Us: Confessions of a Compromised Faith* (Grand Rapids: Zondervan, 2014).

12. Engelsviken, "Reconciliation with God," 86.

inhabitants. Chris Wright points out that the "combination 'heaven and earth' is the typical scriptural way of referring to the whole of creation," and that Jesus is Lord over all of it. He writes, "The Great Commission does not begin with a command, but with an affirmation," referring to Jesus's opening words, "All authority in heaven and on earth has been given to me" (Matt. 28:18).[13] The statement declares the authority or lordship of Christ, not just over humanity, as the church typically thinks, but over the whole created order. Paul makes this abundantly clear when he describes Jesus as "the firstborn of all creation. . . . All things have been created through him and for him. He himself is before all things, and in him all things hold together. . . . Through him God was pleased to reconcile to himself all things, whether on earth or in heaven, by making peace through the blood of his cross" (Col. 1:15–17, 20). With this cosmic truth, Jesus—the Lord of all creation, in whose name God will re-create the heavens and the earth (Rev. 21:1–5)—commissions his followers to make kingdom disciples of all nations.

The realization of creation's inclusion in God's reconciliation project should disturb us, for we have done great violence to the earth and its inhabitants. By assaulting creation we have assaulted ourselves and thwarted God's will for the world. Based on a faulty theology of dominion, the church has helped to perpetuate the idea that the earth and its nonhuman inhabitants are primarily "natural resources" to satisfy humanity's needs and fancies without caution or compassion. Misinterpreting dominion as domination, broken humanity has cleared forests, blown off mountaintops, dumped waste in oceans, hunted animals for sport, created factory farms, and experimented cruelly on monkeys and rats. Such violent crimes against creation describe not just the distant past but the tragic present. Therefore, scientist Lynn White's accusation against the church more than fifty years ago that it has contributed to the ecological crises of our time still holds true.[14] I find humanity's assault upon the earth and its fellow creatures nearly unbearable; the thought of the church participating and even sanctioning it pushes me right over the edge.

When the church does not see the care of God's creation—that is, stewardship—as part of the Great Commission, then it paints a less-than-whole picture of God's mission to reconcile all things. What kind of disciples of Jesus, Lord of all creation, would have no regard for God's physical creation (including creaturekind)? And furthermore, what kind of disciples are

13. Chris Wright, *Five Marks of Mission: Making God's Mission Ours* (Milton Keynes, UK: im:press, 2015), 29.
14. Lynn White, "The Historical Roots of Our Ecological Crisis," *Science* 155 (March 1967): 1203–7.

we making if we do not instill respect, care, and a sense of commitment for the welfare of all that God owns and longs to redeem?

If, for example, a man enters a church and claims to be a follower of Jesus but tracks cakes of mud into the foyer, litters in the sanctuary, carves his name on the pew in front of him, and decorates the bathroom stall with graffiti, would not the ushers do their job and not-so-kindly escort him out? Furthermore, on discovering the man's dog nearly dead from the summer heat because he left it in the car with the windows closed, would not the ushers report him to the authorities for animal cruelty? Indeed, as Peter Harris notes, "If we proclaim Christ the Creator but demonstrate an abusive or indifferent relationship to Creation, we send confused signals."[15] Whole mission requires the world to encounter the church as steward. For as long as God in Christ desires to reconcile all things and not just some things, the church's mission requires the ministry of stewardship, alongside the ministries of evangelism and peacemaking.

Biblical stewardship is the church's posture and practice—its relationship—with the physical order of the universe, which God created. "To be a steward . . . is to be entrusted by God to care for, manage, and cultivate that which belongs to God."[16] God's ultimate ownership of everything holds the key to understanding biblical stewardship. It is one thing to neglect or destroy an object we may believe we own, but to neglect or destroy something that belongs to someone else smacks of irresponsibility at best, reprehensibility at worst. The faithful church's witness to the Lord of heaven and earth includes taking care of all that God owns.

Stewardship constitutes a disciple-being, disciplemaking issue, and therefore a missional issue. "From coins to creation, the call to be good stewards is an integral part of authentic Christian discipleship."[17] To the extent that the church serves the world as steward, it bears witness to the coming day when creation will stop groaning, when the lion will lie down with the lamb, when the trees of the field will clap their hands. The glimpses of God's future certainly include a renewed heaven and a renewed earth, wherein fear will be no more between human and nonhuman creatures (Isa. 11:6–9).[18] Indeed, at the

---

15. Peter Harris, "Living and Serving in God's Creation," in *Down-to-Earth Christianity: Creation-Care in Ministry*, ed. W. Dayton Roberts and Paul E. Pretiz (Wynnwood, PA: Association of Evangelical Relief and Development Organizations and Evangelical Environmental Network, 2000), 167.

16. Al Tizon, *Missional Preaching: Engage, Embrace, Transform* (Valley Forge, PA: Judson, 2012), 106.

17. Tizon, *Missional Preaching*, 106.

18. David P. Gushee, *The Sacredness of Human Life* (Grand Rapids: Eerdmans, 2013), 407. In the context of 2 Pet. 3 and Rev. 21, Gushee contrasts a renewed creation with the notion that God's plan is to destroy the heavens and the earth and replace them with brand-new

end of time, when God in Christ will reconcile all things, we will see not only the redemption of humanity but also a restored ecology. Engaged in the Great Commission, the church as steward bears witness to "the river of the water of life, bright as crystal, flowing from the throne of God and of the Lamb. . . . On either side of the river is the tree of life with its twelve kinds of fruit, . . . and the leaves of the tree are for the healing of the nations" (Rev. 22:1–2).

The circular dimension speaks to nothing less than God's reconciliation project going full circle. The church takes part in this by reflecting reconciliation between God, people, and creation. In the benedictory words of Ruth Padilla DeBorst, "May God's Spirit move among us, renewing relationships, restoring God's image, planting seeds of hopeful yearning in us so that we may all more faithfully live out God's mission as God's people on God's earth."[19]

Discussion Questions

1. Do you agree with this chapter's contention that a church practices the Great Commission as evangelist (vertical), peacemaker (horizontal), and steward (circular)?
2. Discuss how these three dimensions embody the church's mission in the "reconciliation of all things."

---

ones. For our relationship with creaturekind, see Sarah Withrow King, *Animals Are Not Ours: No Really, They're Not* (Eugene, OR: Cascade, 2016).

19. Ruth Padilla DeBorst, "God's Earth and God's People: Relationships Restored," *Journal of Latin American Theology: Christian Reflections from the Latino South* 5, no. 1 (2010): 17.

ELEVEN

Reconciliation and the Great Commission

Peacemaking as Mission, Part 2

· · · · · · ·

If it is possible, so far as it depends on you, live peaceably with all.
—Paul (Rom. 12:18)

When the church serves the world as evangelist, peacemaker, and steward, it proves faithful to its missionary call to fulfill the Whole Commission. In an increasingly fragmenting world, the horizontal dimension of reconciliation—peacemaking as mission—has appropriately received much-needed attention.[1] The church can no longer view peacemaking as optional. The historic peace churches would say it never was![2] In our fractured and fracturing world, the propagation of the gospel of peace can no longer be the task of a small pocket

1. Robert Schreiter, "The Emergence of Reconciliation as a Paradigm of Mission," in *Mission as Ministry of Reconciliation*, ed. Robert Schreiter and Knud Jorgensen (Oxford: Regnum, 2013), 10–12.
2. Willard Swartley, "The Evangel as Gospel of Peace," in *Evangelical, Ecumenical, and Anabaptist Missiologies in Conversation*, ed. James R. Krabill, Walter Sawatsky, and Charles Van Engen (Maryknoll, NY: Orbis Books, 2006), 69–77. The author argues that if the church had taken more seriously the biblical centrality of peace, "its method of witness and expansion would have avoided both coercive tactics in its mission and its too frequent persecution of Jews and Muslims" (70). For a more detailed treatment of peace as core to the mission of God, see Swartley's *Covenant of Peace: The Missing Peace in New Testament Theology and Ethics* (Grand Rapids: Eerdmans, 2006).

of Christian pacifists. The time has come for the global body of Christ to embrace peacemaking as a core part of its vocation to make radical kingdom disciples of all nations—that is, to engage in holistic mission.

Peacemaking means the hard work of overcoming distrust, misunderstanding, bitterness, and even hatred between conflicted parties in the power of the whole gospel. But it goes beyond conflict resolution; it also seeks to restore and maintain harmony.[3] Peacemaking as mission strives in the Spirit to reflect nothing less than the *shalom* of God in social relationships, going beyond the mere absence of conflict to full-on, relational embrace between oppressed and oppressor, victim and victimizer, abused and abuser. "The end toward which the journey of reconciliation leads," Katongole and Rice celebrate, "is the *shalom* of God's new creation—a future not yet fully realized, but holistic in its transformation of the personal, social, and structural dimensions of life."[4]

What does peacemaking look like in a world that, humanly speaking, is hopelessly broken? What principles must be operative for genuine peace to manifest itself? Fortunately for the whole and reconciled church, the growing field of peace and reconciliation studies has been productive in developing both theoretical and practical resources for the missional church. Interacting with and adding to many of those excellent works, I offer as a reflective practitioner what I believe to be the most crucial elements of peacemaking as mission.

A Heart of Peace: Spirituality of Reconciliation

The list begins with a heart of peace. Are we spiritually, mentally, and emotionally (and even physically) ready to be peacemakers, agents of God's reconciliation? Do we have a heart that bends toward the peace of Christ, and does it extend widely, even to those whom we might deem to be enemies of Christ? These heart questions reflect the truth that before people-to-people reconciliation is a theology, a missiology, or a strategy, it is first and foremost a spirituality. The vertical intersects with the horizontal (in an intersection that forms, not coincidentally, the shape of a cross) at the ministry of gospel peacemaking. Therefore, the church's mission of peace should begin, operate, and end in prayer. As Robert Schreiter, who has done extensive work on a spirituality of reconciliation, tells us plainly: "A spirituality that is rooted

3. Rick Love, *Peace Catalysts: Resolving Conflict in Our Families, Organizations and Communities* (Downers Grove, IL: IVP Books, 2014), 42–49.
4. Emmanuel Katongole and Chris Rice, *Reconciling All Things: A Christian Vision for Justice, Peace and Healing* (Downers Grove, IL: IVP Books, 2008), 148.

in deep and ongoing communion with God is essential for any measure of reconciliation to be effected."[5]

Prayer as Warfare

After all, the ultimate enemy of peace is none other than the devil (1 Pet. 5:8). If we must battle, therefore, let us do it in the spiritual realm, putting on the whole armor of God, which includes shoes that equip us to proclaim the gospel of peace (Eph. 6:15). Practically speaking, a commitment to spiritual warfare at least means a commitment to intercede for a world convulsing in violence. As part of the discipline of prayer, individual and corporate, we acknowledge Jesus as the Prince of Peace and pray regularly against hate crimes committed, for example, among African Americans and Middle Eastern Americans in the US; or against the religious wars that have caused destruction and misery in places such as Sudan, Palestine, India, and Syria; or against corrupt and/or inept governments that have caused mass displacement in places such as Colombia and more recently Venezuela. At the time of this writing, tensions have escalated between the US and North Korea, causing once again worldwide fear of nuclear war. In the face of this, the church must intercede for the world, praying against its annihilation.[6]

We pray against such things, but we also pray *for* God's faithfulness, wisdom, and strength. We pray for healing for the suffering, and we pray that God would begin the work of restoring order in these places. We back up those prayers with the church's actions of compassion and justice in solidarity with the afflicted and oppressed there. As we "wage peace" in this way, we believe in faith that "the God of peace will shortly crush Satan under [our] feet" (Rom. 16:20). A heart of peace understands the radically spiritual nature of peacemaking, which should drive us to pray Christ's peace over our cities, nations and governments.[7] Celebrated theologian Karl Barth is credited with saying, "To clasp the hands in prayer is the beginning of an uprising against the disorder of this world."[8]

5. Robert Schreiter, "The Emergence of Reconciliation as a Paradigm of Mission," in Schreiter and Jorgensen, *Mission as Ministry of Reconciliation*, 15.

6. Choe Sang-Hun, "2 Days after North Korea Missile Test, a Show of U.S. Airpower," *New York Times*, August 31, 2017, https://www.nytimes.com/2017/08/31/world/asia/north-korea-south-korea-us-joint-exercises.html.

7. Love, *Peace Catalysts*, 53–55.

8. Karl Barth, quoted in Dirk J. Smit, *Collected Essays in Public Theology: Collected Essays 1* (Stellenbosch, South Africa: Sun Press, 2007), 448. Though this quote is widely attributed to Barth, no sources consulted are able to provide a primary citation for this oft-cited remark.

Anger and Peace

A heart of peace should not just drive us to our knees on behalf of the world; it should also drive us to examine the condition of our own hearts, for the world within is not detached from the world without. If understanding peacemaking as primarily spirituality does nothing else, let it remind us that the condition of the world is but the condition of the human heart writ large. As we set the Spirit free to root out bitterness, prejudice, and arrogance from our hearts, we not only cultivate a heart of peace but also plant the seeds of world peace.

Two related Spirit-probing questions form in my mind regarding this. First, does anger serve or hinder peace? Contrary to pop psychology, anger does have a place; it is not in and of itself evil. It signals to us from within that something does not align with the universal sense of goodness. Injustice *should* anger us. For example, when I began to discover the evils inflicted on colonized peoples—especially *my* people—it was not wrong for me to get angry.[9] Then when I began to discover the church's role in the evils of colonialism, my anger rose appropriately. When injustice provokes us to anger, we reflect the heart of God, which beats for justice (Isa. 1:21–24; Hos. 6:9–13; Amos 4:1–3). Furthermore, we can view anger as that powerful emotion provoked by what McNeil calls catalytic events—experiences that can move us from self-protection and self-preservation mode to a missional life of reconciliation, community, justice, and advocacy.[10]

So anger can play a valid and important role in the peacemaking process, but it cannot reside too long in a heart of peace. Length of time matters, for whereas anger that arises from righteous indignation can ignite transformation, anger that lingers can fester, and when it festers, it breeds violence. After doing its job of provoking us to outrage against injustice and its perpetrators, anger must in time give way to mercy, grace, and forgiveness. Otherwise it will overtake us, making us bitter people who wish harm and destruction on those whom we deem to be offenders and oppressors. Some graduate from wishing to actual killing, . . . and the cycle of violence continues. Moreover, sustained anger has a blinding effect: we work hard to take the speck out of

9. Much has been published about both the Spanish and the American colonization of the Philippines. The most compelling treatment of colonialism in the Philippines from a Filipino nationalist perspective is Renato Constantino's *A History of the Philippines: From the Spanish Colonization to the Second World War* (New York: Monthly Review, 2010).

10. McNeil talks about catalytic events—experiences that shake the foundations of one's assumptions—as the beginning of the reconciliation process, in that they move us from preservation to reconciliation. Brenda Salter McNeil, *Roadmap to Reconciliation: Moving Communities into Unity, Wholeness and Justice* (Downers Grove, IL: IVP Books, 2015), 41–49.

our neighbor's eye while the log in our own eye remains embedded (Matt. 7:1–5). An angry prophet can serve the cause of peace, but a bitter, judgmental, and arrogant one over time, not so much.

Grace and Peace

Second, and related to the first question, how gracious am I toward my enemies or even those I simply find disagreeable? Does my moral outrage prevent me from extending the gift of grace, which God has so freely given to me? Major offenders come chiefly to mind here, such as the corrupt government leader, the colonizer, the slaveholder, the rapist, the terrorist, the racist. But I am also thinking about those who commit lesser offenses out of ignorance. I think, for example, of missionaries who insensitively criticize the lifeways of their hosts as they navigate the waters of a different culture. Majority-culture participants in antiracism workshops who question the concept of "white privilege" also come to mind. Are my own sensibilities so hypersensitive that I cannot extend grace—slack, understanding, and so on—even to those who "don't get it"? If "gracelessness" describes my heart and the church's heart toward others, then do we not foster enmity in the world and not peace?

Peacemaking begins with cultivating a heart of peace. Katongole and Rice describe South African antiapartheid heroes Nelson Mandela and Desmond Tutu in a way that strikes me as depicting activists whose energy was generated by a heart of peace. They write, "While [Mandela and Tutu] carried a great burden about gaps of injustice, they radiated conviction and not condemnation, redemption and not final judgment, embrace and not rejection. The truly prophetic nature of their work . . . was pursing justice with a quality of mercy that shaped a quest for communion with enemies and strangers."[11]

Power of Relationship: To Know and to Be Known

From a heart of peace flows a willingness to submit to the power of relationship. Regardless of the nature of the conflict—whether a hotly disputed social issue, a wall built by ideological differences, or an estranged marriage—when people on both sides demonstrate a willingness to get to know each other, reconciliation between them becomes a tangible possibility. The converse is also true: an unwillingness to know and to be known makes reconciliation an impossibility. If we do not submit to the power of relationship, reconciliation will at best be superficial, at worst a temporary lull that leads to

11. Katongole and Rice, *Reconciling All Things*, 135.

disappointment and even a sense of betrayal, which in turn often leads to greater violence. I think of numerous peace accords that have been publicly lauded, for example, between Israelis and Palestinians or between tribal/religious factions in Sudan through the years.[12] These accords may have reflected political agreement and been signed by both sides of the conflict, but because they seemed devoid of interpersonal relationships, they did not last and in fact intensified the conflict.

It is easy to hate abstractions or to dehumanize those whom we do not know. Yet when we begin to familiarize ourselves with the faces, names, and families of our enemies—and furthermore, when our faces, names, and families become familiar to them—the dividing issues take on a new emotional complexity that opens possibilities of different attitudes and behaviors toward one another.

Dick Cheney, for example, the former Republican vice president of the US and staunch conservative on virtually every issue, has expressed favor toward same-sex marriage since 2009.[13] Could it be because one of his daughters, Mary Cheney, is a lesbian who is married and raising two children with her wife, Heather Poe? The "enemy"—in this case, the enemy of traditional marriage, which to most conservatives undermines the moral foundation of society and should therefore be resisted—was his daughter, whom he knows and loves, and so, concerning this issue, he has landed in a radically different position on the conservative-liberal continuum than he has on almost every other issue. I mention this not so much to comment on the issue of same-sex marriage as to attest to the power of relationship to modify how we interact with "the enemy."

I remember intensely wishing that a small circle of Islamophobic, evangelical friends of mine could meet the peaceful but traumatized group of Fulani (Muslim) women with whom I sat one afternoon in Cameroon. Chased out of the bordering Central African Republic by armed fundamentalist Christians, these women sought safety for themselves and their families on alien soil. If my friends could just get to know them even a little, I found myself wishing, perhaps they could see the error of automatically associating terrorism with Muslims. For, in this case, the Muslims were not the terrorists but the terrorized, at the hands, no less, of those who claimed to be Christians!

12. For Israel-Palestine, see "History of Middle East Peace Talks," BBC News, July 29, 2013, http://www.bbc.com/news/world-middle-east-11103745. For Sudan, see "One Year after Peace Deal, South Sudan 'Worse Off,'" Aljazeera, August 27, 2016, http://www.aljazeera.com/news /2016/08/south-sudan-worse-160826191344694.html.
13. "Dick Cheney on Same-Sex Marriage," C-SPAN, June 1, 2009, https://www.youtube .com/watch?v=E5jefmsqBG8.

I wish these same friends, who have also bought into the narrative that refugees are people to fear and keep away, could have met the refugees from Syria with whom I recently spent time in France and Germany. If they could only hear their stories of tremendous loss, hunger, trauma, suffering, and heroic acts of survival, they would think, feel, and perhaps vote differently about them. I could give other examples. The point is, submitting to the power of relationship with those who would otherwise remain in the abstract changes perceptions, beliefs, rules of engagement, and ultimately behavior toward the other.

The peacemaking process advances significantly when we develop relationships, when we are willing to enter social terrain that up to that point has been deemed to be evil and dangerous by tradition, social prejudice, and/or family upbringing. The invitation to relationship opens the door to experiencing "the enemy" firsthand, which creates the possibility of affirming our common humanity. Peacemakers facilitate the establishing of relationships between two warring factions and thus begin a humanization process essential for reconciliation.

Explicitly or implicitly, every peace and reconciliation organization or initiative I have encountered affirms the crucial importance of relationship. A few explicit ones include Musalaha, a Jerusalem-based organization making peace between Israelis and Palestinians. Founder Salim Munayer identifies six stages of reconciliation, and establishing relationships sits at the top of the list. This "interpersonal approach" is essential, claims Munayer from his vast experience in peacemaking, in order to advance to the "intergroup approach." He explains that "by first working to establish friendships and cultivating a sense of care for the other, there is greater mutual flexibility to discuss contentious issues."[14] In other words, before it tackles the impossibly huge Israel-Palestine issue on the sociopolitical level, Musalaha creates space for Israelis and Palestinians to get to know each other on a personal and human level.

Another program, called Oriented to Love (OTL), which I helped to initiate when I served briefly as president of Evangelicals for Social Action, addresses the seemingly irreconcilable rift between gay and straight Christians. "Dedicated to empowering Christians to better understand their brothers and sisters in Christ who hold sexual/gender identities and theological convictions different from their own, OTL gathers small but highly diverse groups of people for loving, in-depth encounters on level ground at the foot of the

14. Salim J. Munayer and Lisa Loden, *Through My Enemy's Eyes: Envisioning Reconciliation in Israel-Palestine* (Milton Keynes, UK: Paternoster, 2013), 224. See also Musalaha's website at http://www.musalaha.org.

cross."[15] The testimonies of OTL alums speak volumes about how getting to know the other expanded their capacity to love. Musalaha, OTL, and other initiatives that engage in peacemaking as mission across a wide range of issues affirm the power of relationship as foundational to the work of people-to-people reconciliation.

It should go without saying, but establishing relationships requires a long-term commitment. A peace event—whether for a weekend, a week, or a month—has its limitations. The event itself, therefore, requires equipping participants to maintain ongoing contact with the other if lasting peace is to have a chance. For example, the Reconciliation Roadmap model, developed by McNeil, depends on contact theory, "which suggests that relationships between conflicting groups will improve if they have meaningful contact with one another over an extended period of time."[16] To the extent that two conflicting parties sustain meaningful relational contact with each other—whether Israelis and Palestinians, black and white people in North America, Muslims and Christians, or gay and straight people—reconciliation becomes possible.

Real Dialogue: Truth, Love, and Vulnerability

The power of relationship opens the door for reconciliation, but it would be a mistake to think that "the feeling of reconciliation" marks the end of the process and not the beginning. "The problem," Munayer and Lisa Loden explain, "is that once participants have begun to establish a relationship and a sense of appreciation for each other, they hesitate to raise the divisive issues."[17] The divisions must be named and processed, however, if we desire true peace. An important yet risky follow-up step in the peacemaking process, therefore, is to learn how to speak our convictions (what I will call from now on "the truth") in love with one another. This takes courage because vulnerability comes with the high risk of offending and being offended.

If the previous stage stresses the common humanity shared between warring factions, then this stage begins to name the issues that have divided them. Important conversations about personal life, family, and testimony—all of which affirm our common humanity—must at some point advance to the hard work of dialogue over the points of conflict if we desire the peacemaking

15. "Projects and Partners," Evangelicals for Social Action, accessed October 25, 2017, http://www.evangelicalsforsocialaction.org/projects-and-partners.

16. McNeil, *Roadmap*, 33.

17. Munayer and Loden, *Through My Enemy's Eyes*, 224.

process to succeed. Munayer and Loden call this stage "Opening Up." They write, "By increasing their sense of vulnerability and the real possibility of being hurt, participants demonstrate a growing dedication to reconciliation and can begin to discuss issues related to the conflict."[18]

Vulnerability not only takes courage; it also takes skill. And by skill, I mean the art of speaking the truth in love. Truth and love constitute the two sides of vulnerability. When we speak our very different convictions to one another, no matter how well we couch them, we offend one another; but when we speak our convictions in love, the experience of offense can be converted by the Spirit into a broadening of one's perspective—not necessarily a change in conviction or theology but a capacity to embrace someone who believes very differently than we do on any given issue. As the previous step of submitting to relationship creates a safe space, this step of opening up fills that space with truth and love—vulnerability that leads to peace. This takes skill.

Theological Skill

It first of all takes theological skill—the ability to hold in creative tension what Rick Love succinctly describes as the "exclusive truth claims and inclusive love aims" of biblical faith.[19] That is, the Bible teaches universal truths, and one of them is to love all. Elsewhere I similarly argue that the combination of the particularity of Christ and the universal love of his message constitute the scandal of Jesus.[20] He taught that he is the way, the truth, and the life and that no one comes to the Father except through him (John 14:6); it does not get any more exclusive than that. But the exclusive Jesus did not exclude anyone. Instead, by his words, deeds, and life, he demonstrated the unconditional love of God that included all, even those deemed enemies (Matt. 5:43–48).

What then do we do: side with truth uncompromisingly or act with love lavishly? Followers of the "scandalous Jesus" do both. They bear witness to God's Son as the only way to the Father, even as they "extend the indiscriminate love of God toward all—including [and especially] those considered anathema."[21]

Communication Skill

Vulnerability also takes communication skills, beginning with the art of listening. Do we know how to listen to the painful stories of others, especially

---

18. Munayer and Loden, *Through My Enemy's Eyes*, 225–26.

19. Love, *Peace Catalysts*, 144.

20. Al Tizon, *Missional Preaching: Engage, Embrace, Transform* (Valley Forge, PA: Judson, 2012), 144–45.

21. Tizon, *Missional Preaching*, 145.

when we are implicated in their pain? To the extent that we do, we inch closer to experiencing and contributing to reconciliation. Peacemakers know the value and yet the risk of sharing personal stories of pain and tragedy. With this knowledge, they facilitate storytelling between conflicted groups with great care, laying down ground rules aimed to create as safe a space as possible. McNeil mentions using "I" statements, not allowing interruptions, ensuring confidentiality, and being mentally and emotionally present.[22]

As "the other side" tells their stories, we actively listen—that is, we seek to understand the conflict from a different angle, *their* angle; we empathize with their pain; we feel the holy guilt of whatever part we have played in their pain—all this in contrast to getting into a defensive posture. I remember listening in this way as a participant of the OTL dialogue a few years ago. I felt confident, as I entered the OTL weekend, that the empathy I carried for those in the LGBTQ community was real and solid; but as I listened to story after story of how their respective churches ridiculed, ostracized, excommunicated, and barred many, if not most, if not all, of them from fellowship, I realized that I did not know the meaning of empathy. I pledged to learn better how to love my gay/lesbian sisters and brothers in Christ, even as I hold to my traditional convictions regarding homosexuality and same-sex marriage.

Communication skills also include knowing how to tell our own stories well—the other side of the truth-in-love equation. We know how to share easily among those who believe the same way; how do we do it when we are among those who believe fundamentally differently? First of all, we do no favors to anyone by watering down our convictions or by downplaying the pain of our own stories. In an attempt to get along with everyone, some have settled for a shallow ecumenism that avoids differences instead of embracing them. I doubt, however, that Paul called for shallowness when he said, "If it is possible, so far as it depends on you, live peaceably with all" (Rom. 12:18). The phrase "If it is possible" suggests great effort in speaking the truth in love, even at the risk of disturbing the peace.

Rick Love, a self-professed evangelical, shares about a time at an interfaith roundtable when a mainline pastor questioned his presence. The pastor asked why Love chose to participate in the roundtable when everyone knew that he desired ultimately to convert them. To his surprise, a Muslim imam named Ahmad came to his defense, reminding the mainline pastor that, of course, each one desires the other to embrace the other's faith. Love writes, "Both Ahmad and I believed we could pursue peace together and still bear witness

22. McNeil, *Roadmap*, 71–72.

to our respective faiths."[23] Genuine ecumenism (peaceful unity amid differences) requires participants to stay true to their convictions.

Building on our commitment to authenticity, how well do we tell our story? I refer again to my OTL experience. At various points over the weekend, I riskily shared my belief that God's ideal design in human sexuality happens between a man and a woman. I also shared that my fundamental prayer for my gay/lesbian friends is God's transformation. This kind of praying may sound like a version of reparative or conversion therapy, a wrongheaded attempt to change homosexual orientation, which the American Psychiatric Association has rightly condemned.[24] Reported trauma caused by this kind of therapy gives me great pause to speak the language of transformation in this area. However, when I say I pray in this way, I refer to pleading with God, who alone can heal any and all types of sexual disorientations—whether homo- or hetero-. It is all-inclusive praying, including for myself, for God to heal and transform us. I did my best to be clear about my convictions, even as I qualified them.

In humble repentance, I also admitted to my complicity in "gay jokes" and my inaction when I heard about churches that mistreated gay and lesbian members in their pews. I vowed to end my complying ways and to do my part in educating churches to love and embrace the other—in this case, our gay church members, family members, friends, and neighbors—even as I hold fast to what is considered a traditional view of sexuality and marriage. I shared my conviction that in Christ one can truly have the capacity to love those who do not believe the same way, and thus I do not receive the social narrative today that anyone who does not fully affirm all things LGBTQ is a hater. Some in the group pushed back, verifying that my convictions offended some in the room; but for the most part, I felt heard by the gay participants in the group, as much, hopefully, as they felt heard by the straight participants as they shared their stories.

Vulnerability—speaking the truth in love with both theological and communicational skills—requires risk-taking, for the peace process could end at that point. As Munayer and Loden report, "Many times, at this stage . . . participants are hurt by the discussions. Their pain is evident. The honeymoon of friendship is over. Whatever suspicions they may have quietly harbored about the other side are now forcefully confirmed."[25] But if we push through the

---

23. Love, *Peace Catalysts*, 151–52.

24. For more on reparation therapy, see Annesa Flentje, Nicholas C. Heck, and Bryan N. Cochran, "Experiences of Ex-Gay Individuals in Sexual Reorientation Therapy: Reasons for Seeking Treatment, Perceived Helpfulness and Harmfulness of Treatment, and Post-Treatment Identification," *Journal of Homosexuality* 61 (2014): 1242–68.

25. Munayer and Loden, *Through My Enemy's Eyes*, 226.

pain and awkwardness of vulnerability, motivated to persevere by the vision of God's beautiful endgame, then we are poised to experience the fruit of vulnerability: getting one step closer to Spirit-led reconciliation.

Healing Pain: Repentance, Forgiveness, and Lament

We get one step closer because vulnerability has prepared the broken for the healing work of God, which is yet another crucial element of peacemaking as mission. Peacemakers are healers between peoples. Now this may sound warm and fuzzy, but the ministry of reconciliatory healing involves excruciating pain. I liken it to fracture resetting—a surgical procedure that seeks to fix a once-broken bone that set incorrectly over time as it was left to heal by itself. The procedure requires rebreaking the bone—not a pleasant thought. In fact, a shiver just shot through my entire body as I typed this! The ministry of healing, as part of the peacemaking process, breaks bones and resets them en route to genuine reconciliation in Christ.

The problem lies in us getting used to our deformities. To be sure, prejudice, bitterness, and hatred deform the soul—whose bones were improperly set after being broken by injustice, so that we are crippled, disabled from walking toward other people, especially those who broke our bones in the first place. We get used to the immobility, the limp, the alienation from the other. We convince ourselves that the enmity between us and them is just the way it is. The art of peacemaking attempts to convince the deformed to undergo fracture resetting in order to be healed and reconciled in Christ. Of course, peacemakers themselves are also deformed and continue their own healing journey, making them what Henri Nouwen famously described as "wounded healers."[26] With great empathy because we are wounded ourselves, we seek to turn pain into healing pain, to rebreak the broken bones of all involved, and then to reset them in Jesus's name and by the power of the Spirit, so that all can once again walk toward one another as we undergo God's healing.

"Deformity" describes both sides of any conflict, but not in the same way. Different bones need resetting on the two sides, and relational healing toward peace requires knowing the difference. Furthermore, it requires knowing that the difference does not just mean not being the same; it also means not being equal. As Munayer and Loden explain, "In every conflict one side is more powerful than the other."[27] At first I did not agree with this statement, but as I reflected on the various conflicts in which I have been involved (either as

---

26. Henri Nouwen, *The Wounded Healer* (New York: Image/Doubleday, 1990).
27. Munayer and Loden, *Through My Enemy's Eyes*, 225.

participant or mediator), I have experienced the truth of it. Whether a hus-band having the emotional upper hand over his wife in a marital crisis, or a larger tribe having more say in an organizational or church dispute than a smaller tribe, or a majority culture having the political positioning in a racially charged conflict over a minority culture—the conflict, more often than not, has consistently proved the inequality factor. To the extent that peacemakers discern, identify, and acknowledge the power differential, they can help guide the two sides in the healing process.

To Wrongdoers: Repent!

In the case of the more powerful in a broken, conflicted relationship, those who by their power have leveraged advantage at the expense of the weaker, the primary message is this: repent! God calls on oppressors, abusers, terror-ists, colonizers, rapists, johns, and even unknowingly complicit beneficiaries of unjust systems to repent, to turn from their wicked ways, and to confess their sins to God and to the people they have harmed. Repentance rebreaks the bone of perpetration that malformed the powerful into oppressors and resets it toward justice and reconciliation.

Peacemakers cannot water down this message; repentance is the essential part that wrongdoers play in the healing process, not only for the sake of the healing between them and their victims but also for the sake of their own healing. Peace-makers need to call them to repentance, yes, with love and grace, but they cannot mince words here. As mediators, peacemakers encourage both sides of a given conflict to own their part in the conflict. But in light of the power differential, peacemakers must turn into prophets as they call perpetrators to repentance.

For "God is not evenhanded," Desmond Tutu said in a *Time* interview. "God is biased, horribly in favor of the weak. The minute an injustice is per-petrated, God is going to be on the side of the one who is being clobbered."[28] This more than implies God's judgment on those doing the clobbering. René Padilla pulls no punches when he writes, "In any situation in which power is misused and the powerful take advantage of the weak, God takes the side of the weak. In concrete terms, that means God is *for* the oppressed and *against* the oppressor, *for* the exploited and *against* the exploiter, *for* the victim and *against* the victimizer."[29] Nothing less than heart-wrenching repentance of Ninevite proportions would cause God to relent from meting out severe judg-ment on the wicked (Jon. 3:6–10).

28. Desmond Tutu, quoted in Alex Perry, "The Laughing Bishop," *Time*, October 11, 2010, 42.
29. C. René Padilla, "God's Call to Do Justice," in *The Justice Project*, ed. Brian McLaren, Elisa Padilla, and Ashley Bunting Seeber (Grand Rapids: Baker Books, 2009), 24.

When wrongdoers truly do repent, however, God shows mercy, as the story of Jonah clearly demonstrates. As we know, the outrageous extent of God's compassion toward the truly repentant so infuriated Jonah that he preferred his own death than to see God spare the evil Ninevites (4:3, 9). Blinded by hatred, Jonah could not (or refused to) see the Ninevites as human beings, people who bore the image of God and who had most probably been victimized themselves before they became victimizers. As Célestin Musekura, founder and president of the African Leadership and Reconciliation Ministries (ALARM), reminds us, "Abusers are victims before they become perpetrators."[30] In that light, why would God, who desires all to be whole and reconciled, not relent from meting out judgment on the truly repentant (Jon. 4:6–11)? With God's judgment lifted, wrongdoers begin to heal, and they position themselves to contribute to the peace process.

To the Wronged: Forgive!

"Repent!" shouts the peacemaker-prophet to wrongdoers. With equal urgency, they also carry an ultimate message to the wronged. In their direction, the message that leads to peace is this: forgive! Like the act of repentance for wrongdoers, the act of forgiveness for the wronged makes possible both relational and inner healing. Victims of wrongdoing need to forgive not only for the sake of the peace process but also for the restoration of their own souls.

Yet in my kingdom estimation, urging the wronged to forgive is the greater ask. Yes, perpetrators will need the help of God to repent humbly and sincerely; but for the colonized, the abused, the enslaved, the raped, the widowed, and the orphaned to forgive their victimizers requires a double measure of God's intervening presence. We can view it as the need to rebreak and reset multiple bones instead of just one. Loved ones murdered, interrogation, imprisonment, torture, the confiscation of property, the betrayal of a spouse, the sexual abuse of a child, and so on: these memories severely cripple the soul and, for some, the body.

I think of Ruach, a twenty-five-year-old South Sudanese Christian man who, because of his strong faith, was thrown by a Muslim rival in front of a machine that amputated his right leg and crushed his testicles. When our partners in South Sudan notified us of this tragedy, we responded immediately by sending emergency funds to obtain the urgent medical help needed. After months of life-and-death struggle, Ruach survived the attempted murder; he is recovering and getting stronger. But his deformity is permanent. The loss of his leg, his manhood, and the possibility of ever fathering a child will

---

30. Célestin Musekura and L. Gregory Jones, *Forgiving as We've Been Forgiven: Community Practices for Making Peace* (Downers Grove, IL: IVP Books, 2010), 61.

always remind him of the crime committed against him. I see his permanent physical crippling mirroring his emotional, spiritual crippling. And I thought to myself intensely, how dare we peacemakers come to Ruach and his family (his father is a pastor) and tell them to forgive the Muslim man who pushed him in front of that machine. How dare we preach forgiveness toward the pusher and, for that matter, all the misguided Muslims who persecute, maim, and kill Christians in the name of Allah.

Indeed, forgiveness is the harder ask in the peacemaking process. For, humanly speaking, revenge makes much more sense for Ruach and his family. Retributive justice demands retaliation. The wrongdoer must pay. An eye for an eye. A tooth for a tooth. A leg for a leg. A testicle for a testicle. Let us gather an army of vigilantes and avenge our son and our brother. Let us destroy the man, his family, and his whole village in the name of the Lord! And the vicious cycle of violence spins on.

The only power capable of breaking this cycle, and thus defying the logic of revenge, cannot ultimately come from ourselves: the crippling of our souls prevents that. It must come from the Holy Spirit, who alone can empower us to forgive. "Forgiveness from the heart is a supernatural act," says Musekura.[31] Grounded in the radical forgiveness of God in Christ extended toward all—all!—in the Spirit the redeemed learn to love their enemies. Peacemakers preach supernatural forgiveness, hard as it is, because in Christ, God has forgiven us (Matt. 18:21–35; 1 John 4:19). Musekura, a victim himself of tremendous loss of family members and friends in the Rwandan genocide of 1994, declares nonetheless that forgiveness constitutes the heart of the gospel and therefore the core of our identity in Jesus Christ. "As people who have been forgiven, we have no choice [but to forgive also]."[32] Beyond the obligation to forgive, however, our lives in the Spirit produce fruit (Gal. 5:22–23), which renews our hearts, minds, and actions, thus making us capable of forgiving those who have wronged us.[33]

As foundational as this theology may be to the possibility of forgiveness, it feels inauthentic and shaky without the healing of memories. The adage "Forgive and forget" misguides in so many ways, and peacemakers would exacerbate its wrongheadedness if they sought to help victims try to forget what happened to them. Besides, can someone like Ruach really forget the incident that cost him his leg, his testicles, and what undoubtedly will be years of medical complications and emotional anguish? How can the oppressed, the

31. Musekura and Jones, *Forgiving*, 80.
32. Musekura and Jones, *Forgiving*, 36.
33. A new heart, a new mind, and new actions are the result of putting on Christ—that is, of being a Spirit-led follower of Jesus. See Musekura's chapter "Putting On Christ" in *Forgiving*, 59–84.

enslaved, the tortured, the raped, the sold, and the betrayed possibly forget? Psychologically speaking, to forget horrors done to us requires disassociation, which creates disorders such as amnesia, long-term repression, multiple personalities, and so on. Peacemaking cannot be about telling the wronged to simply forget the past based on their new identity in Christ. Peacemaking cannot be about creating a Christ-centered disorder!

The healing of memories, in contrast, does not mean forgetting, but rather "remembering rightly" or redeeming the pain of past wrongs.[34] This goes beyond semantics. Whereas the word "forgetting" conveys the sense of erasing the offense and thus attempting never to think about it again, rightly remembering involves revisiting the horror of the offense and going through the pain again—rebreaking the bone—but this time bringing the crucified and risen Christ into the situation, resetting the bone with radical love toward victimizers. As Miroslav Volf asserts, "To remember rightly wrongs that we have suffered is to remember them through the lens of the memory of Christ's death and resurrection."[35] Remembering rightly means remembering both the suffering and the victory of Christ for the sake of all, even as, and especially when, we revisit those places of deep pain. Only within the framework of Christian hope can we learn and practice the supernatural art of forgiveness.

Of course, I speak only of the theological angle regarding healing from trauma, which is incomplete in and of itself. In addition to remembering rightly by inviting the Spirit of Christ to accompany us back to those painful places, we should also, as a ministry of referral, urge the wronged to be in deep PTSD therapy under the care of qualified professionals. Furthermore, peacemaking involves discerning whether and when the time is right for victims to revisit the past publicly—that is, with their victimizers present. Ideally, on hearing their painful stories, victimizers repent in sackcloth and ashes. Peacemakers want nothing better than to witness the forgiveness-and-repentance dance and thus to celebrate the beginning of genuine reconciliation between the victim and the victimizer.

However, to forgive does not depend on whether wrongdoers repent. The wronged cannot control the response of wrongdoers. If they do not repent, then forgiveness becomes more about the victims' liberation; they have, by the act of forgiveness, freed themselves from tortured memories. This is not insignificant, though admittedly, without the repentance of the wrongdoer, reconciliation cannot happen. Neither can it happen if the wronged do not

---

34. Miroslav Volf, *The End of Memory: Remembering Rightly in a Violent World* (Grand Rapids: Eerdmans, 2006), 11–16. In these pages Volf describes what it means to remember rightly, but he rolls it out in much more detail in the rest of the book.

35. Volf, *End of Memory*, 103–4.

forgive. For the sake of their own healing and for the possibility of people-to-people reconciliation, therefore, peacemakers urge victims of wrongdoing to claim their identity in the crucified and risen Jesus and to extend, by the power of the Spirit, the miraculous hand of forgiveness.

To the Wrongdoer and the Wronged: Lament!

One more element has proved crucial for the healing process and deserves our attention. Peacemakers call victimizers to repent; they call victims to forgive; and then at some point, they call both victim and victimizer to lament, indeed to lament together. "Lament in the Bible," writes Soong-Chan Rah, "is a liturgical response to the reality of suffering and engages God in the context of pain and trouble."[36] It expresses deep sorrow passionately, complains unabashedly, wails loudly, groans deeply, and seethes with words against unjust systems, cruel regimes, great loss of life, crimes against humanity, and the seeming absence of God even as it assumes that hope can be found only in God.

Though lament has both personal and communal dimensions to it, the latter proves most valuable to peacemakers since communal lament enables the shared expression of pain. Further, it provides an opportunity for both victim and victimizer together to bring complaints and petitions to God. As Rah explains, "Communal lament draws from the whole community, and a collective voice rises up in lament."[37] Besides the book of Lamentations, attributed to the prophet Jeremiah, 65 out of the 150 psalms can be considered laments. Most of them are personal laments that David penned either while being chased or hunted down or while in exile, or both; but some decidedly express the anguish of a nation (Pss. 12; 44; 74; 80).

Several years ago I was asked to open a community-development consultation in South Africa to set the tone for a week of partnership-building presentations and activities. At the risk of beginning the event with a downer, I led the participants, composed of both African and North American Christian workers, in a time of communal lament. It did not feel right in a gathering on partnership in development to gloss over the history of colonialism and the part that the Western church played in it, which undoubtedly the African participants continued to experience in one form or another. I named the Western church's centuries-long collusion with the colonial project by way of the missionary enterprise. But rather than simply give a hollow apology on behalf of Western missions, which in my view would have felt ironically colonial

---

36. Soong-Chan Rah, *Prophetic Lament: A Call for Justice in Troubled Times* (Downers Grove, IL: IVP Books, 2015), 21.

37. Rah, *Prophetic Lament*, 167.

(a one-way act initiated and done by the powerful to the less powerful), I offered an alternative—an opportunity to lament the colonial past together.

I facilitated a group recitation of several general postcolonial laments (see sidebar). Then, afterward, I encouraged anyone and everyone to cry out with laments, specific to their contexts. Though there was no crying out, almost everyone spoke. In each other's hearing, participants shared honestly and sincerely. While most of the Africans shared the pain of suffering losses and indignities related to the colonial spirit past and present, those from North America confessed varying degrees of participation in condescending and paternalistic attitudes and/or behaviors. Communal lament created a space ripe for repentance and forgiveness. When it felt right to cap the time, we recited together, "Have mercy on us, O Lord. Empower us to sin no more and to champion the justice and peace of the gospel."

Communal lament has a powerful role to play in the healing process, which can lead to reconciliation since it provides the opportunity to repent, forgive, and come before God together with both honesty and hope. As wounded healers, peacemakers engage empathetically in the hard, painful work of repentance, forgiveness, and lamentation among broken, conflicted peoples.

Postcolonial Lament

For these things, we weep; our eyes flow with tears (Lam. 1:16):

- for the brokenness of humanity that enables one people to think of itself as superior to other peoples;
- for the tremendous loss of life and the dehumanization of black and brown peoples all over the world;
- for the extinction of beautiful, indigenous cultures as part of the colonial project;
- for the church's collusion with colonization, which violated the very nature of the gospel of Jesus Christ as an invitation;
- for the coercive ways in which the church evangelized indigenous peoples;
- for how the colonial legacy continues in different forms today.

Have mercy on us, O Lord. Empower us to sin no more and to champion the justice and peace of the gospel.

Just Peacemaking: "Peace, Peace," When There Is No Justice

Peacemaking as mission requires the practice of justice; otherwise the end toward which we work would be but a facade of God's *shalom*. "They have treated the wound of my people carelessly," the Lord says through Jeremiah, referring to sham prophets and priests, "saying, 'Peace, peace,' when there is no peace" (6:14). The sham of proclaiming a conflict-free community lies in the fact that security and serenity—which often pass for peace—mask a failure to address the injustices that the masses have suffered from in that community. Thus, in false peace situations, the oppressed become repressed, rendering the "peace, peace" proclamation as no peace at all, for peace without justice is not biblical peace. In that light, false prophets and priests essentially declare, "'Peace, peace,' when there is no justice." True peacemakers see peace without justice for what it is: a cover-up, a false hope that comforts the strong and keeps down the weak, that leaves unchallenged the status quo of sociopolitical inequities.

To say this more positively: "To make peace, we must make justice."[38] Peacemaking as mission requires a practical commitment to social justice, which can be defined in biblical terms as God's righteousness, fairness, and love accomplished by right actions for all.[39] Just peacemaking, an empirically based theory (methods that have shown measurable results) that not only seeks to prevent war but also to proactively make peace, proves helpful here.[40] Its very name assumes that peace and justice have an integral, inseparable relationship. Taking this relationship seriously, we discover two important practices for just peacemakers.

Addressing the Why of Human Suffering

First, just peacemakers address the why of injustice—the causes—and do not just treat the symptoms. I am reminded of Ron Sider's famous analogy, which I call the "parable of the ambulance."[41] A group of Christians responded to the frequent accidents that occurred along a dangerous mountain road by purchasing an ambulance to rush those who survived the

38. James Burke, John Langan, Pamela Brubaker, Duane Friesen, and Glen Stassen, introduction to *Just Peacemaking: The New Paradigm for the Ethics of Peace and War*, new ed., ed. Glen H. Stassen (Cleveland: Pilgrim, 2008), 22.

39. I elaborate on God's righteousness, fairness, and love in my book *Missional Preaching* as a buildup to a fuller definition of biblical justice (84–85). See also Mae Elise Cannon, *Social Justice Handbook: Small Steps for a Better World* (Downers Grove, IL: IVP Books, 2009), 31–32.

40. Burke et al., introduction to *Just Peacemaking*, 9–14.

41. Ronald J. Sider, *Rich Christians in an Age of Hunger: Moving from Affluence to Generosity* (Nashville: W Publishing, 2015), 220–21.

crashes to the hospital (many fatalities also occurred). One day a visitor came to town and asked why they didn't just campaign to close down the road and to build a tunnel instead. The Christians came up with all sorts of excuses, including not wanting to upset the mayor, who owned a restaurant halfway up the mountain, as well as believing that God called them "to give a cup of cold water," not to close roads and build tunnels (i.e., address the root cause).

As the perplexed visitor left, "one question churned round and round in his muddled mind. Is it really more spiritual . . . to operate the ambulances which pick up the bloody victims of destructive social structures than to try to change the structures themselves?" In other words, is it really more spiritual to attend to the wounded (compassion) than to prevent the wounding from happening in the first place (justice)? Of course, we must not pit compassion against justice, for both reflect the heart of God for the suffering. Just peacemakers know, however, that the church must move beyond compassion and practice justice, move beyond operating an ambulance on a dangerous road to working toward safer alternatives, perhaps leading a campaign to close down the road and to build a tunnel instead.

Undoubtedly, "injustice is a major cause of war."[42] If justice means God's manifold blessings to be enjoyed by all, then injustice is inequity that deprives people of those blessings, creating pockets of oppression, poverty, and marginalization. These hardships sustained over time cause collective discontent, unrest, resentment, and anger—the stuff of war. Doing justice therefore addresses one of the most deeply rooted causes of conflict.

What does it mean to do justice in a violent world? Just peacemaking offers ten practical principles for proactively making peace in the world (see sidebar). Time and space prevent us from mining the riches of this complex theory. Suffice it here to point out that two of the ten principles speak directly to making or doing justice. While "Advance democracy, human rights, and religious liberty" addresses issues on the political level, "Foster just and sustainable economic development" addresses issues on the economic level. These two principles identify the main social arenas in which people experience injustice: the political arena (oppression, marginalization, and violations of basic human rights) and the economic arena (poverty and little to no access to social services such as health care, clean water, and/or education). Attending to the disadvantaged on these two levels can guide the just peacemaker to identify with the people and thereby discover the root causes of their suffering, and then begin to address those issues.

42. Burke et al., introduction to *Just Peacemaking*, 22.

Ten Practices of Just Peacemaking

1. Support nonviolent direct action.
2. Take independent initiatives to reduce threat.
3. Use cooperative conflict resolution.
4. Acknowledge responsibility for conflict and injustice and seek repentance and forgiveness.
5. Advance democracy, human rights, and religious liberty.
6. Foster just and sustainable economic development.
7. Work with emerging cooperative forces in the international system.
8. Strengthen the United Nations and international efforts for cooperation and human rights.
9. Reduce offensive weapons and weapons trade.
10. Encourage grassroots peacemaking groups and voluntary associations.

From *Just Peacemaking*, rev. ed., edited by Glen Stassen (Cleveland: Pilgrim, 2008).

On the political level, just peacemaking often manifests in advocacy work, which involves, among other things, "unmuting" the socially disadvantaged, or making their voices heard so the advantaged can hear their cries and be given the opportunity to right the situation. For example, during my three-year stint at Waterhole—the squatter community in Quezon City where I was first assigned—several of the leaders of the church with which I worked participated in obtaining land rights for the eighty-plus families that made up the community. The stigma of being squatters weighed on the people's hearts, minds, and lives. So a group of residents, including members of what was then Waterhole Baptist Church (now Acts Integrated Ministries), found the legal owner of the land and let her know the people's desire to have legal land rights. Land rights, though not the same as land ownership, would give the people the legal ability to build houses and own them. Furthermore, on a dignity level, it would eliminate the invisible label of "squatter" that hung over their heads. The community group met with the owner several times, sometimes at the church.

Several obstacles complicated the negotiations, but the long and the short of it is that over a period of about a year, the local government divided up the property into lots and sold them at generously low rates determined by the owner, who was sympathetic to the people. That they transitioned from

being squatters to legal residents was the immediate fruit of the effort. Over
a period of several years, most of the residents were able to build concrete
dwellings they could call their own. Unmuting the voices of the former squatters and negotiating with the landowner to obtain rights for them exemplified
just peacemaking—that is, doing justice that leads to genuine peace.

That victory exemplifies just peacemaking on the political level; the self-
help groups (SHGs) facilitated by the Zimele Wethu Foundation in South
Africa, primarily among women, exemplify it on the economic level. Zimele
Wethu is "a non-profit company committed to creating self-sustaining communities through empowerment." The poor have been told all their lives that
they have little to nothing to contribute to their own betterment, that the only
hope of social uplift must come from the outside.

The power of the SHG concept lies in its radically different messaging—
namely, that together the poor have the resources to increase their capacity to
transform not just their own lives but the lives of their neighbors too. In the
words of Zimele Wethu's cofounder and executive director, Audrey Mukwavi
Matimelo, "We . . . encourage [the poor] to start thinking about how they
can change their poverty situation with what they have." The work of the
Zimele Wethu staff consists of gathering and meeting with small groups of
mostly women, helping them identify the needs of their community, and then
building enough trust among them to begin saving what little each has and let
it accumulate into a resource pool that can address those needs—essentially
the creation of a truly people's bank. "To date," Matimelo reports, "the
SHGs have raised 495,000 rand (almost $40,000) collectively." She continues,

> It is only when we return the economies back to the poor that we will create
> empowerment and wealth. The concept of SHG returns that economic power
> to the poor because it rebuilds poor people's economies through strong social
> networks with weekly savings and access to loans for small businesses and col-
> lective bargaining power for purchase and markets. . . . SHGs run community
> initiatives motivated by *ubuntu* values. With their group funds they run crèches,
> home-based care, and care and support for orphaned and vulnerable children.[43]

Through SHGs, Zimele Wethu creates income generation through local,
asset-based, sustainable systems and by doing so makes peace. How so? As

---

43. Audrey Mukwavi Matimelo, quoted in Omega Moagi, "Turning Poverty Around," News
24, April 4, 2017, http://www.news24.com/SouthAfrica/News/turning-poverty-around-20170403.
For a much more detailed treatment of SHGs and how Zimele Wethu implements this effective
approach to empowerment, see Matimelo, "Mobilizing Community Assets to Alleviate Poverty
among Women: A Case Study of Zimele Developing Community Self-Reliance in Rural Kwazulu-
Natal" (PhD diss., University of Kwazulu-Natal, Pietermaritzburg, South Africa, November 2016).

people begin to contribute to the betterment of their own lives and their communities, the reasons for collective discontent and strife are eliminated, or at least significantly decreased. I doubt that Matimelo and her staff consider themselves peacemakers as they go about creating more just economic and social systems, yet their actions define the "just" in just peacemaking. When the root causes of conflict on the political and economic levels are addressed, social peace, lo and behold, becomes a realistic vision.

Enemies Doing Justice Together

To do justice in both the sociopolitical and economic arenas leads to peace; to do so together across tribal, ethnic, cultural, religious, and/or ideological differences can truly solidify that peace. With sensitive, proper guidance, members on both sides of a conflict can, according to Munayer and Loden, "acquire a shared vision for joint actions and advocacy." The sixth stage of Musalaha's approach to reconciliation, "Taking Steps," refers precisely to working together for the sake of justice, which signifies a genuine readiness to advance reconciliation. "Musalaha participants who have reached this stage," Munayer and Loden explain, "are clearly committed to the process of reconciliation and are able to inspire and invite others to join the cause."[44]

It is not uncommon to encounter people on either side of a conflict who are weary of the direct work of reconciliation—that is, of dealing with the nature of the conflict itself. For example, I remember inviting an African American doctoral student to a workshop I was team-facilitating on the black-white divide in the US. She responded, in essence, "I'm sick and tired of talking about the black-white divide; we all are. Instead of trying to figure out how blacks and whites can get along, why don't you just help us all serve God together?" In other words, instead of trying so hard to reconcile two peoples, we should facilitate unity in a common cause, which could result in reconciliation. From this perspective, reconciliation can be seen not so much as a ministry but as the fruit of justice work.

I still think it is important to directly discuss the issue of racism and other injustices that divide, but the student made a valid point in that she highlighted the importance of doing justice together as a crucial aspect of peacemaking. Just peacemakers find causes to which both sides can commit, even as they continue to facilitate reconciliation workshops and seminars. Can members of rival tribes in South Sudan work together to provide clean water for their communities? Can Christians and Muslims in the Philippines march together

---

44. Munayer and Loden, *Through My Enemy's Eyes*, 232.

in protest against human rights atrocities of an authoritarian government? Can black, white, and brown people in the US work together to improve the educational system of our major cities? Can Palestinians and Israelis stand up together against the indignities that so many Palestinians endure at the checkpoints? These and many other instances of "enemies working together for the sake of justice" do much for the cause of peace. Just peacemakers know this and make it a crucial part of what they do to move people closer to the joy of true embrace.

Nonviolent Action: What Part of "Love Your Enemy" Do We Not Understand?

Peacemaking as mission requires considering one more element—namely, a commitment to nonviolent action. This descriptor may sound like an oxymoron to some, because nonviolence has come to be associated with words such as "inaction," "passivity," "nonresistance," "submission," and even "complicity." Not only should the teachings of Christ—not to mention the cross of Christ—tell us otherwise; they should also tell us that nonviolent action reflects the way of God to overcome evil. Besides, what part of the commands to love our enemies (Matt. 5:43–44), turn the other cheek (Matt. 5:39), and overcome evil with good (Rom. 12:17–21) do we not understand? To the extent that we *do* understand and practice them at face value, we position ourselves as peacemakers in the world.

Nonviolent Action

Sider defines nonviolent action as "an activist confrontation with evil that respects the personhood even of the 'enemy' and therefore seeks both to end the oppression and to reconcile the oppressor through nonviolent methods."[45] John Cartwright and Susan Thistlethwaite provide a more vivid, if not ironically militant, picture of nonviolent direct action as "a strategy that lances the festering boil of violence and produces healing without resort to war."[46] Peacemakers need not claim to be pure pacifists to commit to nonviolence.[47] A true just-war perspective, in fact, places the use of violence at the very end of its tactical list, meaning that we should try all ways nonviolent before

---

45. Ronald J. Sider, *Nonviolent Action: What Christian Ethics Demands but Most Christians Have Never Really Tried* (Grand Rapids: Brazos, 2015), xv.
46. John Cartwright and Susan Thistlethwaite, "Support Nonviolent Direct Action," in *Just Peacemaking*, 42.
47. Sider, *Nonviolent Action*, xv.

reluctantly resorting to violence. The call to nonviolent action, therefore, goes beyond the just-war and pacifism debate and beckons the whole church to testify through our actions to both the justice and the love of God in Jesus Christ for all, which includes the people on both sides of any given conflict. Mahatma Gandhi in India, Rosa Parks and Martin Luther King Jr. in the US, Benigno and Cory Aquino in the Philippines, Óscar Romero in El Salvador, and Desmond Tutu in South Africa represent high-profile examples of non-violent action that effectively changed the course of their respective nations.[48]

From their examples we learn what this aspect of practical peacemaking as mission can look like. It can involve participating, encouraging, and even facilitating boycotts, strikes, and marches to bring mass attention to and public mobilization against an evil, while at the same time and with equal intensity discouraging mean-spiritedness, retaliation, and of course killing. An anti-gun-violence protest I helped to organize several years ago in north Philadelphia comes to mind. Before marching to the storefront of a gun shop where the demonstration was to take place, a co-organizer from The Simple Way gave instructions to the few hundred demonstrators gathered in a nearby Salvation Army church. Speaking from years of activist experience, he warned us of the guaranteed presence of counterdemonstrators, and he instructed us not to engage them in the same way they would likely engage us. It is best not to engage them at all, and certainly do not initiate anything, he said. But when it is unavoidable, we must respond to meanness with kindness, provocations with self-control, and words of hate with words of love. In other words, a peace demonstration needs itself to demonstrate peace if it is going to be effective. Some of us did better than others in following the instructions! Unfortunately, a few from our group counterattacked with loud, harsh words, thus attesting to the difficulty of maintaining a heart of peace. Insofar as we can, however, echoing Romans 12:18, we bear witness to the power of nonviolence to effect change.

For a more recent example, also from the US, at the time of this writing a group of African American pastors is boycotting the National Football League (NFL), committed to continue this action until former quarterback Colin Kaepernick has a job again. Believing that Kaepernick is no longer employed because he took a knee during the national anthem at the beginning of each game in 2016 to protest police brutality, these pastors have "blacked out the NFL." Although lifelong avid football fans, these pastors have chosen to stand

---

48. In *Nonviolent Action*, Sider draws out the principles and practices of nonviolence through historical examples. It is a kind of miniencyclopedia of peacemakers in history, compiled in one volume to demonstrate the effectiveness of nonviolent action.

in solidarity with Kaepernick by refusing to support the NFL in any way—not buying season tickets, not watching games on television, not buying any NFL paraphernalia, and so on—and encouraging others to join the boycott.[49] They may not view themselves as peacemakers, yet that is exactly what they are, as they challenge a social evil by way of nonviolent action.

These types of actions have proved to be effective in drawing attention to an injustice and garnering mass support, to the point that perpetrators must take the movement seriously. The trick is sustaining a practical spirit of nonviolence throughout any protest or boycott. Insofar as we can do that, the movement bears the mark of Christ, for we know the peace of Christ when oppressors are won over, not defeated and destroyed. "We can persist in this costly love even for oppressors," Sider asserts, "because we know 'the universe is on the side of justice.'"[50]

Faithful unto Death

Marches, boycotts, and the like represent nonviolent actions; there are also *radical* nonviolent actions. The tactics of Christian Peacemaker Teams (CPTs) come to mind. "CPT seeks to reduce violence by 'getting in the way,'" Sider explains. "Well-trained teams intervene in situations of conflict, accompany endangered persons, document human rights abuses, and provide information that helps supporters at home advocate with policy makers."[51] Peacemakers get in the way of violence, even if it costs them their lives.

Kathleen Kern, who has chronicled the history of CPT since its inception, tells the story of the CPT serving in Iraq during the first decade of the twenty-first century. She writes, "By 2006, the Iraq team would experience two serious auto accidents, have friends and colleagues die in violence that spiraled out of control after the invasion of the Multinational Forces in 2003, be tied up and robbed by armed men, and have a delegation kidnapped. Two trained CPTers would die in Iraq, one in an accident [George Weber] and one in an execution-style murder [Tom Fox]."[52] The founders of CPT expected that radical peacemaking would mean this kind of fate for some. CPT training of personnel, in fact, includes planning for their memorial services and making out their wills.[53] I think again of pastor-peacemaker John Kiruga,

---

49. "NFL Blackout," August 17, 2017, https://www.youtube.com/watch?v=HuEY9imwkfU.

50. Sider, *Nonviolent Action*, 31. The quote within the quote comes from Martin Luther King Jr.

51. Sider, *Nonviolent Action*, 148.

52. Kathleen Kern, *In Harm's Way: A History of Christian Peacemaker Teams* (Eugene, OR: Cascade, 2009), 417.

53. Kern, *In Harm's Way*, 416.

whose story of "peace at all cost" I told at the beginning of chapter 10. These modern-day martyrs, of course, have merely continued the legacy of committed peacemakers throughout history whose blood was spilled for the sake of the integrity of the gospel, the growth of the church, and the testament of peace in a fragmented, violent world.

We cannot, however, view martyrdom as a tactic, as if it were the ultimate tool to pull out of the peacemaker's toolbox. God does not call us, for instance, to set ourselves on fire or to attach bombs on our person to blow ourselves (and others) up for Christ. God calls us, rather, to be faithful to the gospel, which means at least three practical, intertwined commitments. "Faithful to the gospel" means at once (1) a sacrificial commitment to others, loving our neighbors, including our enemies and especially the downtrodden (Luke 10:25–37); (2) a resolute, if not absolute, commitment to nonviolence, overcoming evil with good (Rom. 12:20–21); and (3) a commitment to bearing witness to Jesus, whose death on the cross paved the way to abundant life for all who believe.

Whereas the previous section, on just peacemaking, encourages people on both sides of a conflict to work together for justice, nonviolent action emphasizes that that unified work truly demonstrates peace, not just as an end but also as the means toward that end. By engaging in nonviolent action together for justice, people of the two sides of a conflict practice the very peace that they strive to experience between each other. That is, nonviolent direct action indirectly shows the way of peace for and between conflicted parties.

This long-winded chapter warrants a summary of the elements of peacemaking as mission. I have proposed, for the sake of horizontal people-to-people reconciliation in Christ, that peacemakers facilitate

- *a cultivation of a heart of peace* or a spirituality of reconciliation;
- *submission to the power of relationship* across differences;
- *engagement in real dialogue*, characterized by vulnerability, truth, and love;
- *healing pain*, which requires repentance on the part of the oppressor, forgiveness on the part of the oppressed, and lament on the part of both;
- *just peacemaking*, which affirms practical justice as the road to true peace; and
- *nonviolent action*, which affirms peace as both the means and the end of the peacemaking process.

To the extent that these elements interact with one another in any effort at peacemaking, the church bears witness to the peace of Christ in a fragmented world.

What would happen if the church understood and practiced these elements as part of the Great Commission? What would happen if God's people sought to make peace in these ways between women and men? Between races, ethnicities, and tribes? Between the rich and the poor? Between religions? Between family members? Between all the above? As the church forges pathways of peace in a world fragmented along these and many other lines, it would be demonstrating a key aspect in radical, holistic, authentic discipleship. In this way, the church would position itself to live out its vocation to make radical, holistic, authentic disciples among the nations.

Discussion Questions

1. Do you have to be a pacifist to be a peacemaker? Why or why not?
2. What is the relationship between peace and justice?
3. Of the six elements of peacemaking as mission, did any of them strike you as particularly true or untrue? Are there any you would add to the list?
4. Do you know any peacemakers? How would you describe their attitude, demeanor, and interactions with people? How do they practice their faith in the world?

Conclusion

Waging Reconciliation

As averse as I am to bumper stickers in general, I confess to smiling when a car goes by sporting one that says "Wage Peace." This simple phrase, taken from a poem by Judyth Hill, captures for me not only a vision of God's coming *shalom* but also the church's present call to fight for it, to be as proactive, diligent, and sacrificial unto death for peace as a soldier is for war.[1] As we saw in the last few chapters, we are called to *make* peace, not just keep it, and this "demands courage and daring of the highest order," Sider writes with sobering honesty. "It requires discipline, training, and willingness to face death."[2] I imagine God's people faithfully and passionately waging peace in the world to make way for God's future, and I smile grittily.

I encountered another phrase that actually widened the smile even further; in fact, it made me laugh out loud with joy when I first encountered it. On September 26, 2001, just a few weeks after the infamous 9/11 attack that took down the Twin Towers in New York City and claimed the lives of almost three thousand people, the House of Bishops of the Episcopal Church issued a statement expressing profound grief and calling God's people everywhere to "wage reconciliation." That's it! Why just wage peace when we can wage reconciliation! "Let us therefore wage reconciliation," the statement reads more fully. "Let us offer our gifts for the carrying out of God's ongoing work

1. Judyth Hill, "Wage Peace," Voices Education, 2001, http://voiceseducation.org/content /judyth-hill-wage-peace.
2. Ronald J. Sider, *Nonviolent Action* (Grand Rapids: Brazos, 2015), 176.

of reconciliation, healing, and making all things new. To this we pledge ourselves and call our church."[3]

This book has sought to reshape our understanding of the church's holistic
mission in the world by seeing it through the lens of biblical reconciliation.
Throughout these pages I have claimed that holistic mission must mean more
today than simply affirming the integration of evangelism and social concern.
In our fractured world, it must mean including the work of mending, healing,
and reconciling people to people—women and men, black, white, and brown
people, rich and poor, young and old, warring tribes, clashing religions, and
estranged family members.

Of course, holistic mission thinking and practice have not been void of
reconciliation over these last fifty years, but because of the state of our world
today (part 1), it must occupy the center of what it means to engage in holistic
mission. Without a commitment to horizontal reconciliation—what I have
called peacemaking as mission in chapters 10 and 11 to avoid confusing it
with God's larger mission of reconciling all things—we cannot claim to be
doing holistic mission. Or—as I said in the introduction—we need to embrace
the ministry of reconciliation (peacemaking as mission) as the new whole in
holistic mission.

Beyond redefining holistic mission by emphasizing the peacemaking aspect
of reconciliation, I found the broadness of the biblical vision of reconciliation
to be a powerful framework for holistic mission altogether. Holistic mission
can be defined as the church's commitment to reconciliation between God and
people (evangelism), between people and people (peacemaking), and between
God, people, and creation (stewardship). As we understand and practice our
ministry in the world in these terms, we are engaged in holistic mission.
The call of the whole and reconciled church, therefore, is to bear witness to
God's wholeness—God's coming *shalom*—through the vertical, horizontal,
and circular ministry of reconciliation, and thus live out its vocation to make
kingdom disciples among the nations.

The Church as Reconciler: On Calling and Credibility

Redefining holistic mission in terms of reconciliation has served as the basic
premise of this book; regaining the credibility of the church as an agent of
reconciliation has built on that premise by doing a hard reset of our understanding of gospel, church, and mission in a fractured and fracturing world. In

---

3. "On Waging Reconciliation," in *Waging Reconciliation: God's Mission in a Time of
Globalization and Crisis*, ed. Ian T. Douglas (New York: Church Publishing, 2002), xii.

chapter 10, I described the whole and reconciled church as evangelist, peace-maker, and steward. Together these three identities create the one identity of the church as reconciler.

A faithful rendering of the Scriptures leaves no doubt that God has called God's people, the church, to serve the world as reconciler, to wage reconcilia-tion on the earth. God has commissioned us to be a—if not *the*—major player in the divine project to reconcile all things in Christ. The Bible makes crystal clear both our identity (who we are in Christ) and our mission (what we are supposed to do in the power of the Spirit).

Equally crystal clear, however, is the reality that the church has not lived up to its calling over these last two millennia. The church-in-mission has been as humanly flawed as it has been divinely conceived and called. The many sins of Christendom, including the Crusades, colonialism, the genocide of native cultures, witch hunts, and slavery mar the many bright accomplishments of the church through the ages in areas of education, art, ethics, ministry among the poor—not to mention the global spread of the faith through genuine gospel encounter. Indeed, the church through the ages—the great good it has done notwithstanding—has often found itself on the wrong side of racism, sexism, classism, homophobia, and other injustices.

We can argue about how much good versus how much bad the church has done in its history, but we cannot deny that due to its underside, the church has lost much of its credibility as a viable global reconciler. The hope of this book has been that, by doing a hard reset of our understanding and practice of gospel, church, and mission, the whole and reconciled church will be able to recommit to the whole of its missional calling and thus bear the fruit of seeing "more disciples among more populations in a more caring and just world."[4] Nothing will regain the church's credibility more than for it to faith-fully serve a lost, needy, and warring world with bold humility.

Toward that end, we needed to reconsider "gospel," "church," and "mis-sion," for the living truth of these powerful words tends to go astray in our heart and minds. We constantly need to be realigned and renewed, not only because of our fallen propensity to go astray but because our ever-changing world requires it. For the sake of renewal, we have reconsidered the nature of the whole gospel—what it is and what it isn't (part 2). The good news is certainly not about the bad news of judgment and hate, not about the "good news" of prosperity and comfort, and not about the bigger-is-better ideol-ogy of empire building. The good news also means more than the gospel of

---

4. This is part of the mission statement of the Evangelical Covenant Church, accessed October 25, 2017, http://www.covchurch.org/mission.

personal salvation and more than the gospel of social liberation. The whole and reconciled gospel of Jesus Christ, rather, testifies to the good news of the kingdom of God, an invitation extended to all to experience God's reign of mercy, peace, justice, freedom, and love now and in the life to come. The gospel of the kingdom that Jesus preached, and that the church must also preach in the creative power of the Spirit, points to nothing less than God's promise to reconcile all things, to restore *shalom* on the earth.

To the extent that the church bears witness to this whole gospel, it moves toward becoming the whole church (part 3). We saw that reconciliation "begins with me"; that is, it begins with the pursuit of the reconciliation of self, of becoming whole persons. "The whole church" at least means an assembly of persons on their way to becoming whole in Christ. It means much more, however, than a mere collective of whole persons; to be the whole and reconciled church means reflecting the community, diversity, and love of the Triune God. As the Father sent the Son, and the Father and the Son sent the Spirit, so too the Father, Son, and Holy Spirit have sent the church to participate with them in the ministry of reconciliation (2 Cor. 5:18–20).[5] We saw that to be the whole and reconciled church also means cultivating its spirituality—which makes it distinct among other human institutions—growing in "dangerous worship," meaning worship that kills us and our puny, selfish pursuits and then resurrects us in Christ as people poised to participate in God's redemptive purposes in the world.

We then reconsidered the nature of the church's whole mission, whose various aspects grow out of the church's vocation to make radical kingdom disciples of all nations. We revisited the history of holistic mission and how God used a handful of brave theologians and missiologists to again bring together the activities of evangelism and social justice, which were split apart by theological controversies that plagued most of the twentieth century. We reaffirmed that this integration is essential to the church's whole mission and defines the greatness of the Great Commission. With evangelism and justice reintegrated, we saw that the Great Commission can be better described as the Whole Commission. We saw how the Whole Commission consists of evangelism, peacemaking, and stewardship. We also necessarily focused on the peacemaking aspect, as the world continues its downward spiral in intensifying divisions, conflict, and violence. We saw how the church as peacemaker needs to cultivate a heart of peace; submit to the power of relationship; engage in vulnerable dialogue; facilitate healing through repentance, forgiveness, and

5. David J. Bosch, *Transforming Mission*, 20th anniv. ed. (Maryknoll, NY: Orbis Books, 2011), 399.

lament; do justice to make real peace; and commit to nonviolent action at all cost.

If this book has helped in the missional renewal of the church through these fresh understandings of gospel, church, and mission, then it will have accomplished its objective. Of course, renewal only reignites the missional call; we now must live it out faithfully, passionately, humbly, and boldly. Now more than at any other time in the history of our broken world the church needs to wage reconciliation on the earth.

Afterword

I really have nothing to add except AMEN! This is a superbly written, thoroughly holistic, solidly biblical, globally oriented, and creatively relevant statement of what faithful Christian mission is and demands today.

Tizon embraces biblical balance rather than a one-sided emphasis on one important theme to the neglect of others. He calls us to worship and action, biblical study and costly obedience, dependence on the Holy Spirit and immersion in Christian community, personal and social holiness, local and global mission, and of course evangelism and social action.

Rightly and brilliantly, Tizon locates the important task of combining evangelism and social action (which my generation worked so hard to accomplish) in the larger task of reconciliation. He does that with a firm grasp of the brokenness of the global world and an honest confession of the way the church has so often contributed to, rather than helped to overcome, that brokenness. And he describes the goal of reconciliation as right relationship with God, neighbor, and earth—embracing a wonderful biblical balance. Showing how reconciliation lies at the heart of biblical mission is one of the great contributions of this book.

I have devoted most of my life to pleading with Christians to embrace holistic mission and biblical balance. Now, as I approach my eightieth year, I experience great joy in seeing how a younger generation of Christian leaders is taking up that task with biblical fidelity and creative vigor. Knowing that the future mission of the church is in the hands of gifted, faithful leaders like the author of this book, I anticipate witnessing a wonderful flowering of biblical Christianity as I watch from my rocking chair and then from the other side of the Jordan in the presence of our Lord.

Ronald J. Sider
St. Davids, Pennsylvania

Author Index

Adam, Karla, 13n26
Adeney, Miriam, 60n3, 164
Aldredge-Clanton, Jann, 125, 125n32
Alexander, Paul, 62
Alexander, Ruth, 138n18
Al-Rohdan, Nayef, 6, 6n1
Aquino, Maria Pilar, 117n16
Arias, Mortimer, 78, 78n2, 79–80, 79n4, 79n6, 80nn7–8, 81n11
Asamoah-Gyadu, Kwabena, 70, 70n18

Babcock, Maltbie, 131n4
Bacon, Hannah, 117, 117n15
Bagwati, Jagdish, 3n5
Bailey, Sarah Pulliam, 26n14, 50n33
Baker, Heidi, 163
Baker-Fletcher, Karen, 117, 118n17
Baldwin, Lewis V., 127, 127n36
Balmer, Randall, 59n2
Banda, Joshua, 163
Barber, Leroy, 30, 30n23
Barna, George, 26n13
Barnes, Jonathan S., 54n41
Barth, Karl, 185, 185n8
Bediako, Kwame, 31, 164
Benson, Bruce, 69n14
Bergen, Jeremy, 48–49, 49n26, 49n28, 49n30
Berger, Peter, 9, 9n14
Bevans, Stephen B., 52, 52n37
Boesak, Allen Aubrey, xxn9, xxn13
Boff, Leonardo, 113n5
Bolger, Ryan, 94, 94nn6–7
Bolz-Weber, Nadia, 9, 94n9

Bonhoeffer, Dietrich, 68, 68n13, 137–39, 138n17, 152, 152n20
Bonino, José Miguez, 161
Bonk, Jonathan, 51, 51n35
Borquist, Ann C., 162n18
Borthwick, Paul, 55, 55n43
Bosch, David J., 43, 43n13, 45n20, 75, 75n31, 92–93, 92n4, 93n5, 114, 114n7, 147, 147n3, 149n12, 157n2
Boyd, Gregory A., 24, 24n9, 81n10
Bria, Ion, 143, 143n29
Bright, John, 82n14
Brimlow, Robert W., 14, 14nn30–31
Brubaker, Pamela, 201n38, 201n40, 202n42
Bruckner, James K., 99n6, 102–3, 102n12, 103nn14–15, 106
Brueggemann, Walter, 85
Brunner, Emil, 145, 145n1
Budde, Michael, 14, 14nn30–31
Bühlmann, Walbert, 31, 31n27
Burke, James, 201n38, 201n40, 202n42
Burrows, William, 31n27

Camp, Lee, 151, 151nn17–19
Campolo, Tony, 132, 132n6, 135, 135nn12–13, 136n15
Cannon, Mae Elise, xvn1, 26n12, 49n29, 50n32, 178n11, 201n39
Cardoza-Orlandi, Carlos F., 32, 32n31, 33, 33n33
Carter, Craig A., 22–23, 23n4, 23nn6–7
Cartwright, John, 206, 206n46
Castleman, Robbie F., 166n34

219

Césaire, Aimé, 39, 40n5
Chia, Edmund Kee-Fook, 33n32
Choge, Emily, xx, xx*nn*10–11
Christian, Jayakumar, 127
Claiborne, Shane, 62, 62n8, 143n30
Clarke, Sathianathan, 47, 47n25
Cochran, Bryan N., 193n24
Collins, Nick, 10n15
Congar, Yves, 117n16
Constantineanu, Corneliu, 122n28, 174n3
Constantino, Renato, 186n9
Corbitt, Steve, 54, 54n42
Corrie, John, 175n7
Costas, Orlando, 127, 158, 158n6, 161, 164
Crossing, Peter F., 91n1
Cuellar, Gregory Lee, 45nn18–19

Darling, Mary Albert, 135, 135nn12–13, 136n15
Davies, J. G., 130n1
DeBorst, Ruth Padilla, 12, 12n22, 162n19, 181, 181n19
Dempster, Murray A., 162n22
DeYoung, Curtiss, xx*n*9, xx*n*13, 119, 119n19, 120n22, 121n24
Dilley, Andrea Palpant, 43n15
Driver, John, 29, 29n19
Duhigg, Charles, 70n16
Dwyer, Mimi, 13n25

Engelsviken, Tormod, 87nn21–22, 88, 88n24, 103n13, 173n2, 175n6, 178, 178n12
Eppley, Harold, 107, 107n21
Escobar, Samuel, 44, 44n16, 161, 164

Farhadian, Charles, 141, 141n25
Fernando, Ajith, 75–76, 76n32
Fikkert, Brian, 54, 54n42
Flentje, Annesa, 193n24
Frame, Randall, 97n1, 159nn7–8, 161n13
Franke, John R., 113, 113n2, 115, 115nn9–10, 117, 117n14
Franklin, Robert, 66–67, 66n8, 67n10
Friedman, Stan, 168n36, 171n1
Friedman, Thomas, 3n5, 7, 7n5
Friesen, Duane, 201n38, 201n40, 202n42
Friesen, Dwight, 20n45

Gallagher, Sharon, 61n7
Garcia, Jacobo, 49n27
George, Sam, 17n40, 18n41
Gingrich, Newt, 26n13
Gitari, David, 164

Gonzalez, Justo L., 32, 32n31, 33, 33n33
Gordon, Wayne L., 83n16, 120n21
Gornik, Mark, 31n27
Graham, Billy, 160n14
Green, Joel B., 99, 99n4
Greenman, Jeffrey P., 150n16
Gregory of Nazianzus, 115
Grenz, Stanley J., 113, 113nn2–3
Groody, Daniel G., 11, 11n19, 131, 131n2
Gushee, David P., 86, 86n20, 100–101, 100nn7–9, 101nn10–11, 104n17, 180n18
Gutiérrez, Gustavo, 60, 60n3

Hanciles, Jehu, 11–12, 12n21
Harper, Lisa Sharon, xv*n*1, 26n12, 49n29, 134, 134n9, 178n11
Harris, Peter, 180, 180n15
Hart, Addison Hodges, 22, 22nn2–3
Haugen, David, 7, 7n7
Hawk, L. Daniel, 2n3
Heaney, Robert S., 38n3
Heck, Nicholas C., 193n24
Heltzel, Peter, 69n14
Hennessy-Fiske, Molly, 152n22
Heward-Mills, Dag, 71, 71nn19–20
Hickman, Albert W., 91n1
Hill, Judyth, 211, 211n1
Hirsch, Alan, 95, 95n10
Hocking, William F., 75, 75n28
Hoekendijk, J. C., 160n11
Hornsby, Donald, 3n5
Howell, Kellan, 28n16
Huang-ti, Shih, 39
Hughes, Richard T., 25, 25n11
Hunter, James D., 11, 11n20
Husby, David, 171n1

Jackson, Troy, xv*n*1, 26n12, 49n29, 178n11
Janis, Sharon, 131n3
Jayakaran, Ravi, 162n21
Jenkins, Philip, 31, 31nn25–26, 32, 32n29
Johnson, Elizabeth, 117, 118n17
Johnson, Todd M., 91n1, 92n2
Jones, Kirk Byron, 108, 108n22
Jones, L. Gregory, 196n30, 197nn31–32
Jones, Meldon, 6n1
Jongeneel, Jan A. B., 1n1
Jorgensen, Knud, 126n34

Katongole, Emmanuel, xviii, xviii*n*6, 89, 89n26, 98, 98n2, 184, 184n4, 187, 187n11
Kennedy, D. James, 26n13

Kern, Kathleen, 208, 208nn52–53
Khor, Martin, 11, 11n18
Kim, Grace Ji-Sun, 125, 125n32
King, William M., 159n10
Kinnaman, David, 165
Kiruga, John Njaramba, 171n1
Kivisto, Peter, 40n7, 41, 41n8
Klaus, Byron D., 162n22
Klingenschmitt, Gordon, 28
Koenig, John, 112n1
Kuzmic, Peter, 163, 163n23, 164

Labberton, Mark, 140, 140nn22–23
LaCugna, Catherine, 115n12
Ladd, George Eldon, 59, 60n3
Laffert, Karen, 77n1
Laing, Aislinn, 10n15
Lalitha, Jayachitra, 2n3, 148n7, 166nn32–33, 166n35
Lane, Davie, 28
Langan, John, 201n38, 201n40, 202n42
Lee, Hak Joon, 127, 127nn37–38
Leithart, Peter, 24n8
Leupp, Roderick T., 113n4, 116, 116n13, 123, 123n30
Loden, Lisa, 189n14, 190–91, 190n17, 191n18, 193, 193n25, 194, 194n27, 205, 205n44
Long, Thomas G., 139n20
Love, Rick, 184n3, 185n7, 191, 191n19, 192–93, 193n23
Lucco, Dick, 148
Luther, Martin, 58, 58n1
Lynton, Michael, 9, 9n13
Lyon, JoAnn, 164

Ma, Julie, 133, 133n8, 163
Ma, Wonsuk, 133, 133n8, 163
Mach, Rachel, 7n7
Madeira, Phil, 64, 64n1
Maggay, Melba P., 51, 51n34, 60n3, 127, 164
Mantyla, Kyle, 28n16
McGavran, Donald, 121, 121n23
McNeil, Brenda Salter, xviii, xviiin5, xix, xixn8, xx, xxn10, 142n28, 186, 186n10, 190, 190n16, 192, 192n22
Medhat, Omar, 152n22
Melander, Rochelle, 107, 107n21
Moagi, Omega, 204n43
Moberg, David O., 159n9
Moffitt, Robert, 88, 88n23, 176, 176n9
Mombo, Esther, 158n5
Moody, Dwight L., 59

Munayer, Salim J., 189, 189n14, 190–91, 190n17, 191n18, 193, 193n25, 194, 194n27, 205, 205n44
Murray, Stuart, 22n1, 28, 28n17
Musekura, Célestin, 196, 196n30, 197, 197nn31–33
Myers, Bryant, 9, 9n12, 14, 14n29, 17, 17n38, 127

Nassar, Makarios, 152n22
Newbigin, Lesslie, 23n5, 81n11
Ng, David, 148n9
Ng'weshemi, Andrea M., 1–5, 99, 99n5, 105n18
Nikolajsen, Joseph Back, 23n5
Niringiye, David Zac, 92n3, 96, 96n13
Nouwen, Henri, 194, 194n26
Nuñez, Emilio A., 161

Okoro, Enuma, 143n30
Okyere-Manu, Beatrice, 38n1, 53, 53n38, 177n10
Olson, Philip N., 164, 165n28
Omeire, Nnanidi Emanuel, 175n7
Ott, Craig, 146, 146n2

Padilla, C. René, 6, 6n3, 14–15, 15nn32–34, 16, 16n35, 82n13, 161, 162n21, 164, 195, 195n29
Padilla, Catherine Feser, 161
Page, Melvin, 39, 39n4
Pereira, Arun, 17, 17nn36–37
Perkins, John M., 60, 60n3, 83n16, 120n21, 164
Perry, Alex, 195n28
Petersen, Douglas, 162n22, 163
Petersen, Rodney L., 53, 53nn39–40
Platt, David, 73–74, 73n24
Polston, Woodrow, 26n13

Rah, Soong-Chan, xvn1, 26n12, 30, 30n22, 49n29, 178n11, 199, 199nn36–37
Rainer, Thom, 165, 165n29
Rawson, Katie J., 149, 149n14
Reimer, Reg, 152n21
Rennie, David, 70n15
Reznick, Alisa, 60n5
Rhoads, David, 119, 119n20
Rice, Chris, xviii, xviiin6, 89, 89n26, 98, 98n2, 174n5, 184, 184n4, 187, 187n11
Richardson, Rick, 142n28
Rieger, Jorge, 38, 38n2
Ringma, Charles, 135, 135n10
Rivera, Luis, 42, 42n10
Robert, Dana L., 2, 3n4

Rohr, Richard, 114, 114n6, 115n8
Royce, Josiah, 126

Salinas, Daniel, 162n18
Samuel, Vinay, 164
Sang-Hun, Choe, 185n6
Sankofa, 125–26
Saracco, J. N., 67n11
Schmit, Clayton J., 139, 139n21
Schreiter, Robert, xvii, xviin3, 7n4, 126n34,
    183n1, 184–85, 185n5
Searcy, Edwin, 29–30, 29n20, 30n21
Sharpe, Matthew, 67n12
Sider, Ronald J., 59–60, 60n3, 62, 72, 72nn21–22,
    81n9, 83nn16–17, 120n21, 164, 164n26, 165,
    165n28, 201, 201n41, 206, 206n45, 206n47,
    207n48, 208, 208nn50–51, 211n2, 215
Sine, Tom, 7, 7n6, 11, 11n17, 19, 19nn42–43,
    20n44, 60, 60n3
Smit, Dirk J., 185n7
Smith, Efrem, 121, 121n25
Smith, Kay Higuera, 2n3
Smith, Mitzi J., 44n17, 148n7, 157–58, 158n4,
    166, 166nn32–33, 166n35
Smith, Timothy L., 159n9
Snyder, Howard A., 79n5
Soerens, Tim, 20n45
Sparks, Paul, 20n45
Stanley, Brian, 2n2
Starnes, Todd, 26n13
Stassen, Glen, 201n38, 201n40, 202n42
Stetzer, Ed, 175n8
Stiglitz, Joseph, 3n5, 12n23
Stott, John, 121n26, 164, 168, 168n37
Stoudman, Gerard, 6, 6n1
Sugirtharajah, R. S., 38, 38n3
Suico, Joseph, 163
Sunquist, Scott W., 43n12
Sussman, Robert W., 41, 41n9
Swartley, Willard, 183n2

Tamez, Elsa, 60n3
Taylor, William D., 152n21
Tejedo, Joel, 163
Thiessen, Elmer, 75n27
Thistlethwaite, Susan, 206, 206n46

Tinker, George "Tink," 40n6, 42–43, 43n11,
    45, 46, 46n23, 47, 47n24
Tizon, Al, 2n2, 17n39, 51n36, 61n6, 75nn29–
    30, 81n10, 82n15, 83n16, 96n12, 98n3,
    120n21, 130n1, 135n11, 136n14, 144n31,
    149n13, 161n16, 163n24, 164n27, 166n31,
    180nn16–17, 201n39, 215
Tolstoy, Leo, 138, 138n19
Toon, Tarmo, 115n11
Twiss, Richard, 46, 46n22, 148, 148n8

Unruh, Heidi Rolland, 164, 165n28

van der Meer, Antonia, 152n21
van Oort, Johannes, 117n16
Van Opstal, Sandra, 142, 142nn26–28
Vethanayagamony, Peter, 33n32
Villafane, Eldin, 163
Visser 't Hooft, W. A., 160, 160n12
Volf, Miroslav, 89, 89n25, 122n28, 198,
    198nn34–35
Von Welz, Justinian, 166
Vorster, Jakobus, 49, 49n31

Walls, Andrew, 24n10, 31, 31n27, 33–34,
    34nn34–36
Walter, Joanna, 13n27
White, Lynn, 179, 179n14
Willard, Dallas, 81, 81n12, 147, 147nn4–6, 148,
    148n10, 149n15
Williams, J. Rodman, 132, 132n5, 132n7
Wilson, Jonathan R., 137, 137n16
Wilson-Hartgrove, Jonathan, 143n30
Winfield, Nicole, 49n27
Woodberry, Robert D., 43–44, 43nn14–15
Woodley, Randy S., 45nn18–19, 86, 86n19
Woolnough, Brian, 155n1
Wright, Christopher J. H., 161n12, 179, 179n13
Wright, N. T., 73, 73n23

Yaconelli, Michael, 95, 95n11
Yates, Joshua, 11, 11n20
Yeh, Allen, 31, 31n24
Young, Robert J. C., 46n21
Young, William Paul, 122, 122n27

Zurlo, Gina A., 91n1

Subject Index

abortion, 65
Adam and Eve, fall of, 85, 87, 99
adultery, 63
advocacy work, 203–4, 205
Advocate, Spirit as, 138. *See also* Holy Spirit
African Americans, 41
African Leadership and Reconciliation Ministries, 196
Alexander the Great, 39
alienation, 116, 175
All Native Circle Conference, 49
all tribes and nations, 141, 169–70
al-Qaeda, 12
ambassadors, xviii
America
    Christian America, 24–27, 141
    economic dominance of, 11–12
    and globalization, 25
    as new Israel, 24
American Renewal Project, 28
Americas, conquest of the, 39
Anabaptists, 23, 27
anger and peace, 186
Anti-balaka, 65
antiglobalization, 12–14
anti-gun violence protest, 207
anti-Semitism, 23
Anyang City (South Korea), 129–30
apartheid, 127
"Apology for the Transatlantic Slave Trade," 49
"Apology to First Nations," 48–49
Aquino, Benigno and Corey, 207

Asian School of Development and Cross-Cultural Studies, 15
assimilation, xx, 12
Attila the Hun, 39

baptism, in the Holy Spirit, 132–33. *See also* Holy Spirit
Baptist World Alliance (Ghana 2007), 48–49
Barna Group, 165
Beatitudes, 167
blessed, 134
body-soul unity, 98–99
bold humility, 92, 95, 105
boldness, 94–95
Bonhoeffer, Dietrich, 27
breathing, inhale-exhale motion of, 108
British and Irish Association of Mission Studies, xvii
brokenness, 105, 116
"brown-on-brown racism," 61
burning fire analogy (Brunner), 145
burnout, ministry, 106–7
Bush, George W., 70
"buy local" campaigns, 13

Cain and Abel, 39, 104
Cape Town Commitment, xix, 103, 123, 157
capitalism, 7, 11
catalytic events, 186
catechisms written for slaves, 44
Center for the Study of World Christianity, 91n1

Cheney, Dick, 188
child abuse, 93
Christendom, x, 4, 21–24, 44, 147, 151, 213
   Christian America as, 24–27
   decline of, 27–28
   post-Christendom, xxi, 4, 22, 24, 94, 158
Christian America, 24–27, 141
Christian counterculture, 168
Christian hospitality, 17
Christianization, 40, 42–45
Christian Peacemaker Teams (CPTs), 208
Christus Victor, 84
Chung, John, 96n12
church, xv
   colonial past of, xx, 47, 48–50
   as community of broken people, 92–94
   decentered, 29–31, 34
   as diverse community, 111–12
   global, 92
   and healing of the nations, xii
   and intercultural formation, 120
   loss of credibility, 213
   marginalization of, 28
   as missional, 92, 94–95
   moves toward wholeness, 116
   nonwhite, 30
   in power, xix
   as reconciler, 212–14
   spirituality of, 214
   in Western cultural captivity, 148
   whole church, 91–96, 112, 214
   and whole gospel, 95–96
church and state, unholy marriage of, 27. See
   also Christendom
church-in-mission, 213
church planting, 121–22
circular reconciliation, 87, 89, 103, 173–74,
   178–81
City Harvest Church (Singapore), 67
civilization, 40, 45
civil rights movement, 125, 127
classism, 61, 122, 125, 178, 213
Cold War, end of, 7
colonialism, x, xvi, 2, 23, 38–44, 46, 93, 213
   and assimilation, 45
   and racism, 40–41
   reform of, 43–44
colonization, from Manifest Destiny, 25
Columbus, Christopher, 39
Columbus Day, 14
comfort, gospel of, 68–69
Comforter, Spirit as, 138. See also Holy Spirit

commerce and crown, 39–40, 45
Commission on World Mission and Evangelism
   (World Council of Churches), xvii
communal lament, 199–200
communication skill (vulnerability), 191–94
communion, 7
community, and plurality of God, 114–16
compassion, 136, 202
confidence, 137
conquest, 147
Constantine, 22
Constantine's Sword (documentary), 27
Constantinianism, 151
contact theory, 190
contentment, 137
contextual "Christianities," 44
contextualization, 2–3, 177
conversion theology, 75
Copeland, Kenneth, 67
corporate humility, 50–51
corporate repentance, 48–50
courage, 137
Craig, Tom, 70
creation, reconciliation with, 103–4, 179
"cross-cultural," 118n18
Cru (formerly Campus Crusade for Christ),
   50n33
Crusades, 23, 213
cultural arrogance, 50, 152
cultural identities, protection against assimilation, 13

dangerous worship, 140, 214
Darwinism, 40
decentered church, 29–31, 34
deconstruction projects, 50
Deeper Life Christian Ministry (Nigeria), 67
development, 163, 176
dialogue, 17, 190–94
disciplemaking, 169, 176, 180
   as vocation of the church, 145–47
discipleship, 146, 168
   in community, 149
   definition of, 148–52
   as lifelong process, 150
   and whole mission of the church, 152
diversity, 9
   and distinctions of God, 116–18
   vs. interculturality, 125
   in leadership, 143
Dollar, Creflo, 67
dominant/subservient positions, 55

domination, 47
dominion theology, 179
Donatists, 27
Dove World Outreach Center, 65
Dumont, Alf, 49

ecclesiology, xxi
economics, and globalization, 7
Edict of Milan (313), 22
education, as indoctrination into white religion, 45
Egyptian Bible Society, 167–68
empire, gospel of, 69–70, 71
English as a Second Language classes, 16
English Puritans, 25
Enlightenment, 11, 40
"Ephesus moment," 34
equality, 53
eschaton, 11, 20, 105
ethnocentrism, 47, 120
ethnocide, 45, 147
Evangelical Covenant Church in North America, 23n4, 125–26
Evangelical Covenant Church of Kenya, 171–72
Evangelicals for Social Action, 75, 165, 189
evangelism, xxi, 59, 75, 135–36, 165, 174, 175, 212, 214
evangelism and social justice, xvii, 145, 155–56, 164, 214, 217
evangelism-only approach to mission, xvii, 59, 157
every nation, tribe, and people, 141, 169–70
evil, 86
extreme poverty, 10

fall, the, 85, 87, 99, 102, 104, 116
false gospels, 64–71, 82
false peace, 201
Falwell, Jerry, 25
fascism, 93
Fellowship of Reconciliation, 126
First Nations Christian leaders, 46
First Nations peoples, 23, 25, 41, 42, 45, 48–49, 53, 125
flag of the US in church sanctuaries, 141
"forgive and forget," 197–98
forgiveness, 87, 196–99
fornication, 63
Fox, Thom, 208
Francis, Pope, 49
free-market capitalism, 7
"from everywhere to everywhere," 33

fundamentalism, 66
fundamentalist-modernist debate, xvii, 155, 156, 158–59, 163

Gandhi, Mahatma, 207
gay and straight Christians, 189–90. *See also* homophobia; homosexuality; LGBTQ community
Generation Z Christians, 164
generosity, 74
Geneva Centre for Security Policy, 6
Genghis Khan, 39
genocide, 126
  cultural, 45, 47, 213
  of native peoples of the Americas, 23
global capitalism, liturgies of, 11
global church, 92
global fragmentation, xvi
globalization, xvii, xxi
  backlash against, 12–14
  and church-in-holistic-mission, 14–20
  as colonization, 25
  definition of, 6–8
  of the gospel, 19–20
  as ideology, 10–12
  as process, 8–10
globalizationism, 19–20, 68
global partnership, 54–55
Global South Christianity, 9, 32, 92
Gnosticism, 73
God. *See also* kingdom of God
  distinct persons of, 116–18
  image of, 100–102, 115, 117
  intratrinitarian love of, 115, 122
  love of, 123, 124
  masculinity and femininity of, 117–18
  plurality of, 114–16
  power of, 132–33
  ultimate ownership of everything, 180
  as unity-amid-diversity, 119, 122
God's Justice (study Bible), 74n26
good news for the poor, 136
good works, 155
gospel, xv, xxi, 82–85. *See also* false gospels
  globalization of, 19–20
  whole gospel, 57–62
grace and peace, 187
gracelessness, 187
Graduate Theological Union, 37
Graham, Billy, 160
Great Appeal (Romans 12:1–2), 170
Great Commandment, 176

Great Commission, 38, 146–48, 152–53, 157–58, 214
  in Africa, 53
  greatness of, 166–70
  origin of the term, 166
  as the Whole Commission, 174–76
Greatest Commandment (Mark 12:28–30), 170
Great Mission Statement (Luke 4:18–19), 167
Great Nation (Genesis 12:1–3), 170
Great New Creation (Isaiah 65), 170
"Great Omission" (Willard), 147
Great Reconciliation (Revelation 7), 169–70
Great Reversal, 159
Great Sacrifice (death of Christ), 168–69
Great Sermon (Matthew 5–7), 167–68
"great world house," 126–27
Guam, 25
guns, 42
  anti-gun violence protest, 207

Hagin, Kenneth, 67
half gospels, 71–76, 82
Harris, Alice Seeley, 43
Hartford Institute for Religion Research, 70
Harvest Time Christian Fellowship (HTCF), 16
hate, gospel of, 64–66
Hawaii, 25
healing of memories, 197–98
healing of the nations, xvii, 2, 84, 120
healing pain, 194–200
hellfire-and-brimstone preaching, 65
heretics, burning of, 23
Heward-Mills, Dag, 71
Hispanic peoples, 125
HIV/AIDS, 136
holistic health, 106
holistic mission, xii, xvii, 91, 135, 159, 173, 184, 212, 214
  and globalization, 14–20
holistic transformation, 132
holistic worship, 140
Hollywood, 9
Holocaust, 23
Holy Land, 53
Holy Spirit, 114
  baptism in, 132–33
  creative source of God's transforming work, 131
  empowers forgiveness, 197
  as feminine dimension of God, 117–18
  holistic transformation, 134–36
  mission energy of, 144

Pentecost, 84
  power of, 132–33
  and reconciliation, 124
  supernatural power of, 163
Homogeneous Unit Principle (HUP), 121–22
homophobia, 61, 178, 213
homosexuality, 63, 65, 192, 193
horizontal reconciliation, 87, 88, 89, 103, 124–25, 126, 173–74, 177–78, 212
hospitality, Christian, 17
House for All Sinners and Saints (Denver), 94
human flourishing, 67, 68
humanitarian mission, 169, 176
humanitarian partnership, 17
humanity, ecologically connected to earth, 103–4
human nature, 98–100
human-rights abuses, xx
human worth, 100–102
humility
  bold, 92, 95, 105
  and postcolonialism, 50–51
Hutus, 53
hyperindividualism, 48, 101

idols, 152
image of God, 100–102, 115, 117
immigrant churches, 30
incarnation, 123
"Indians," 25. See also First Nations peoples
Indigenous People's Day, 14
individualism, 116
Inhabit Conference, 20
injustice, 60–61, 94, 186, 202, 213
Inquisition, 23
integral mission, 161–62, 163, 164
integrity of mission, 158
Interchurch World Movement (IWM), 159–60
intercultural competence, 16
intercultural koinonia, 118–22, 125, 142
intercultural learning, 9
intercultural worship, 141–42
interdependent team, in mission, 55
intergenerational competence, 17–18
International Association of Mission Studies, xvii
International Congress on World Evangelization (Lausanne 1974), 160
International Convention on the Elimination of All Forms of Racial Discrimination, 53
International Missionary Council, 54
International Monetary Fund, 12

internet, 7–8, 18
interreligious competence, 16–17
"invisible people," 119
Invitation to Racial Righteousness, 125–26
Islamophobia, 178, 188
Israel, as light to the nations, 83
Israelis and Palestinians, 53, 206

Jesus Christ
    as "Afro-Asiatic Jew," 119
    crucifixion of, 123
    as embodiment of the kingdom, 80–81
    human development of, 106
    incarnated the kingdom, 83
    lordship over all cultures, 141
    preaching of the kingdom of God, 79–80
    resurrection of, 84, 102, 123
    substitutionary death of, 84, 87
John Paul II, Pope, 49
John the Baptist, 80
Jones, Jim, 21
Jonestown massacre (1978), 21
Journey to Mosaic, 125–26
joy, through suffering, 136–39
judgment, gospel reduced to, 65
justice, 53, 74, 136, 197, 202
Justinian, 22, 26
just peacemaking, 201–6

Kaepernick, Colin, 207–8
keepers-of-the-gate mentality, 26
Kennedy, D. James, 25
Kenyon, E. W., 67
Kierkegaard, Søren, 27
King, Martin Luther, Jr., 126–27, 207
kingdom generosity, 51
kingdom of God, 14–15, 77–80, 127
    gospel of, 82–85
    reductions of, 79
    as vision of God's shalom, 85–89
Kiruga, John Njaramba, 171–73, 177

Lakewood Church (Houston), 67
lament, 199–200
Las Casas, Bartolomé de, 43
Latin American Theological Fraternity, 75,
    161–62
Lausanne Movement, xvi, xvii, 103n16, 123n31,
    157n3, 162
Lausanne statement on the prosperity gospel,
    66–67
lepers, 136

LGBTQ community, 192–93
liberation language, 161, 163
liberation theology, 155
Lighthouse Chapel International (Accra,
    Ghana), 71
"liturgy after the liturgy," 143
Local First (Grand Rapids), 13
lordship of Christ over all cultures, 141
love, 96
    for enemies, 206
    for God, 130
    for neighbor, 88, 104, 130, 144
Luwum, Janani, 152

Mackenzie, John, 43
"Make America Great Again," 26
Mammon, 15, 152
Mandela, Nelson, 187
Manifest Destiny, 25–26
marginalized, 30, 74, 136
market systems, 9
martyrdom, 138, 209
Marxism, 161
Matimelo, Audrey Mukwavi, 204–5
"McWorld," 19
megachurches, 70–71
Meyer, Joyce, 67
Micah Network, 162
migration, 17
military, dependence on, 27
Millennials, 164–65
ministry, stress and burnout, 106–7
misión integral, 164
missio Dei, 70
missiology, 1–2, 37
    of suffering, 136–39
mission, xv. See also holistic mission
    in context of global racism, 53
    fragmentation of, 28
    integrity of, 158
    spirituality of, 129–44
    tied to colonialism, 2, 4
    as transformation, 161
    as unidirectional, 33
missional worship service, 143–44
missionaries, with teacher complex, 51
missionary condescension, 50
money, and power, 51–52
money scams, 93
monocultural communities, 119
Montezuma, 39
Moody, D. L., 175

multiethnic church movement, as project of
    dominant class, xix
multiethnicity, 120n22
multinational corporations, 13
Musalaha, 189–90
Muslims
    interaction with, 172, 177, 188
    love for, 17
Mustard Seed Conspiracy (Sine), 19–20
mysticism, 135
"myth of race," 41

National Football League, 207–8
nationalism, 120, 152
National Liberation Front of Tripura, 65
"Native Americans," 25. *See also* First Nations
    peoples
natural resources, 179
Nee, Watchman, 152
new creation, 176
new heavens and new earth, 84
new monastic church movements, 20
"Nones" (religiously unaffiliated), 29
nonviolent action, 206–9
non-Western thinking as naturally holistic, 156
nonwhite church, 30
now-and-not-yet, 80

Obama, Barack, 25
Occupy Movement, 13
Old Testament, kingdom of God in, 82
One Day's Wages, 10
opportunism, 69–70
Opportunity International, 15
Oriented to Love (OTL), 189–90, 192–93
Osteen, Joel, 67

pacifism, 184
Palestinians, 53, 206
Palmer Theological Seminary, 97, 159, 160
parable of the ambulance, 201–2
Paraclete, 138
Parish Collective, 20
Parks, Rosa, 207
parochialism, 141
partnership in mission, 55
Pasadena Statement, 121
paternalism, 47, 50, 52, 54, 147
patriarchal system, 118
"patriotic theology," 28
patriotism, 27
Pax Christi, ix

Pax Romana, ix
peace, 85
    false, 201
    waging, 185
Peace Corps, 169
peacemaking, xxi, 145, 174, 177–78, 183–84,
    212, 214
    as healing, 194–200
    and justice, 201–10
    as mission, 173–74, 212
peace of Christ, ix
Pentecost, 84
Pentecostal/Charismatic tradition, 162
Pentecostals and Charismatics for Peace and
    Justice (PCPJ), 163
perichoresis, 115, 122
persecution, 138
personal lament, 199–200
personal piety, 134
personal salvation, 58
    gospel of, 72–74
personal-social gospel debate, 155
Pew Research Center, 29, 31–32
pharisaical legalism, 65
Phelps, Fred W., 65
Philippines, 25, 156, 186n9
piety, personal, 134
pneumatology, and missiology, 131–32
polycentric mission, 4
poor, the
    good news for, 136
    and the oppressed, 15, 72–73, 74, 136
post-Christendom, xxi, 4, 22, 24, 94, 158
postcolonialism, xxi, 4, 34, 38, 94
    and humility, 50–51
    and power, 51
    and repentance, 48–50
    and lament, 200
    and missiology, 46–47, 52–55, 158
    theologians, 2n3
postmodernism, debunked total academic ob-
    jectivity, 1
poverty
    extreme, 10
    and wealth, 51
power, 60, 152
power dynamics, 51–52
power evangelism, 164
power of relationship, 187–90
prayer, as warfare, 185
preaching, hellfire-and-brimstone, 65
Price, Fred, 67

privilege, 60
prosperity
  gospel of, 66–68
  and comfort, 213
Providence, 40
Puerto Rico, 25
"pure water/Kool-Aid" analogy, 21, 23

race, categories of, 41
racial injustice, 61
racial righteousness, 53–54
racism, x, 48, 53, 120, 122, 125, 178, 205, 213
  "brown-on-brown," 61
  and colonialism, 40–41
radical discipleship, 151
radical nonviolent actions, 208–9
Reagan, Ronald, 25
reconciliation, xi, xii, xviii–xix, 3, 205
  of all things, 169–70, 173–74
  as central to mission, xvi–xvii
  circular dimension, 87, 89, 103, 173–74,
    178–81
  competencies in, 16–18, 20
  defines the gospel, 86–87
  horizontal dimension, 87, 88, 89, 103, 124–
    25, 126, 173–74, 177–78, 212
  and intercultural worship, 142
  and love of God, 122–23
  as "non-final" and "final," 89
  in postcolonial missiology, 158
  as project of dominant class, xix
  and racial righteousness, 53–54
  and reign of God, 78
  of self, 98–102, 214
  spirituality of, 184–87
  stages of, 189
  vertical dimension, 87, 88, 89, 103, 124, 126,
    173–74, 175–77
  waging, 211–12
  as "wholeness project" of God, 99
Reconciliation Roadmap (McNeil), 190
Red Cross, 10, 169
refugees, 189
reign of God, 78
relationship, power of, 187–90
relief efforts, mobilization of, 9–10
religious wars, 17
reparative or conversion therapy, 193. See also
  homophobia; homosexuality; LGBTQ
  community
repentance, 195–96
  corporate, 48–50

Requerimiento (1513), 42
restitution, 50
resurrection, 102
retributive justice, 197
revelation, and context, 3
rich-poor divide, 15
Robertson, Pat, 25
Roman Empire, 22, 24
Romero, Óscar, 152, 207
Rwanda, 53, 92n3, 197

salt and light, 95
salvation, personal, 58, 72–74
same-sex marriage, 188, 192. See also homophobia; homosexuality; LGBTQ
  community
"Sand Creek Apology," 48
saving souls, 59
Scudder, Ira Sophia, 43
"Seek Ye First" (song), 77–78
segregation, 177–78
self-care, 105–7, 108
self-centeredness, 105
self-denial, 107
self-donating, 122
self-help groups (SHGs), 204
self-love, 104–8
self-sacrifice, 107–8
sending worship, 142–43
September 11, 2001, terrorist attacks, 12, 211
Sermon on the Mount, 167
"Service of Memory and Reconciliation," 48
sexism, 61, 117, 122, 125, 213
sex scandals, 93
sexual disorientation, 193
sexual sin, 63
Shack, The (allegory), 122–23
shalom, xviii, 14, 20, 78, 80, 82, 84–85, 116,
  175, 184, 201, 211, 212, 214
  shalom kingdom, 85–89, 91
Shema, 103n15, 106
"signs and wonders," 164
simple living, 51
Simple Way, The, 207
sin, as absence of shalom, 85–86
Sine, Christine, 20
Sine, Tom, 19–20
singleness, 99
slavery, 41, 126, 213
  catechisms written for slaves, 44
social concern, 155
social gospel–only approach, 157

social justice, xvii, 157, 158
social liberation, 74–76, 214
sociology of humankind, 99
South Africa, 53
Southern Baptists, 165
Soviet Union, collapse of, 7
Spirit. *See* Holy Spirit
Spirit baptism, 132–33
spirituality, 128
spirituality of mission, 129–44
spirituality of reconciliation, 184–87
spiritual warfare, 185
stewardship, xxi, 51, 174, 178–81, 212, 214
stress of ministry, 106–7
suffering, 68, 201–2
    and joy, 136–39

Taylor, Hudson, 166
teacher complex, 51
ten Boom, Corrie, 152
territorial expansion, 25, 33–34
theological liberalism, 159
theological skill (vulnerability), 191
theology of religions, 17
Tizon, Al and Janice, 19–20
traditionalism, 18
transformation, 161, 163, 164
    holistic, 132
transformational development, 164
transformation of the world, xviii, 134
tribalism, 178
Trinity, the, 108, 112–18, 214
    feminine dimension of, 117–18
    mystery of, 114
triple reconciliation, 174
Trump, Donald, 26
Tutsis, 53
Tutu, Desmond, 187, 195

United Church of Canada, 30, 48–49
United Methodist Church, 48
United Nations, 169
United States
    flag in church sanctuaries, 141
    and globalization, 25
unity-amid-diversity, 118, 119, 122
Universal Church of the Kingdom of God
    (Brazil), 67
University Hill Congregation (Vancouver),
    29–30
unmuting the socially disadvantaged, 203–4
unwholeness, 107, 165–66

Upper Darby (Pennsylvania), diversity of, 5–6
US flag in church sanctuaries, 141

Vancouver School of Theology, 30
vertical reconciliation, 87, 88, 89, 103, 124, 126,
    173–74, 175–77
violence, 47, 116
violent evangelism, 42–43, 52
vulnerability, 191–95

waging peace, 185
waging reconciliation, 211–12
Waldensians, 27
Waterhole Baptist Church (Quezon City), 203–4
wealth and poverty, 51
Weber, George, 208
Westboro Baptist Church (Topeka, Kansas), 65
Western Christianity, 32
Western cultural superiority, 40
white colonial assimilation, 45
white privilege, 187
white superiority, myth of, 41
whole church, 91–96, 112, 214
Whole Commission, 157–58, 174, 183, 214
whole gospel, 57–62
"whole-life stewardship," 51
whole mission, 145–53, 166, 170
wholeness, 102–3
whole persons, 97, 103–7, 112, 214
whole world, xxi, 3, 97, 116, 119, 126–27, 134,
    160
"wholly Spirit," 134–36. *See also* Holy Spirit
WindListener (blogger), 75
witch hunts, 23, 93, 213
word, deed, and sign, 162–63, 173
world, transformation of, 47
World Bank, 12
world Christianity, 31–32
World Council of Churches (WCC), 75, 160
World Relief, 10
World Trade Organization, 12
World Vision, 10, 15
worship, 139–44
    dangerous, 140, 214
worship songs, in different languages and in-
    struments, 143
worship wars, 139
wounded healers, 194
wrongdoers, 195–99
wronged, 196–99

Zimele Wethu Foundation (South Africa), 204